"patria ante politica"

DIPLOMARINE

TERRORISM, TURF WARS, COCKTAIL PARTIES
AND OTHER PAINFUL JOYS
MY FIRST THIRTY YEARS OF FOREIGN AFFAIRS

*For Ed Jacko,
With special regards.*

Timothy C. Brown PhD

CONSUL GENERAL (RET.)
MARINE, DIPLOMAT, SCHOLAR

patria ante politica
DIPLOMARINE

Marine

Diplomat

Scholar

Dr. Timothy C. Brown, PhD, Consul General (ret.)

Dr. Brown is on his third career. He was an enlisted Marine for ten years from 1954 to 1964; a Foreign Service Officer (FSO, career diplomat) for twenty-seven years, from 1965 to 1992. Since 1992, he has been a scholar, author and conference speaker.

During his first Marine enlistment he was an Embassy Guard in Managua, Nicaragua. During his second, he was a Thai and Spanish Intelligence Linguist.

From 1965 to 1992, he served as a Foreign Service Officer successively in Israel, Spain, wartime Vietnam, Mexico, Paraguay, El Salvador and Amsterdam, in the State

Department in Washington, DC as Paraguay/Uruguay Desk Officer, Deputy Director of European Political/ Economic Affairs and Deputy Coordinator for Cuban Affairs. Returning abroad, he served as United States Consul General in Martinique (France), as Senior Liaison Officer (SLO) to the Nicaraguan Democratic Resistance (the Contras) in Central America and was a Senior Border Research Fellow in New Mexico.

He retired from the Foreign Service in 1992, returned to college and completed doctoral studies in four disciplines—Political Psychology, International Economics, Foreign Relations, and History and, in 1997, was awarded an interdisciplinary PhD by New Mexico State University. He has since been a free-lance writer, lecturer, academic researcher, and conference speaker.

During each of his careers Dr. Brown received numerous honors. While a Marine he received Letters of Commendation from three Ambassadors and a future Assistant Commandant of the Marine Corps. During his Foreign Service career he received three Meritorious Honor Medals, two Superior Honor Medals, was recommended for a Citation for Heroism Under Fire and was nominated for the National HUMINT (Human Intelligence) Award. While a scholar, Dr. Brown was honored as one of only eighty-seven former Marines profiled in *Above and Beyond: Former Marines Conquer the Civilian World* (Turner, 2003), alongside six Generals, three United States Senators, a former Secretary of State, and more than thirty top business leaders; listed in *Who's Who Among America's Teachers* and *Who's Who in the West*; honored as the Annual Distinguished

Graduate of the University of Nevada-Reno in 1982; and, in 2010, inducted into the Hall of Fame of his *alma mater,* Sparks High School.

In *Diplomarine,* Dr. Brown draws on personal experiences from his first thirty years as Marine and diplomat to take the reader deep inside the largely secret worlds where foreign policies designed in Washington are transformed into realities by those charged with implementing them in the field.

He has published four other books: *A Guide to Thailand* (FMFPAC, Hawaii, 1962); *The Causes of Continuing Conflict in Nicaragua* (Hoover Press, 1995); *When the AK-47s Fall Silent: Revolutionaries, Guerrillas, and the Dangers of Peace,*(Hoover Press, 2000); and *The Real Contra War: Highlander Peasant Resistance in Nicaragua* (Oklahoma University Press, 2001).

He has also published numerous peer reviewed articles in the *Annals of the American Academy of Political and Social Sciences, Journal of American Popular Culture, Policy Studies Review,* the *International Journal of Intelligence and CounterIntelligence,* Stanford University's Hoover Digest and other professional journals. He has also published numerous editorial commentaries in the *Wall Street Journal, Washington Times Weekly,* and in newspapers throughout Latin America and been a guest speaker at numerous international and academic conferences, including in Paris, Mexico City, The Hague, Lima, Peru, in Washington, DC, at Stanford University, the United Nation's Peacekeeping Training Center in Canada, the Joint US Special Operations University (JSOU) and aboard cruise ships, including the *Queen Elizabeth II.*

Dr. Brown is a founding Director of the Paris-based *Centre International de Reserches et d'Études sur le Terrorisme et l'Aide aux Victimes de Terrorisme (CIRET-AVT),* the think tank of the former Director of France's Direction de la Surveillance du Territoire (DST) Yves Bonnet. He has been a Research Fellow at Stanford University's Hoover Institution, taught at New Mexico State University, Western New Mexico University and Sierra Nevada College and been a Member of the Board of Bentley Enterprises, a privately owned corporation.

He has been married since 1958 to the former Leda Zúñiga Fernandez of San José, Costa Rica and they have four children, eight grandchildren, and four great grandchildren — and counting.

BOOKS IN PRINT
AVAILABLE ON AMAZON

The Real Contra War – Highlander Peasant Resistance in Nicaragua Oklahoma University Press, 2001

When the AK-47s Fall Silent – Revolutionaries, Guerrillas and the Dangers of Peace, Hoover Press, Stanford University, 2000

The Causes of Continuing Conflict in Nicaragua Hoover Press, Stanford University, 1995

SELECTED ARTICLES

"Women Unfit for Combat? Au Contraire!" *Wall Street Journal*, Sept. 30, 1997

"The Fourth Member of NAFTA—The US-Mexico Border," *Annals of the American Academy of Political and Social Science*, 1997, v. 550

"Nahuas, Gachupines, Patriarchs and Piris," *Journal of American Culture*, Winter 1997, 20/4

"Realist Revolutions," *Policy Studies Review*, Summer 1998

"A Business Model for Foreign Labor," *Hoover Digest*, 2007, 3

"Identity Wars", *International Journal of Intelligence and CounterIntelligence*, December 2012

ISBN-13: 9781481134743
ISBN-10: 1481134744

Library of Congress Control Number: 2012922955
CreateSpace Independent Publishing Platform
North Charleston, South Carolina

This book is dedicated to my friend and mentor,
former Nevada Governor Donal Neil "Mike"
O'Callaghan, and to his lady Carolyn

author's collection

Carson City, Nevada, 1972. Governor and Mrs.
O'Callaghan in the Governor's mansion
(photo courtesy of Michael Neil O'Callaghan)

author's collection

Las Vegas, Nevada, 1998.
The author with Governor O'Callaghan at
wedding of his second daughter, Rebecca.

author's collection

The author with Senate Majority
Leader Harry Reid (D-NV)

I met Dr. Timothy Brown decades ago through our mutual friend and mentor, the late Nevada Governor Mike O'Callaghan. Mike believed in Dr. Brown's work for the State Department, and it was not long before I, too, came to appreciate his service to our country. Dr. Brown dedicated his life to protecting and strengthening American values and *Diplomarine* is the fascinating story of his experiences as a Marine and diplomat. His was an unusual career and I did not always agree with the foreign policies he was implementing. But his unique experiences and 'boots-on-the-ground' insights provide a valuable, if not unique, window on the international relations field in which he worked.

Senator Harry Reid, (D-NV)
Senate Majority Leader, Washington, DC, 2013

...and to Nevada, my home

author's collection

Washington, DC: Author and wife, with
daughters Tamara and Barbara, Nevada's 1983
Cherry Blossom Princess.

"To some who hurry along Nevada's highways, the country through which they pass seems almost barren of life. But to those who know it, the desert is the home of a myriad of living things.... A few stopped and settled along the way, and eventually others returned to share the harvest of the desert's wealth."

Sessions S. Wheeler, *The Nevada Desert*

"And for me, as for them, it is home. From its piñon-laced desert ranges, through wide-ranging valleys, past ranches and farms, world-renowned cities, hidden oases, azure lakes, and distant Indian haunts, Nevada is both dream and reality. My home and, if you will it, yours."

Barbara Frances de Gerardo Zúñiga-Brown

ACKNOWLEDGEMENTS

Many friends, colleagues and fellow denizens of the world of foreign affairs contributed to this book, some knowingly, including Ambassadors George Landau, Myles Frechette, Lyle Lane, Everett Ellis "Ted" Briggs, and Cresencio "Cris" Arcos, and Foreign Service professionals John Penfold, Bill Meara, David Lindwall and Fran Kendrick, each both a consummate professional and personal friend. Special thanks also to Larry Pippin, my undergraduate advisor at the University of Nevada, and Jose Garcia and Ray Sadler of New Mexico State University. Still others come from other walks of life, Eugene Choy and Tom Fee, my close friends since high school (Tom even allowed me to plagiarize part of my book title from his own book of poetry, *Love and Other Painful Joys*), Tom's sister Nancy and cousin Mary Kay Conwell, who read and critiqued earlier versions of this book from the perspective of well-informed readers, as did the late Dr. Bill Ratliff of Stanford's world-renowned Hoover Institution, Dr. Elizabeth Burgos Debray, Ambassador Myles Frechette, Robert Morton, my former editor at the Washington Times, Juan Tamayo of the Miami Herald, Dr. Paul Manoukian and Clay Brust of Robison, Belaustegui, Sharp and Low, my legal counsel. All provided me with invaluable advice, suggestions, and support, as did Watchara Ruisanthai Lizama, who helped me with my forty-year-old and very rusty Thai. Gabrielle Peterson Newman, Michael Nelson and Robert

Macias of Grafx8 Media Group (www.graphx8.com) in Minden, Nevada were especially helpful, as were my publishers, Createspace. Others not named here, belong to the world of secrets and know who they are, or who they told me they were. Any merit this book has is thanks to all of them and many more not named here. As for any errors, mistakes, or misstatements that remain despite their diligence, those are and forever will be mine, and mine alone. And last, but by far the most important, I must thank the one person that has contributed the most, not just to this book, but to my life throughout the decades, my beloved wife, Leda. Without her, all of this would lose its meaning.

TABLE OF CONTENTS

ILLUSTRATIONS

FOREWORD
BY
AMBASSADOR MYLES R.R. FRECHETTE

The United States, rightly and proudly, honors its military veterans as heroes for their wartime sacrifices in the service of our country, as we should and, God willing, will always do. But there are others that also serve, sometimes in combat alongside our soldiers, more often as quiet sentinels manning daily, year on year, decade on decade, the front lines of America's national security. They serve in virtual silence; unsung and unrecognized, except when the bombing of an Embassy or murder of an Ambassador makes the headlines. They too are heroes, and they too, deserve the thanks of a grateful nation. *Diplomarine* opens a rare if not unique window into the work they do, the lives they lead and the sacrifices they and their families make, in a world few know, and even fewer understand.

That *Diplomarine* is a great read, a series of rollicking good tales of adventures, irreverently told by a distinguished former diplomat, Tim Brown, I've known as a friend and colleague for more years than I care to count, is just the icing on a delicious cake. His readers join him on a roller coaster ride that takes them to eighteen countries on four continents and into five war zones during the hottest three decades of the Cold War, usually with his wife, Leda and their four growing children in tow. Each tale entertains. But each also carries a message, often pungently stated. A bullet fired at him through an Embassy window by an anonymous sniper during his very first tour abroad as a teenage Marine Embassy Guard in Nicaragua, almost ending his life before it began, introduces his reader to the always present dangers inherent in practicing the career of foreign affairs abroad. His second Marine enlistment finds him on an intelligence mission in remote rice villages in northeast Thailand, sleeping in Buddhist temples to escape roaming Pathet Lao insurgents. A few years later, having left the Marine Corps for the Foreign Service, he's in war-torn Vietnam, a civilian with a military command, clearing artillery fire missions and risking his new career by opposing a Phoenix assassination. And so it goes, even in places the world assumes are perfectly safe. While in Amsterdam his wife and children are threatened by a convicted terrorist whose repeated telephone calls prove he has them under constant surveillance. In Martinique, an island the world sees as an idyllic Caribbean paradise, his office is bombed and he's marked for assassination by a terrorist group. In Tegucigalpa, Honduras, his wife is teargassed. And in between he does his job, protecting Americans, issuing visas, interviewing political refugees, representing his country in foreign ministries, at swank "working" cocktail parties, and in remote villages on horseback. And from each of these experiences Tim draws lessons for all of us. Vietnam teaches him to question the wisdom of involvement in foreign wars we don't really understand; experiences in Israel and Spain teach him that prejudice knows no borders; policy battles in Washington teach him that sometimes political battles are as fierce as those fought with guns. Diplomarine is a fun read that opens a new window on America's first line of national security. Read it, and you'll discover new worlds, new challenges, new opportunities and, above all, new heroes. Enjoy.

Ambassador Myles R. R. Frechette

United States Ambassador to Cameroon and Colombia

&

Assistant United States Trade Representative, The White House

THE NEW DIPLOMACY IN ACTION

author's collection

Baghdad, Iraq, 2007. In the world of diplo-wars it can be hard to tell the soldiers from the civilians. Here, personnel of the State Department-led 1st Embedded Provincial Reconstruction Team (1st ePRT), wearing full "battle rattle," are in Baghdad, standing in front of their official vehicle, an MRAP (Mine-Protected Ambush Resistant Armored Vehicle). Commanded by a senior State Department officer, the 1st ePRT was an integral part of the 2007 "surge" of American forces into Iraq in tandem with the Army's 4th Infantry Brigade. Its commanding officer, a graduate of the National Defense University and a career Foreign Service Officer since promoted to the rank of Minister-Counselor (Major General equivalent), is in the middle. Iraq was his third diplo-war. The first came in Panama during the ouster of dictator Manuel Noriega; the second in South Africa. His fourth diplowar may come in Afghanistan. He's also the author's son.

INTRODUCTION

I finally stopped procrastinating and began writing this book one freezing winter's morning back home in Nevada, where I was licking my wounds after a lifetime roaming the globe, first as a Marine and then as a Foreign Service Officer, a career diplomat. A great deal of what I've written has been reconstructed from decades-old memories, so I apologize in advance if others remember events differently. But one memory is especially vivid in my mind. I was sitting in my favorite rocking chair in my end-of-life sanctuary, an enclosed porch with a spectacular view of the Sierra Nevada Mountains, my decades of tramping through the twisted vineyards of foreign affairs, and maybe even my life, over — or so I thought. The stately poplars just outside my window were clad in pogonip, the freezing fog the Shoshone call "white death"," and sparkled in the winter sun like statues robed in diamonds. A wedge of Canada geese would occasionally break the silence as they honked their way westward to their winter feeding grounds. I was sitting as still as possible trying to avoid the jolts of pain that came whenever I moved, hopefully recovering from nearly taking life's permanent off-ramp. I had a thick blanket wrapped tightly around my shoulders, but I was still freezing, probably because of the blood thinners.

The dash by medevac helicopter across Washoe Valley to Saint Mary's Hospital in Reno, during which I lost my undershorts, Lord knows how, had been very different from my dozens of earlier 'chopper flights. Those were in the service of my country, and many of them involved dodging air ambushes in Vietnam or insertions into jungle clearings elsewhere. My most recent ones had been quick dashes in and out of remote Contra camps along the Nicaragua-Honduras border, many of them in the Lady Ellen, a rickety helicopter named for the wife of former CIA Director Bill Casey. During those flights I held a tin can to catch the hydraulic fluids leaking from its rotor shaft while simultaneously praying we wouldn't get popped by a SAM-7 surface-to-air missile. This one was very different, and very, very personal, a dark-of-night race to Reno to have an emergency triple bypass at the crack of dawn the next day, lest my next heart attack kill me. This was followed by several days in intensive care hovering between life and death. My favorite cardiologist, Dr. Sri Challapalli, told me later my adventure had cost me a few brain cells. Raw, ruby-red gashes from groin to ankle marked the long surgical incisions in my left leg where the surgeons had harvested the veins they used for the grafts. But it was the one in my chest where they'd cracked open my sternum to get at my heart, that hurt the most. It had been touch and go. But I'd survived.

Leda, my Costa Rican bride of more than fifty years, and the gaggles of brats and grand-brats we'd produced, not to mention my ninety-year-old mother; all had bigger scares than I did. For me it had been just one more "when you hear the bomb explode it's too late to duck" moment like so many others I'd experienced over the decades. All in all, it seemed a good time for retrospection. And besides, I needed to exercise the few brain cells I had left.

As I sat there enjoying the painful joys of recovery, I silently began to ask myself deep existential questions like, "How in hell did a PK, preacher's kid, that almost flunked high school Spanish end up with three careers centered on Central America, of all places? And how did Nevada and a bunch of Nevadans like Mike O'Callaghan, Gene Choy, Harry Reid, Paul Laxalt and Tom Fee end up playing major roles in my life when I wasn't even in Nevada ninety-nine percent of the time?"

I was just eleven years old in 1948 when my parents divorced and my mother took me with her from Fresno, California, to Reno, Nevada and, at first, I hated Nevada with a passion—dry, dusty, depressing. But over the years, I've sunk roots so deep it's hard for me to believe I'm not native-born. Nevada is that sort of place, mostly because Nevadans are that sort of people. I've never voted anywhere else; my wife became an American citizen there; our youngest and oldest were both born in the same maternity room with the same doctor in attendance in Saint Mary's, the same hospital where, decades later, I had the triple bypass that saved my life.

There are dozens, perhaps hundreds, of books on America's foreign policies as seen from virtually every angle save one - that of the poor bastards charged with trying to make them work. In *Diplomarine* I try to fill this gap, at least partially, by telling what the world of foreign affairs looked like to me from the bottom up over a course of thirty years, first as an enlisted Marine and then as a career diplomat.

My baptism into the foreign affairs community came in 1956 in Managua, Nicaragua during my first Marine enlistment. The Cold War was in full swing; Nicaraguan *caudillo* Anastasio "Tacho" Somoza García had just been assassinated; revolutionaries were preparing to launch armed insurgencies throughout Central America; and I was a wide-eyed innocent on his first adventure abroad. After re-enlisting in 1959, I switched worlds, studied Thai at the Army (now Defense) Language Institute in Monterey, California, and basic intelligence skills at the Army Intelligence School in Fort Holabird, Maryland. For the next four years I was to be a Thai Intelligence/Linguist and flit back and forth between Fleet Marine Force Pacific (FMFPAC) headquarters in Hawaii and Thailand, Laos and the Philippines as an interpreter, intelligence collector and analyst. In my not-so-copious spare time I tried to take care of my growing family and prepare for our future by taking night courses at the University of Hawaii.

In 1964, toward the end of my second Marine enlistment I took and, to my surprise, passed the Foreign Service Officer Written and Oral Entrance Examinations and was offered a commission. Had I immediately accepted I would have become the only officer in the Foreign Service without a college degree, and that would have put me at a severe competitive disadvantage. So, at the State Department's urging, in June of 1964 I decided to leave the Corps, go back home to Reno, and try to finish the last three semesters of my undergraduate studies in nine months. My long-suffering wife, Leda, now expecting for the fourth time, went ahead with Barbara, Rebecca and Tamara, our three daughters, to fix up a small house my mother had agreed to let us live in. I gave her our last $100, with which she managed to buy enough Salvation Army furnishings to make it habitable. Despite being six months pregnant, she even managed to paint its interior. After that, the least I could do was finish my undergraduate studies, which I did. Ten months later in June of 1965, degree in hand, I received my FSO commission.

For the next twenty-seven years I was to be a Foreign Service officer, a career diplomat. During the first fourteen, I served consecutively in Israel, Spain, wartime Vietnam, Mexico, Paraguay, El Salvador, and the Netherlands. In 1978, when our oldest daughter, Barbara, graduated from the International School in Amsterdam and was appointed to West Point by former Governor of Nevada, then Senator Paul Laxalt, we returned to Washington, DC. Over the next five years, 1978–83, I was to serve in three very different positions inside the Department of State in Washington, DC, as Desk Officer for Paraguay/Uruguay Affairs, then as Deputy Director of European Regional Economic/Political Affairs, and finally as Deputy Coordinator for Cuban Affairs. By 1983 all three of our daughters were married, and our son was studying at American University. So, when I was assigned to Martinique as Consul General, we had to leave them behind. As our son Tim keeps reminding us, even after all these years, we were the ones that left home, not our children. Still, a job's a job. And as jobs go, being Consul General in the French Antilles/Guiana, responsible for France's three *départements*, or provinces, in the Americas—Martinique, Guadeloupe and French Guiana, ain't bad.

During my three decades as a practitioner of Machiavelli's dark arts, I spent more time in war zones as a diplomat than Marine. If my readers take away just one lesson from the tales told in *Diplomarine*, I hope it will be that implementing foreign policies in the field, whether in a Marine uniform or a diplomat's suit and tie, is exceptionally complex, always challenging and, on occasion, very dangerous. During my diplomatic years, the gourmet dinners, swank cocktail parties and quiet afternoons on topless beaches, for which diplomacy is best known, were repeatedly interrupted by wars, terrorist bombings, assassinations, narco-mobs, partisan confrontations, bureaucratic turf wars, politics, and other forms of organized mayhem. As they say in rodeo, it was one hell of a ride. One hell of a ride, yes: But not the wildest. That one was yet to come.

Diplomarine ends with my departure from Martinique for what was to be by far the most sensitive, dangerous, and controversial assignment of my diplomatic career, as Senior Liaison Officer (SLO) to the Nicaraguan Contras in Central America. The United States was convulsed with political controversies as impassioned as those that surrounded the Vietnam War, the Iran-Contra imbroglio was in full swing and Ollie North was the hero/villain of the day. And yet, despite the raging scandals, President Reagan asked Congress for, and received, funds to continue covert CIA support for the Contras. But Congress, in its infinite (or finite) wisdom imposed as a condition precedent, that the Secretary of State take personal responsibility for how it was spent. No more Iran-Contra style White House end runs around its authority.

As part of the State Department's response to this, I was transferred from Martinique to Tegucigalpa, Honduras to head up a secret, compartmentalized office unique in the history of the State Department. For the next two years it would be my job to keep a hawk's eye on the United States' relationship with the Contras, including the Central Intelligence Agency's covert operations. When Congress replaced the CIA's covert program with a decidedly overt one of "humanitarian assistance" managed by the Agency for International Development (AID) I would spend two more years trying to keep a hawk's eye on that program instead. During those last two years, Nicaragua held its very first more-or-less honest national election, and the Contras were demobilized, disarmed, and repatriated, almost half returning to homes in seventeen Segovian highlander peasant villages from which they came. That story, and the series of all-but-unbelievable intelligence failures that had led the United States deeper and deeper into the morass of the Contra War, I've reserved for another book.

With the Contra War over and the Contras demobilized, I believed my job was done, and spent the last two years of my Foreign Service career decompressing at the Border Research Institute in Las Cruces, New Mexico. I then left the Foreign Service, went back to college, spent the next several years completing doctoral studies in four disciplines—Political Psychology, Economics, History, and International Relations—and, in 1997, received an interdisciplinary PhD from New Mexico State University. My dissertation, since published as *The Real Contra War* (Oklahoma, 2001), was, not surprisingly, on the Contras. What was surprising was that during my four years working intensively with them, during which I had access to the best intelligence available to the United States government, I hadn't even known who they really were. That I had to learn by asking Contras, not my country's intelligence experts.

While Special Liaison Officer (SLO) to the Contras in Central America I had depended on major studies of them written by the intelligence community that were not merely dead wrong but reached conclusions that were the precise opposite of the truth. One study, prepared for inclusion in a National Intelligence Estimate (NIE) by the State Department's Office of Intelligence, was so far off the mark that it might as well have been written in Havana or Managua by the Contra's enemies, not in Washington by its supposed friends. Other earlier, but equally erroneous reporting, may well have misled President Reagan, CIA Director Bill Casey, Congress, and many others, just as later reporting misled me, for one simple reason. They believed, as I did, what they were told by the intelligence community.

During my post-Foreign-Service doctoral research, I was able to thoroughly document that, far from the murderous thugs of the "Black Legend of the Contras" painted by the media and anti-Contra activists during the Contra War, almost 98 percent of the Contras were just *"un atterro de campesinos bien encachib'aos,* (just a whole bunch or *really* pissed off peasants). This was exactly the opposite of what our intelligence community believed they were.

This made me wonder if we might not have been as wrong about the other side of Central America's recent civil wars as we had been about the Contras. If we hadn't even known who our own allies were, were we also wrong about our enemies? So, once I had my PhD in hand, I launched on yet another quest for understanding that took me back, of all places, to my wife's childhood home in San José, Costa Rica to talk with one of her closest neighbors, Plutarco Hernández Sancho. I'd met Plutarco during our September 12, 1958 wedding reception. But, since he was just fourteen years old at the time, I hadn't paid much attention to him other than to notice that he kept making goo-goo eyes at my bride.

During the intervening years, Pluti, as I now call him (we have since become close friends), had gone on to become a major player on the revolutionary side of Central America's civil wars, especially Nicaragua's Sandinista revolution. In fact, Manuel Jirón, in his 1986 *"Quién es Quién en Nicaragua"* (Who's Who in Nicaragua, Radio Amor, San José, Costa Rica), dedicates more space to Plutarco than to Nicaraguan President Daniel Ortega and his brother, General Humberto Ortega, combined. During my years as Thai Intelligence Linguist, Plutarco was organizing Costa Rica's first Communist Youth League. During my years as a junior diplomat, he spent several years studying at Patrice Lumumba University in Moscow, a year being trained in guerrilla warfare at Campamento Cerro, just outside Havana, Cuba, and an additional six months in North Korea, doing advanced studies in how to subvert a country under the personal tutelage of Kim Il. And during my years as a mid-career diplomat he spent sixteen years as a National Director of Nicaragua's Sandinista National Liberation Front (Frente Sandinista de Liberación Nacional, FSLN).

After giving me a fairly candid oral history of his life as a revolutionary, which I dutifully videotaped, Plutarco then went the extra mile and introduced me to five key members of his Cold War cell. Each, in turn, allowed me to videotape their oral history. And therein lays yet another story I'm reserving for the future. With that, let us begin.

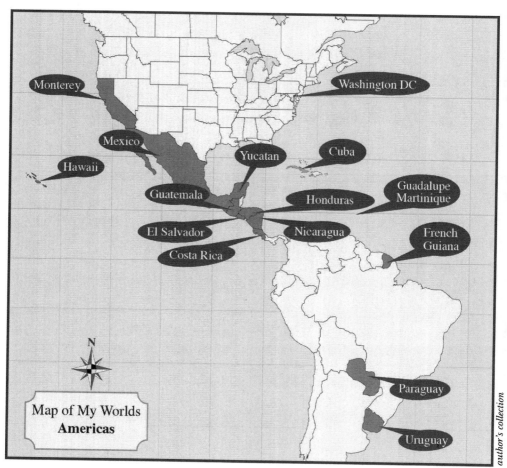

Monterey

Washington DC

Mexico

Hawaii

Yucatan

Cuba

Guatemala

Honduras

Guadalupe
Martinique

El Salvador

Nicaragua

French
Guiana

Costa Rica

N

Map of My Worlds
Americas

Paraguay

Uruguay

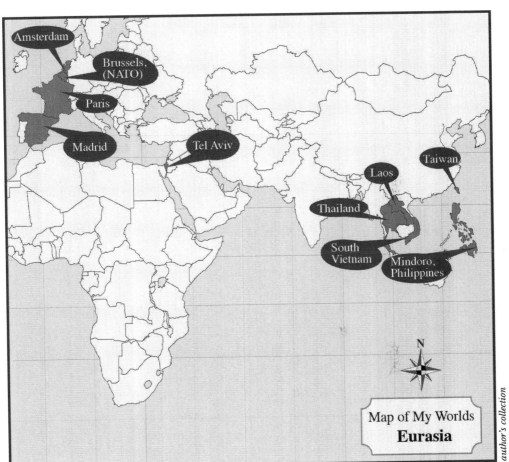

Amsterdam

Brussels, (NATO)

Paris

Madrid

Tel Aviv

Laos

Taiwan

Thailand

South Vietnam

Mindoro, Philippines

N

Map of My Worlds
Eurasia

ONE

IN THE BEGINNING

Unlike Bridey Murphy, I have no memories of former lives. As far as I know my life started when I was born, although it's rumored it began when I was conceived in the middle of a Kansas wheat field. What I do know, because my mother told me and I always believed her, is that I was hatched into this world in the small Kansas town of Anthony. While both of my parents were raised in Fresno, California, I was born there because, at the time, my father was serving as the assistant pastor at Anthony's Pentecostal Church of God church while studying at divinity school in nearby Enid, Oklahoma. This made me the only Jayhawker in a family of Prune Pickers. Not that I remember much about my birthplace, as my parents headed back to California when I was just two and insisted I go along. They later told me that during my short sojourn in the Kansas wheat fields I'd enjoyed the usual run of babyhood experiences—setting the house on fire by pulling a Christmas tree down on my head, taking a swig of kerosene so I could enjoy having my stomach pumped, being tossed about by a tornado while riding in the car in my baby basket. My own memories begin at about age three, when we arrived back in Fresno, where I stayed until I was eleven. I remember getting caught on my bike in a sudden hail storm and taking shelter in an abandoned house I absolutely knew was haunted, cheerily chewing globs of asphalt plucked from the street in front of our house on a balmy 110–115 degree summer day, shooting my brother in the gut with my Red Ryder BB Gun, and dousing the next-door neighbor brat with whitewash when he tried to steal some of my comic books.

From Fresno, my mother hauled me off to northern Nevada, where I was to attend five schools in six years, Billinghurst, Northside and Central Junior High Schools in Reno and Reno then Sparks High schools, finally graduating in 1955 from Sparks. While at Sparks High, I managed to con my congressman, Cliff Young, into nominating me for appointments to West Point, Annapolis and the brand-new Air Force Academy, only to flunk all three of their entrance medical exams thanks to a nose flattened one too many times on the football field. The University of Nevada, Reno and several private colleges also accepted me. But none offered me the financial help I would need to attend them. This left me with as a third option, joining the Cold War, which was fine with me.

A voracious reader of history and current events, I had concluded while still in high school that neither Woodrow Wilson's "war to end all wars" nor the MAD-ness of the mutually assured destruction Cold War doctrine born at Hiroshima and Nagasaki, had lessened man's thirst for making war on his fellow man. They'd just made wars sneakier affairs conducted by proxy—instigated insurgencies, surrogate revolutions, sponsored subversions, covert operations, and so forth. In those days, most of these wars involved efforts by Marxists to share with the rest of the world the blessings of the Russian Revolution. With the naïve optimism of the young, I was in a hurry to join in the fray before it ended.

author's collection

Reno, Nevada, 1953: "The house at the top of the hill," my home while in high school. The ladder leaning against the house on the right was the only way in and out of my attic bedroom. At right, the biggest little outhouse in Washoe County, Nevada. The house, since remodeled and now surrounded by modernization, is still there; not so the outhouse.

My older brother, Billy, had joined the Marines a couple of years earlier, was stationed in Okinawa, and seemed to be enjoying himself, and I wanted to follow him into the Corps. So, after accidentally misstating my age as seventeen when I was really just sixteen, I joined the Marines and became a Private in the 49th Special Infantry Company, Marine Corps Reserves, since morphed into a detachment of the Corps' 4th Force Recon Battalion.

Rather like the Ghost of Christmas Future, my very first outing as a Marine set the tone for my life to follow. Early in the summer of 1954, sporting the virgin arm of a peon-no-class, or Private, I clambered aboard a creaky twin-engine

DC-3 for my very first airplane ride and flew to San Diego for two weeks of combat training. The highlight of this joyous summer-camp experience came when, after being thrown into a swimming pool carrying a full combat load and surviving, I found myself scrambling down the boarding nets of a troop ship as a member of Boat Team 1-1, a participant in an amphibious warfare extravaganza that involved recapturing San Diego's five-star Coronado Island luxury resort from the "bad guys," whoever they were. Off we went at flank speed for the beach where, the instant our boat touched bottom, the Navy coxswain dropped the front ramp and invited us to leave. With helmets strapped on tight, gas-operated, clip-fed, semiautomatic, M-1 rifles at port arms, and fierce looks on our faces, we did our very best imitations of John Wayne in *Sands of Iwo Jima,* as we charged ashore - to find an entire artillery battalion sitting there wondering where the hell we'd been.

Almost a year later, I graduated from my alma mater, Sparks High School, by skipping my senior year. So, still sixteen years old, but now with the single stripe of a PFC (Private First Class) on my arm, I left my reserve unit and joined the regular Marines. But I wasn't the only wet-behind-the-ears kid throwing himself into the vortex of the Cold War with gusto. Other equally enthusiastic teenagers were also entering the fray, albeit on the other side. Decades later several of them were to become my friends. But before becoming the bosom buddies we are today, we were to spend a few delightful decades trying to kill each other, usually in someone else's country.

I began my active duty Marine career with the traditional first bump in every Marine's life, an exercise in legalized sadism known as boot camp. In May of 1955, the bus carrying me to the Marine Recruit Depot in San Diego stopped in front of the most colorful collection of summer camp counselors I'd ever seen. The Marines call them DIs, Drill Instructors. Their job is to take motley young brats like me, strip them of their civilian identities, and remodel them into moving parts of the Marine Corps' well-oiled "Mean Green Fighting Machine."

author's collection

Reno, Nevada, 1954: Marine Corps Birthday Ball at the El Cortez Hotel. I'm second from the right and the only Marine not in Dress Blues. My unit thought I was seventeen years old when, in fact, I was just sixteen. But either way, I was being honored as the youngest Marine at the ball. The gentleman at the back in coat and tie is former Nevada Governor Grant Sawyer.

Bereft of my greasy blue-jeans and cowboy shirt, shorn like a sheep and issued some cow chip green uniforms, I was ready to join in the fun and games, cleaning toilets, raking dirt in an orderly fashion and learning how to sleep with the pieces of a disassembled M-1 rifle without having its bolt end up in the wrong aperture of my anatomy. We also learned how to stroll in step, Marine-style, took midnight walks on the wild side of the Grinder with our roommates, and played with our guns—excuse me, rifles - all on three hours sleep a night. I didn't find most of this much of a problem, since I'd had my very own over-and-under 410/.22 cal. rifle/shotgun since I was ten, roamed the hills around Reno by myself for days on end, and had some experience in an elite Marine Reserve unit and a stripe to prove it. So mostly I just went along with the program until, one day, the DI's called me in to complain that I was spoiling their efforts by having too much fun. From then on, they promised, they would make a special effort to make me as miserable as everyone else, so I would feel like I belonged. They even arranged a special birthday surprise for me. On the morning of June 9, 1955, my seventeenth birthday, I was invited to a ceremony at which I was asked to sign a sworn affidavit revealing my true age or go to the brig—my choice. I chose to sign it. They even gave me a copy I still have as a souvenir. From boot camp I headed off to Camp Pendleton for combat training via a month of mess duty and was then assigned to the 7th Marine Regiment. Little did I imagine that within months I'd be off to greener, muggier climes.

T W O

THE IMPORTANCE OF
BEING STUPID

In high school I vaguely knew where Central America was. But I didn't spend time thinking about it. Football and girls, track and girls, glee club and girls, even debate and girls, (you should have seen my debate partner!). But Central America? No way! So, little did I suspect that even as I panted and sighed my way through several adolescent infatuations, the fickle middle finger of fate was flipping me off in that direction. Or at least that's the only explanation I can come up for my being the youngest Marine at the Marine Corps Annual Birthday Balls in Nicaragua in 1956, '57, and '58, , and then the oldest at the Ball in Honduras in 1987, '88, and '89, with assignments in Guatemala and El Salvador sandwiched in between. Who cares, you may ask. Well I do, for one, as does every Marine. At a Marine Ball the first slices of the birthday cake are traditionally given to the youngest and the oldest Marines present, who then gives it to his lady. For four of those Balls, my lady was the lovely Costa Rican lass who's still my wife.

My Central America-centric, life-long odyssey began when I was promoted to Corporal at the tender age of seventeen while with the 7th Marines at Camp Pendleton, the unit to which I'd been assigned after boot camp and combat training. The promotion made me the youngest noncommissioned officer (NCO) anyone had ever seen. The other NCOs in the regiment, all eons older than me, joyously welcomed me into their ranks in time-honored fashion by "pinning on" my stripes with their fists, one blow to my shoulder per stripe, an experience that was to be a life changer. In agony from the pounding my arms had taken, I was wandering around the base semi-comatose when a flyer caught my eye. It read, "Wanted: Volunteers for Embassy Guard Duty. Must be NCO and have at least three years remaining on enlistment." It sounded like a great way to get the hell out of the infantry, although when I mentioned it to my squad-bay buddies, they looked at me like I was nuts.

I remember my Sergeant, with a sad shake of his head, screaming at me in his usual dulcet tones, "You stupid asshole! You ain't @#*ing qualified for that shit. They use that shit to con real Marines into re-upping, not boot assholes like you!" (Note to my readers: Throughout this book, @#* stands for a Marine term of endearment.)

When I pointed out that the flyer said nothing about reenlisting, he answered, "Well, you ain't gonna get it, that's for @#*ing sure! But if you want to piss off the Gunny, go ahead and ask him."

So I did—piss off my Gunny, the Marine name of a platoon sergeant, who stared at me in disbelief and shouted at me in his usual dulcet voice, "You dumb shit! Are you out of your @#*ing mind? You gotta reenlist to get that shit!"

When I showed him the flyer, he too said, "Well, if you want to piss off the Sergeant Major, go ahead." And I did—piss off the Sergeant Major that is.

And so it went up the chain of command until I found myself standing at attention before the Regimental Commander, a

Bird Colonel, who said, "What the hell. I don't think you'll get it. But there's no reason for you not to apply." (Expletives diminish and grammar improves, slightly, up the chain of command.)

So off went my application signed by the Colonel and then, silence, and yet more silence, until one day the Gunny called me in and said with an evil grin, "Brown, you just got orders to Oki. Your plane leaves in two weeks." So much for Embassy Duty: Or so I thought.

Thankfully, I was saved by the bell. Just days before I was to fly off to Okinawa, a second set of orders arrived that trumped the first, ordering me to report to Fox Company, Headquarters, Marine Corps (HQMC), for training as a Marine Security Guard (MSG). That's how I, a newly minted seventeen-year-old boot Corporal, came to be standing rigidly at attention, orders in hand, straight off the Greyhound bus from California, reporting in to one of the gruffest Old Corps Marine Sergeant Majors in captivity, who looked balefully up at me and greeted me with a cheery, "Who the @#* are you, and what are you doing standing in front of my desk? Get out of my @#*ing light!"

When I handed him my orders, he stared at them, at me, and back at my orders in disbelief. "Who the @#* gave you these? You write them yourself? You gotta be at least twenty-one to be a Marine Embassy Guard!"

But after some thought, he said in the analytical way of all Sergeant Majors, "What the @#*. You're already here, so you might as @#*ing well join the incoming class. But I guarantee your ass is gonna wash out, and then it'll be mine, and I'll hand you a toilet brush and make you 'Captain of the Head' (Marine-ese for chief toilet cleaner) for the rest of your @#*ing enlistment."

To some this may not sound like a particularly warm and fuzzy welcome. But for a Marine it was pretty typical. Besides, after that greeting, I wasn't about to wash out. If there was one thing I'd already learned to hate, it was cleaning toilets.

About halfway through MSG training, I found out the truth, revealed here for the very first time. One evening at the slop chute (Marine-ese for beer hall) I was downing a cool coke (I was too young to buy beer), when a Sergeant I'd known at Pendleton appeared before my very eyes. Sometime before I made Corporal, he'd been transferred to Headquarters Marine Corps (HQMC), where he was in charge of preparing the volunteer packets for Embassy duty.

"Hey, Brown!" he said, "I see you made it. You know you're really not old enough to be here, and I was supposed to reject you. But the @#*ing shave-tail Lieutenant I work for is a real shit, so I stuck it to him by slipping your package into a big stack of stuff. The dumb ass signed off on it without reading it. Congrats! His balls are really gonna be caught in a crack when someone finds out. You know you're about ten years younger than anyone else over there." He was exaggerating, of course—there was one just nine years older than me.

To the Sergeant Major's surprise, if not pleasure, I made it through. He was even more surprised when, after perusing the list of available billets, I asked if I could go to Managua, Nicaragua, "Please, sir, pretty please?" He clearly thought I was out of my mind. But since I was the only graduate of Marine Security Guard School ever to volunteer for Managua, he agreed, because, as he so kindly responded, "Why not reward stupidity?" The rest is, as they say, history.

THREE

MANAGUA, NICARAGUA, IS A WONDERFUL PLACE

After a three-day trip with stopovers in Guantanamo Bay, Cuba and the Panama Canal Zone, I reported in to the Gunny in charge of the Marine Security Guard detachment in Managua, who looked at me like I was a freak that should still have been in high school, which, of course, I was. But I was getting used to that sort of reaction. Besides, a few months later I received a third stripe, making me, at age eighteen, possibly the youngest Sergeant in the Marine Corps. That forced everyone but the Gunny to shut up, and he was usually too otherwise occupied to care. Years later, after making Sergeant a second time, I nearly became the oldest Sergeant in the Marine Corps, but that's another story.

Once in Managua, it quickly became obvious that life in the field was somewhat less formal than it had been in the 7th Marines. Situated not too far from the Embassy, the Marine House was a two-story structure on a side street just down from Parque Lilliam, about five hundred square feet of weeds and dead grass named after the sister of Nicaraguan President Luis Somoza. Among the house's more delightful architectural features was an intermittent waterfall that cascaded from the second floor down the stairs into the living room when it rained, which was about every other day, turning it into a swimming pool for the biggest cockroaches I'd ever seen. The neighbors were also interesting. Right across the street was a thriving establishment the Gunny once delicately described in a report to Washington as an "open-air sporting house." A favorite pastime of my fellow Marines and their guests was to sit quietly on the second-floor balcony watching the entertainment. And on a quiet night, while standing guard, I could hear the screams of the poor bastards being tortured in the prison behind the military headquarters on top of the hill above the Embassy and hear the roars of the lions that patrolled its perimeter.

Washington, DC had been the first exotic city I'd ever visited. But at least the people there spoke peculiarly accented but somewhat comprehensible English, you could drink water straight out of the tap, and the sewers worked. But Managua was *really* foreign, a new world of different customs and foods where the natives spoke a different language, lived in strange houses, and it was hot as hell all the time, not just in the summer. I'd been Spanish Club President at Sparks High, but when I arrived in Managua I couldn't even order a cup of coffee, since no one there spoke "Nevado-Spanglish." But, then, I also had a hard time understanding some of the Americans at the Embassy, especially those from the south or down east. Still, and despite the heat and humidity, neither anything like Nevada weather, I spent much of my spare time walking around the city to get a feel for the place. In 1972, many years later, Managua was to be almost entirely flattened by a strange, urban-only earthquake. But in those days the architecture of central Managua was still Spanish, and the city was laid out along classic colonial lines, with a central plaza bordered on three sides by a Governor's Palace, Army head-quarters and a cathedral, each representing one of colonial Spain's three centers of power—the Crown, the Army, and the Catholic Church. Just one side was available to civil society and it was occupied by a grand old hotel called, rather unimaginatively, the Gran Hotel.

Managua lies on the southern end of Lake Managua, also known by its pre-Conquest name, Lake Xolotlán, the smaller of Nicaragua's two giant freshwater lakes. Like Washington, DC, Managua became the nation's capital as a compromise between the country's two older, more traditional power centers, León and Granada. When I arrived in 1956, the cathedral and Gran Hotel still stood on the central plaza near the lake or, as Nicaraguans say, *al lago* (towards the lake). But Army headquarters and the *Palacio Presidencial*, the Presidential Palace, had been moved about ten blocks *a la montaña* (towards the mountain) and now sat on the rim of the (hopefully) inactive Tipitapa volcano crater, benevolently smiling or malevolently glowering down on the citizenry beneath, depending on your political opinion. At the time, the Palace was occupied by Luis Somoza Debayle, the second of three Somoza strongmen.

Managua was laid out in a grid made up of stone-paved avenues lined with small businesses and traditional homes of leading families, all built right up to the sidewalk. Prone to tropical deluges, a phenomenon totally alien to Nevadans like me, Managua's streets sat two or three feet below the sidewalks. This allowed them to double as storm drains by turning into instant rivers that carried the water of the torrential rain storms down to the lake. The homes of the relatively wealthy occupied the interior of many of the city's downtown blocks. But, since they faced inward and not outward, with only their carriageways or small entrance doors visible, they were largely masked from public view.

As they still are, the Nicaraguans were very hospitable, and within a few months, I'd visited several of their homes. My first visit to one of them came when I tagged along with another Marine to a party at his girlfriend's home, that of the Amador family, just outside the city center. Only years later did I learn that Don Fausto Amador, the host family's patriarch, was the natural father of Carlos Fonseca Amador, the most famous leader of the Sandinista Front during its revolutionary efforts to oust the Somozas from power. (As used here and throughout this *opus magnum* Don, or the feminine Doña, are honorific titles, not first names.) I still have a signed invitation Don Fausto sent me to an Aviation Day event. At the time I was more interested in a young lady I met there, Ilieana Tunnerman, who invited me to visit her family's more traditional home in the city center.

I was fascinated both by Ilieana and her home. The Tunnermans were German-Nicaraguan descendants of foreign administrators hired generations earlier by elite Spanish-colonial families to manage their business affairs. Towards the end of the colonial period and during the earlier years of Nicaragua's independence, the country's elites considered administrators of European descent as both socially more acceptable and politically safer that teaching the local lower classes management skills. So there were a number of prominent German or French families in the country. The Tunnerman family patriarch, Don Carlos, was a prominent member of the German-Nicaraguan community and President of the Central Bank. (There's that Don, again!)

In sharp contrast to its rather austere exterior, the interior of Iliena's home was built around a central patio alive with greenery, flowering plants, and murmuring fountains, with its rooms ranged along all four sides of a colonnaded porch looking inward toward them. The home's walls were of seemingly ageless adobe, an extraordinarily effective barrier to both the intense heat and the hustle and bustle of life outside, making it a cool, quiet sanctuary from the world beyond.

Not that I was ever free to wander around inside her home even though, or maybe precisely because, my entrée had been through Ilieana. The family was understandably careful with the young American Marine who began to call on their daughter. So mostly we just sat and visited under the watchful eyes of a chaperon, usually her younger brother, Carlos, who grew up to be a secret gunrunner for the Sandinistas and later became Nicaragua's Ambassador to the United States. A bit slow on the uptake, at first I assumed "Carlillos" just happened to be hanging around whenever I visited Iliena—until he went with us to the movies for the third time.

I also became friends with a young Nicaraguan engineer named Remy Rener. Remy was the son of Don Pablo Rener, President of the National Assembly and a close confidant of the Somozas. Of French origin and originally from the Atlantic port of Bluefields, the Reners lived several miles *a la montaña* in the relatively cool hills to Managua's south. Toward the end of my years in Managua, Remy would be a best man at my wedding, and decades later he would be the executor of the estate of then President Luis Somoza. But in those days he was just a young buddy. It didn't take long for me to realize that Managua was really a tale of two cities, the genteel, elegant city of the well-to-do and a much grittier one where the poor lived.

FOUR

HARVESTING THE FRUITS
OF IMPERIALISM

As I mentioned earlier, life in the Marine House in Managua was rather less formal than it had been in the 7th Marines. The Gunny in charge of the detachment set the tone. It took me several weeks to realize that he wasn't married to the young lady who came out of his room every morning and had breakfast with us. Each Marine also had his own room and was allowed to close its door when entertaining company. That resulted in some interesting moments. The house also had an echo, which became especially resonant one evening when one of my Marine colleagues let out the most blood-curdling scream I'd ever heard. He'd been circumcised just that morning and had stitches in his you-know-what, so this may have had something to do with his being—to paraphrase the immortal words of Mae West—happy to see his girlfriend, who was in his room consoling him.

Among the more colorful house traditions were weekly bachelor nights designed to delight Marines and other males with hornier-than-thou attitudes. These usually took the form of both films and live entertainment by young professional ladies and a select group of "friends of the Marines" who were regulars at them. In fact, they were the ones who usually brought the porno flicks. Among the dignitaries in attendance one evening was the Military Attaché, an Army Colonel who, in the spirit of the occasion, was helping one of the young ladies divest herself of her bloomers just as his wife walked in unannounced. But, rather than join the party, she did a smart about-face and left, effectively ending the evening's revelries.

I learned the details when former Commandant of the Marine Corps Lemuel C. Shepherd—wearing his hat as Commanding General of the Inter-American Defense Board (IADB)—arrived in Managua to visit the Nicaraguan battalion assigned to him. Oblivious to the gathering storm, and since I'd never seen a real live four-star General, I was rather looking forward to making his acquaintance and was pleased when the Gunny invited us to fall out in full Dress Blues to greet him.

The scene is still etched in my memory. There we were, standing at attention in the Embassy's foyer as the General arrived, escorted by both the Ambassador and the Military Attaché's wife, who had insisted on riding from the airport with him without her husband in attendance. After greeting the civilian staff, General Shepherd and Ambassador Whelan sidled over to our side of the Embassy foyer to say hello. In true Marine tradition, the General then proceeded to give us—quietly, so the civilians standing on the other side of the foyer couldn't hear him—one of the most colorful royal ass chewings I've ever enjoyed. Being somewhat attuned to conversational nuances, I quickly gathered that he was annoyed by something the Military Attaché's wife had told him. He first commented, rather emotionally I thought, on the goings-on at the Marine House. He then suggested that the whole lot of us might want to pack our sea-bags as we'd soon be receiving orders to rejoin the real Marine Corps as Privates. That was interesting enough. But what happened next was even more memorable.

After General Shepherd finished, but before he could move on to other more pressing matters, like making a head call, Ambassador Whelan, also speaking just loudly enough for us but not the staff across the foyer to hear, engaged the General in what Congress calls a colloquy.

"General," said the Ambassador, "You know, I was a Marine myself during World War One."

"Really, Mr. Ambassador? Semper fi! Once a Marine always a Marine! What unit?"

When the Ambassador told him, the General seemed perplexed. "That's strange, Mr. Ambassador. We were in the same unit, but I don't recall meeting you."

At that point, Ambassador Whelan's smile was replaced by a glare. "I'm not at all surprised General. I went in as a Private in 1917 and came out as a Private in 1919. But one thing the Corps taught me was the chain of command. And these are my Marines!"

Personally, I thought Ambassador Whelan had a point. But what most fascinated me was watching a former Commandant of the Marine Corps, second in importance to a Marine only to their mother and God, get chewed out. Orders did arrive the very next day transferring the Gunny and the two MSG's that had been at the house back to the real Marine Corps, which I thought was rather drastic, since if Marines agree on anything, it's that sex is essential to the well-balanced life. I also couldn't believe that the Military Attaché's wife hadn't known her husband enjoyed it. But then maybe she'd also learned of the photos of his secretary he'd left in his lower right-hand desk drawer where one of my fellow Marines had found them during a security check. At least, having been on duty at the time, I was spared the indignity of being ordered back to the real world.

Being a Marine in Nicaragua in the 1950s was a rare treat in other ways as well. The Somoza's had been put in power by the Marines during their 1930s campaign there, and they loved us for it. So, even though we were only NCOs, Nicaraguan soldiers were under orders to salute us as though we were actual officers and gentlemen, a practice that served me as a constant source of amusement.

The Ambassador, Tom Whelan, a North Dakota Republican, had been appointed by Harry Truman, a Democrat, to get him out of the country lest he defeat Harry's pet Republican Senator, Bill Langer. Whelan wound up staying on as Ambassador until finally being replaced by Kennedy a decade later. It was a colorful learning experience that took place while I was on duty that set me on the path to my future diplomatic life. At the time, a few somewhat churlish scholars, and the occasional nun, were insisting that the United States was a bit too cozy with the Somozas, who were, admittedly, rather short on democratic virtues. But I was on my first diplomatic excursion as a lend-lease Marine, so I had little with which to compare the Somozas except, perhaps, my DIs during boot camp. And compared to them, the Somozas were paragons of liberalism. True, it struck me as odd that the commander of Nicaragua's Customs Service was an American Army Colonel seconded to the Nicaraguan National Guard, in which he was also a Colonel, making him a Double Colonel. I recall one memorable instance when his sudden appearance at a US Air Force base in Texas wearing his Nicaraguan, not American, uniform, complete with the three silver stars of a Nicaraguan Colonel, wreaked protocolary havoc. I also found it a bit curious that the chief of President Somoza's personal bodyguard detachment was a US Secret Service agent and that his confidential secretary was also an American. But I just assumed that was the way we ran things in countries we considered our own backyard. Even the direct, no-dial telephone linking Whelan's desk to that of the President seemed perfectly natural—until "Uncle Tom," as Luis Somoza privately called Ambassador Whelan, used it one evening to stop a war.

Given all that's happened in the region since, it may be hard for some to believe that Central America had problems even before their foreign advisors began insisting that if they gave the region's revolutionaries real guns they should fight real wars. But up until the mid-1950s, unlike the region's more recent Cold War-era civil wars, dustups between Central American countries tended to be rather desultory affairs. And so it came to pass that in late 1956, ostensibly because of unauthorized Honduran incursions into Nicaraguan territory, Honduras and Nicaragua began to throw shadow punches at one another. The Managua media was full of reports of impending war, and day after day the local newspapers were reporting that columns of heavily armed Nicaraguan Guardia Nacional troops were advancing on the enemy and heroes were being made by the hour.

As a budding analyst I had some doubts, since Nicaragua's troops had reportedly been trying to get to the border for more than a week, even though it was just a few hours by bus. So I couldn't help but wonder what was taking them so long and decided to ask a friend, a Managua-based international press stringer. A semi-professional saloon crawler, even though the war was supposedly heating up, he hadn't budged from his corner stool at the bar of the Gran Hotel, then Managua's premiere watering hole. So I walked downtown to ask him why he wasn't at the front covering the war. His answer taught me a lesson in journalism that has stayed with me ever since. First, he patiently explained, they didn't have ice at the front. And besides, American journalists weren't expected to report what was really going on. The editors back in the states decide what the facts about foreign events were, not mere eyewitnesses. A stringer's job was just to provide local color that would lend credence to whatever the papers decided to publish. Staffers in his organization's New York offices would then write the story, sometimes even using some of his input, to fit editorial policy. So if he sent them facts that clashed with what they wanted to publish, he would simply sow confusion and generate animosities toward himself that might shorten his drinking career. And that was an outcome he considered hardly worth the risk. Besides, he added, there was no war underway. It was all *pedos y resbalones*, a delightful Spanish phrase I promptly added to my vocabulary, meaning roughly "farting into a hurricane."

Later that starry eve, as the breezes off Lake Managua sent the temperature plunging into the low nineties, I headed for work at the Embassy. Since it was raining cats and dogs, this involved a rather invigorating after-dark excursion, wading knee-deep through open-air rain drains wearing the upper half of my summer Dress Blues, shower shoes, and a bathing suit, while holding my trousers and spit-shined shoes over my head beneath my umbrella. Once there and suitably attired, I relieved the Marine on duty and took my place of honor at the entrance.

By and large, guarding an empty Embassy is pretty boring, not least because most employees avoid the place after work like the plague. Once in a while, a sympathetic staffer would slip by with coffee, or a military attaché would race in to get his porno collection. On occasion, even the Ambassador Himself would show up, as was the case the night "Long Tom" Whelan taught me my first major lesson in cutting-edge foreign policy implementation.

Always a delight, Whelan arrived unexpectedly that evening, holding a rather tall rum and coke in each hand. Normally, neither Marines standing guard duty nor eighteen-year-olds drink alcohol. And I was both. Plus, to paraphrase John Paul Jones, I had not yet begun to drink. But I had learned to obey orders. So when the Ambassador handed one of them to me and ordered me to drink it, I tried my best to obey. He then headed upstairs to make a phone call to deliver what diplomats daintily call a *démarche*. For those unfamiliar with diplo-speak, *démarche* is a Frenchified diplomatic term for anything from the mildest of milquetoasty remonstrations to a royal ass chewing delivered via diplomatic channels by a representative of one country to another. Since Whelan left his office door open as he proceeded to deliver one of the latter, I was about to learn, rum and coke clutched tightly in hand, how real diplomacy is conducted. I already knew, since I'd overheard other conversations between them, that when using their direct line, both the Ambassador and the President tended to be fairly informal with one another. Whelan usually addressed President Luis Somoza as "Louie," and Somoza usually addressed Whelan as "Uncle Tom." So that part of this particular conversation came as no surprise.

author's collection

Managua, 1957: I'm standing guard by sitting at a desk next to the main entrance to the American Embassy in Managua protected by the selfsame plate glass window a sniper put a hole through trying to kill me. If the sniper had been a better shot, I wouldn't be writing this book.

But it quickly became obvious that, this time, their conversation would be more than just a friendly chat. Apparently, Washington was less than entirely pleased with the ongoing dustup between Nicaragua and Honduras because it was disturbing the tranquility of a region we consider our private reserve. And if anyone was going to disturb the region's tranquility it was going to be us, not some Central Americans. I was about to hear one side of a masterful, if somewhat indelicately delivered, forceful *démarche*.

At first Whelan spoke so softly I couldn't follow the conversation. But, apparently, Somoza made the mistake of arguing that, because Honduras had started the whole damn thing, Nicaragua shouldn't be held responsible. If so, Whelan wasn't buying. To be precise, America's pro-consul-esque Ambassador, a former Marine, raised his voice and told Nicaragua's President (and I quote from memory), "Goddamn it, Louie, that's *pura mierda*. I don't give a shit if the @#*ing Hondurans did start the @#*ing war! You get your @#*ing troops off the border or I'm going to shove a battalion of Marines right up your ass!"

Since there was, in fact, a Marine battalion afloat nearby on its way to Panama, Louie got the message, the war ended, and I was able to add a word in French to my burgeoning foreign affairs vocabulary. The expletives I already knew. On his way out, Whelan winked and ordered me to finish my drink. Then and there, I began to fantasize about becoming a diplomat one day.

FIVE

PRESIDENTIAL POOL PARTY

Of course, being a Marine Security Guard was not just a matter of standing post inside the Embassy in a military manner. During his first inspection visit to Managua, a new Marine Regional Officer made a serious attempt to suck up to the Ambassador by telling Whelan that he could also use us as ceremonial guards. And so, about three weeks after his visit, I found myself standing at attention at the entrance to the Ambassador's swimming pool, saluting distinguished invitees as they arrived for a poolside soirée. At least the uniform of the day wasn't full Dress Blues, as they're hotter than a horse blanket laid over a mare in heat. Instead, I was wearing tropical Delta Blues. Not that my relatively comfortable attire made it in easier to keep a straight face.

Whelan, being a well-practiced if not consummate diplomat, greeted each guest and whoever they had with them with a warm, plastic smile and a booming welcome. Then, as soon as they were out of earshot, he would make a snide side remark only I could hear. When one Ambassador arrived with his particularly horse-faced wife, Whelan greeted him with open arms, then turned to his wife, and said, "My dear, you're more beautiful than ever tonight." As they moved on, he then commented under his breath, in an aside only I could hear, "Which isn't a compliment. She's uglier than his horse."

When another appeared with a stunning young lady on his arm, again he greeted them with a warm smile and said essentially the same thing, "My dear, you're more beautiful than ever this evening." Then, as they too moved along, he added, "She should be. She's his mistress. But what the hell, he has good taste."

After greeting the Ambassador of Mexico, who arrived with his two daughters in tow, Whelan turned to me and said, "They're yours," which is when I learned that I was not there just to serve as a ceremonial guard. I was also there as a working member of the Ambassador's staff and had an assigned mission.

In addition to numerous Ambassadors, the guests included the Foreign Minister and both the then President of Nicaragua, Luis Somoza, and the country's future President, Luis's younger brother, Anastacio "Tachito" Somoza, who was, at the time, the Commanding General of Nicaragua's armed forces. While I'd been to a number of Embassy parties since arriving in Nicaragua, this was my first reception at the official residence. So, after the last guests arrived, Whelan dismissed me from my post, and I began to circulate. I found almost all of the conversations the guests were having with one another to be inane, or at least deadly boring, until I reached the Mexican Ambassador's daughters. They had apparently been primed in advance, and we immediately became good friends. Between their company, and an occasional lingering glance down the décolletage of a passing ambassadorial mistress, the evening passed rather quickly.

When the reception began to break up, the Ambassadors and assorted lesser mortals, including the American

Embassy officers that were there, began taking their leave. Regrettably, this included both of the Mexican Ambassador's daughters and all the prime examples of feminine pulchritude, leaving only paunches, uniforms, and wrinkled shirts. But apparently their departure signaled the beginning of the real festivities, as everyone still present promptly made a beeline for the bar, where the evening's serious drinking began. As the hour advanced, it became evident that I was the only person around the pool not getting soused out of my mind, not counting the servants. And even some of them were taking the occasional nip. This gave me a new source of carefully masked amusement as I watched Whelan, the President, his brother General Somoza, and the Foreign Minister become more and more animated and less and less coordinated.

I'm still not sure why, but Whelan decided to end the evening's revelries with a bang, or more precisely, a splash, by pushing the Commanding General of the Nicaraguan Army into the swimming pool, uniform and all. Being quite a large man, he made quite a large splash. Not to be outdone, the President, on seeing his brother take an unexpected swim, sidled over to Whelan and gave him a shove that propelled a second rotund body into the pool. That left only three dry guests, the Foreign Minister, the President, and me. Being a consummate diplomat, the Foreign Minister joined them by leaping into the pool unassisted. Not certain how to react, and too junior in rank to join the august assembly in the pool anyway, especially not while wearing Dress Blues and carrying a pistol, I snapped to attention and gave a smart hand salute as the President joined the fray. After splashing around awhile, they all then climbed out of the pool and headed for the bar for another drink.

At that point Whelan, perhaps slightly sobered by his unexpected swim, came over, looked me straight in the eye, and asked, "Did you see anything?"

"No, sir!"

"Good. Then get the hell out of here."

And I did.

SIX

(Milton) Eisenhower Panics Panama

My tour in Nicaragua coincided with the Eisenhower presidency although, as a lowly Marine NCO, he was a bit above my pay grade, as was almost everyone else, including his brother Milton. Besides, I was a teenager, and more interested in girls than politics. Still, some things did catch my attention. The Cold War was quickly getting into full swing nearby, and I began hearing more and more about what was happening. Fidel Castro and his merry band had left Mexico for the Cuban Sierra Maestra to begin the Revolution that would put him in perpetual power, and other revolutionary groups were getting it on in Nicaragua, El Salvador and Guatemala. All this effervescence had made my Commander in Chief, Ike, rather antsy. So Ike named his brother Milton "Special Ambassador of the United States for Latin American Affairs" and sent him to the region on a fact-finding trip. Milton began his tour in Panama where, at the time, we controlled a piece of real estate known as the Panama Canal Zone. His visit took place well before the displacement of casts of thousands became a routine part of the travels of every truly senior official on an official trip abroad, so the arrangements were not quite up to today's standards.

In the 1950s, trips of that sort involved mere dozens, not the hundreds they do today. But even back then no one wanted to lose President Eisenhower's brother, at least not on their watch, which led to a fascinating but little reported incident. When Milton arrived in Panama, someone in his entourage suddenly realized they had forgotten to provide for his personal security during his tour. Given the growing effervescence in the region—assassinations, coups, counter-coups, mobs, the occasional armed insurgency and so forth—when someone mentioned their concern for Milton's safety to the Commander in Chief, Southern Command, (CINCSOUTH), the CINC said he'd be happy to provide a platoon of troops. Milton's escort replied that, while a platoon would be nice, they would have neither the training nor the security clearances needed to perform the mission.

The CINC then became creative, "Not to worry. The Marines at the Embassy have both. So we'll just send them."

The screw-up in charge of Milton's visit apparently replied, "Sure, why not?" which is when things got interesting.

Realizing that stripping Embassy Panama of its Marine Security Guards would leave it unguarded, the CINC ordered the nearest Marine unit, the ready platoon at Coco Solo Naval Base, to go protect the Embassy—*now!* Of course no one told the Marines what to protect it from. But then, no one ever does. So they just slapped on their helmets and grabbed their rifles, a few bandoliers of ammunition, some grenades and a machine gun or two and, loaded for bear, boarded a convoy of trucks and roared out of the Canal Zone and across Panama City to the Embassy. It was a holiday weekend, so no one was there to greet them except for one Marine Guard.

No problem. The officer in command of the platoon told the guard to tell the Non-Commissioned Officer in Charge (NCOIC) of the MSG detachment to order all of his Marines to report immediately, and in civilian clothes, to Eisenhower's entourage to serve as his protective detachment during his tour of Central America.

When the detachment Gunny received this order (or so I was told later), he blanched and responded, "Sir, I'll do my best. But that will leave the Embassy completely unguarded, except for me."

"No problem, Gunny. I'll just have my men stand guard for you inside."

"Sorry, sir. Can't do that. Your Marines don't have the right security clearances."

"Really?" the commanding 2nd Lt. replied, "Then I'll just have them hang around outside." And that's exactly what he did by setting up a hasty defensive perimeter around the Embassy, including triple strings of concertina wire, sand-bagged machine gun positions, snipers on the roof, anti-vehicle barriers, the usual stuff.

All in all, it was a rather good show, except for one tiny problem. No one had bothered to tell the Ambassador what was being done. This might not have bothered him too much, until Panamanian President de la Guardia called him and asked, "Mr. Ambassador is something going on I should know about?"

"Why do you ask, Mr. President?" said the Ambassador.

"Because there are a whole bunch of your Marines with guns and stuff, setting up all sorts of stuff around your Embassy, so I thought maybe you know something I don't." (President de la Guardia spoke Dartmouth not Marine English.) This revelation caught the Ambassador totally off

guard. But by the time the Embassy's Security Officer, or anyone else, managed to unscramble the mess, Milton's plane
was already wheels up.

I didn't catch onto any of this until I went up to the Casa
Grande, the Ambassador's residence in Managua, to take a
dip in the pool. Whelan always kept cold beer (and cold Coke
for me) in his fridge and let his Marine Guards use his pool
pretty much any time we wanted to, except when there was
an official reception going on. So I jumped on a bus, (literally, since Nicaraguan buses rarely stop when picking up passengers), swimming trunks in hand, jumped off it at the stop
nearest the residence, and headed up the hill. The walk up
from the Pan-American Highway seemed perfectly normal
until I arrived at the house and saw one of my buddies from
MSG school standing at the door in civilian clothes and carrying a weapon, which seemed rather odd. Not the weapon—I
was used to those. It seemed odd for him to be in Managua in
civvies (civilian clothes) carrying one. But I just said hi, went
into the Casa Grande, got into my trunks, and was almost in
the pool when I caught a glimpse of President Eisenhower's
brother talking with the Ambassador. At that point, I executed a smart about-face, jumped back into civvies, and ran
back down the hill as fast as I could before someone could put
me to work.

SEVEN

THERE BE DRAGUNOVS!

One of my more interesting excursions from Nicaragua took place late in my tour when secret orders arrived for me to put on civvies, leave my uniforms behind, and grab the next plane to Guatemala for unspecified duties. It was the first of many classified sets of orders I received as a Marine, and very intriguing. I dutifully hung my uniforms in the closet at the Marine house, packed my bags with clothes two sizes too small, and hitched a ride to Managua's airport. Once there, it was difficult for me to remain incognito since, from time to time, damn near everybody at the airport had seen me pick up the diplomatic pouch from couriers as they passed through. But I did my best to look like an ordinary visitor with a short haircut, light skin, blue eyes, and, since I was still a growing teenager, pants two inches too short.

When I boarded the flight for Guatemala I found three other short-haired Gringos already aboard who looked a hell of a lot like people with whom I'd gone through boot camp. They were also in civvies, sitting in economy and looking much like I did, both excited and bewildered. One was from the detachment in Panama City, and the other two were from the detachment in Costa Rica. When we arrived in Guatemala City, we tried our best to blend in with the local brown-skinned, four-foot-two Maya Indians, since no one from the Guatemala City Embassy was there to meet us, and none of us knew where it was located. So at first we just milled around inside the terminal waiting for someone to show up, which they didn't. Eventually we realized that was getting us nowhere, so we decided to take the initiative, went through immigration and customs using our official passports, and began to mill around outside instead.

After about half an hour, a taxi driver came up to us and asked, "Are you the new Marines for the American Embassy?"

"No," I said, "But take us there anyway." So much for secret missions!

At the Embassy, we were greeted by a couple of Marines from the Guatemala detachment as well as a more mature gentleman who turned out to be a Secret Service agent from Washington. Apparently, while stumbling around the colonial-era aqueduct behind the Ambassador's residence, someone had tripped over a loaded Soviet-made Dragunov sniper rifle, complete with scope, aimed at his dining room window. Although there was no sniper attached to it, the Embassy Security Officer still leaped to the conclusion that someone just might have been interested in killing him.

At first Ambassador Sparks pooh-poohed the problem, insisting that no one would want to shoot him. Since this was before killing American diplomats became an international sport, had the sniper succeeded Sparks would have earned his place in the *Guinness Book of World Records* as the first American Ambassador to have his head blown off by a bullet from a Dragunov. Ten years later the honor of being the first American Ambassador to Guatemala to be killed by terrorists went to one of his successors, John Gordon Mein. But since Sparks couldn't imagine anyone wanting to single him out for such an honor, he initially refused to have bodyguards.

That changed when the Secret Service agent arrived in Guatemala City unannounced, walked past the guards into the Embassy without being challenged, took the elevator to the Ambassador's office, walked past his secretary, slapped a pistol down on his desk, and said, "If I were an assassin, you'd be dead now, Mr. Ambassador." At that, and despite his sense of invincibility, Ambassador Sparks agreed, which is how I found myself carrying a carbine, dressed in a lightweight, tropical suit, spending night after freezing night "snooping and pooping" around the Ambassador's carefully manicured garden, waiting for the next sniper to appear.

Although I could not have known it at the time, several experiences in Central America were to be sneak previews of events to come decades later. One of them took place at the residence of the Spanish Ambassador to Guatemala. One evening I accompanied Ambassador Sparks to a diplomatic reception as his bodyguard. We arrived in an Embassy car in which I sat in the back pretending to be the Ambassador while he sat in front next to the driver pretending to be me, making me the prime target should someone try to shoot the Ambassador. By then I spoke Spanglish fairly well. But I was not yet the sort of striped-pants cookie pusher one invites to a diplomatic soirée. My job at the reception was just to stand near the Ambassador to take any bullets that might come his way.

The guest of honor was Guatemalan Army Colonel Miguel Ydigoras Fuentes, at the time the momentary President of Guatemala. After greeting Ambassador Sparks, much to my surprise, Ydigoras reached back to greet me as well, asking me my name which, of course, I gave him. A few months earlier, Ydigoras had become President in the time-honored Latin

American tradition by riding into Guatemala City astride a tank, driving to the Presidential Palace, and suggesting to the sitting President that he might want to take a break from his arduous duties. Long after Ydigoras became an ogre in the eyes of many for helping the United States with preparations for the Bay of Pigs invasion, this encounter was to be the key to one of my more interesting experiences in El Salvador midway through my diplomatic career.

But perhaps the most portentous incident had taken place in Managua earlier, shortly after I arrived. One evening, while attending a lecture by a visiting American professor of philosophy at the Centro Cultural Nicaragüense-Norteamericano, a tall, fortyish Nicaraguan gentleman sat down beside me. Waiting for the speaker to begin, I struck up a conversation with him in my inimitable broken Spanish. I don't remember what we talked about. But I do remember that during the question period, he asked the lecturer what he thought of Marxism. I also remember the lecturer's response. "I don't think about Marxism at all. I'm a philosopher not a politician. Dogmas don't interest me." The next morning the Legal Attaché at the Embassy, one of the spooks-in-residence, told me that the man seated next to me at the lecture was a member of the Central Committee of the clandestine Communist Party of Nicaragua.

Fast forward: Forty-odd years later in Mexico City in June of 2000, eight years after I retired from the Foreign Service, earned a PhD, and became a post-doctoral scholar of sorts. As part of my ongoing research into the revolutionary side of Central America's late Cold War travails, a tall, slender Nicaraguan named Noel Guerrero Santiago was to give me his oral history. Jose "Pepe" Puente, a post-Foreign Service friend who had been the key liaison between Central America's revolutionaries and the Soviet KGB and Cuban DGI stations in Mexico City, brought us together. During the early years of both the Cuban and Nicaraguan revolutions, Puente had been taught guerrilla warfare tactics by Guerrero, whom he called *El Patriarca,* the Patriarch.

Guerrero had never before allowed himself to be photographed, much less interviewed on camera, and it took a number of meetings for me to convince him to give me his oral history. In the end he agreed, but only after extracting from me a promise from me not to make any of what he told me public until after his death.

What Guerrero told me blew my mind. He explained that he'd been a founding member of Nicaragua's Communist Party and an active Communist agent since the 1930s and early 1940s. He spent several of those years in the United States when such activities were controlled by Earl Browder, General Secretary of the Communist Party USA. In effect, although it wasn't the label he used when describing himself, Guerrero had been in the United States working as a COMINTERN labor organizer. Guerrero also told me that he'd been in Nicaragua during the run up to the 1956 assassination of the first Somoza strong man, Anastasio "Tacho" Somoza García. When I asked if he'd had a hand in its planning, he just smiled.

Guerrero also confirmed something Puente had told me that after the triumph of the Cuban revolution: He'd been "Che" Guevara's top confidential aide in Havana after Fidel Castro's victory. I found his story fascinating, but one of his most counter-historical claims especially hard to believe. The prevailing story is that the Sandinista Front was created in Central America by a small group of young Nicaraguan idealists under the leadership of Carlos Fonseca Amador. Guerrero told

author's collection

Mexico City, 2007. Jose Obidio "Pepe" Puente, a Cold War enemy turned good friend. While he was a college student, Puente served first as a personal aide to Noel Guerrero and then to Fidel Castro; participated in the meeting in Havana at which the Nicaraguan Sandinista Front, the FSLN, was organized; went on to manage the Front's safe house in Colonia Linda Vista, Mexico City, where I've recently stayed several times as his guest; and served as its liaison with Cuban intelligence and the KGB until 1979, when he temporarily became the tenth member of the Sandinista's ruling junta. In 1965, Puente was best man at the Mexico City wedding of Carlos Fonseca, the best know leader of the revolutionary era FSLN, to Maria Hayde Terán. Puente tells his story in Chapter 2 of my *When the AK47s Fall Silent,* Hoover, 2000.

me that this version of when and how the Sandinista Front's was founded was a cover story invented to hide how it has really been created. He insisted that he, not Carlos Fonseca, had been the first leader of the Sandinistas, and that the Front had been created in Havana under the watchful eyes of Cuban Intelligence, not in Central America, his being "Che" Guevara's "watchful" eyes. When I mentioned this to Puente, he seconded Guerrero's version, and added that he had also been present in Havana at the Front's creation, and that Guerrero had, indeed, been its first leader. But, even then I wasn't completely convinced until, in 2004, when Guerrero's role as the Front's original leader was definitively confirmed by, of all people, General Humberto Ortega, the brother of Nicaraguan President Daniel Ortega, and former Commander in Chief of the Sandinista People's Army (Ejercito Popular Sandinista, EPS), in his monumental *La Epopeya de la Insurrección* (Managua, LEA Grupo Editorial, 2004 —pages 101, 125, 129 and 131-133 - for those as incredulous as I was).

Guerrero also confirmed that he was an expert in guerrilla warfare and, during Che Guevara's tenure as President of Cuba's Central Bank, was Che's top advisor on fomenting revolutions elsewhere. He also confirmed that in the early 1960s he'd spent well over a year in Tegucigalpa, Honduras, training the first group of Sandinistas in guerrilla warfare and that Carlos Fonseca and Pepe Puente were among those he trained. Again, and contrary to Cold War-era legend, this raised the possibility that it may have been Guerrero, not Spanish Civil War General Alberto Bayo y Giroud, who taught Guevara guerrilla warfare. He also confirmed to me that he was the man I'd met in Managua.

Noel Guerrero – Santiago - El Patriarca

author's collection

Near the Glorieta Riviera, Mexico City, June 22, 2000: Noel Guerrero Santiago, a founding director of Nicaragua's Communist Party, was once a labor union organizer in the United States. A guerrilla warfare expert, he was a confidential aid of Ernesto "Che" Guevara. Guerrero, not Carlos Fonseca Amador, as is widely believed, was the first leader of Nicaragua's Sandinista National Liberation Front as has now been acknowledged by General Humberto Ortega, the brother of Nicaraguan president Daniel Ortega. Guerrero, who passed away recently, was arguably the most important Latin American revolutionary the world has never heard of. In Mexico City in 2000, Guerrero, allowed me to videotape his oral history interview on condition that it not be made public during his lifetime. This picture of Guerrero, taken from his oral history interview video, may be the first picture of him ever published.

EIGHT

THE BAY OF PIGS: A LOVE STORY

For me personally, the most important event I attended during my years in Managua was a birthday party. The party was for Jack Starbird, a US Agency for International Development (USAID) employee, thrown for him by his Costa Rican wife, Bruni, and most of those invited were Jack's friends or colleagues. But, since her seventeen-year-old niece, Leda, was living with them at the time, she decided to invite someone more her niece's age as well. Being the only sober Marine in Managua, I was the chosen one (sobriety does have its virtues). When we first met, Leda was singularly unimpressed, but I was star-struck. And since she spoke very little English, I immediately began studying Spanish with a vengeance.

After I spent several months of valiant efforts to woo her, Leda returned to her home in San José, Costa Rica. But I wasn't about to give up. In those days, there was no internet, much less Skype or Facebook. Leda's family didn't even have a telephone. The nearest one to her was an old, hand-cranked one in Don Basilio's corner store across the street from where she lived. So I was left with a choice - abandon the chase or visit Costa Rica whenever I could scrape up enough money and con the Gunny into a couple days of leave. Pan American Airways, now defunct, soon became my commuter of choice, the San José Marine House my crash pad, and a downtown juice bar my hangout when I couldn't be with Leda (I was *still* too young to drink!). Thankfully, because Leda's family was very traditionally Spanish, her father saved me from going broke by flat out refusing to let us go on dates. No movies, no dinners, no dances, only short visits with her in her home under the watchful eyes of her mother, father, two brothers, grandmother, a couple of aunts, and as many cousins as her family could scrape together. In fact, and probably to the shock of my readers, Leda and I didn't go out on our first date until after we were engaged, and then just once, and with a chaperone. I later learned that even that concession was made only after a heated family argument settled in the traditional Spanish manner, not by her father or mother, but by her grandmother, Doña Luisa, the family matriarch. A clueless Gringo, I didn't understand just how much chaos my courting caused or how many unforgivable social mistakes I made. But we're still together more than fifty-six years later, so it must have worked.

I began the Costa Rica campaign of my courtship of Leda by simply showing up unannounced at her home in Barrio Santa Lucía, San José, an especially egregious example of my cluelessness. The very first time I went to her home to see her, her brother Carlos opened the door, and I simply walked in and found her sitting in the living room in her bathrobe, her face painted with a dozen or more bright red iodine spots. To their credit, her parents didn't just throw me out (which is what they probably should have done). Instead, while Leda fled to her room to make herself presentable, her mother Doña Maria, politely offered me a cool glass of buttermilk, flavored with strawberry syrup. I duly quaffed it down, albeit with a pained smile on my face, since I hate the stuff and it gives me a bellyache, and worse.

From then on I tried to forewarn her of when I planned to visit by leaving a message with Don Basilio, although between her weak English, my miserable Spanish, the bad phone connection, and my complete lack of understanding of how such things should be handled, she didn't always get the word. Still, her family slowly became more or less resigned to my random appearances at their door and managed to tolerate the strange foreigner that kept showing up. A couple of times we even played games, one of which involved everyone there that was under twenty-one holding hands while the person first in line stuck one of their fingers in a light socket. It was, I must admit, a rather unusual form of entertainment. But since it was one of the few times that her family would let me hold her hand, I looked forward to it with relish.

During the long hours between visits, I took to wandering around central San José getting to know the city, its churches, neighborhoods, stores, plazas, parks, and museums. It didn't take long for me to realize that there was more going on than just the usual city life. In nearby neighborhoods, I saw women in house after house busy sewing. That wouldn't have seemed unusual, since sewing was a daily task for many *Josefinas*, except that they were sewing olive-green uniforms. I also noticed that a small *pensión*, bed-and-breakfast, just a few doors down from Leda's home, housed some young men with dark beards who bustled in and out at all hours of the day and night wearing furtive looks and chattering away in a Spanish dialect that was all but incomprehensible to me. Other young men with beards and accents were manning small kiosks on the Avenida Central side of the Costa Rican Central Bank in downtown San José, talking with other young men lined up in front. And at night, on my way back to the Marine house, I sometimes saw covered trucks race by. Many years later, Plutarco Hernández confirmed that the *pensíon* near Leda's home had been the local safe house where both Fidel Castro and Che Guevara stayed during visits to Costa Rica. He also confirmed that the clothes being sewn were uniforms and that the kiosks were recruiting stations.

As the end of my tour in Managua approached I began to realize that, once I left Nicaragua, it would be all but impossible to continue my courtship. So I had to make a decision. I was still a minor, as was Leda, so we were much too young to get married. But it would be almost impossible for me to commute from the United States to see her. Besides, she had any number of better-qualified, local gallants just waiting to court her. So I decided to ask her to marry me. With that settled, at least in my own mind, I began my preparations. During one of my visits I secretly went into her room, measured one of the rings on her vanity, and sent off for a mail-order engagement ring. When it arrived, I went back to San José, showed her the ring, and asked her to marry me—or at least that's what I thought I asked her. She looked at the ring, smiled sweetly, handed it back to me, and said, "That's nice. Who's it for?" Needless to say, I was devastated. I put the ring back in my pocket, executed a hasty retrograde movement (Marines never retreat), and fled back to Managua as depressed as I'd ever been in my life. But after a few weeks of moping around, I worked up the courage to make one last try. Only this time I would be better prepared.

My first step was to ask my friend Remy Rener what I'd done wrong. Appalled, he told me, "Pretty much everything."

To begin with I hadn't asked her father for permission to call on her, much less marry her. I'd also never declared my intentions to her, at least not in comprehensible Spanish. And when I showed her the ring I'd screwed up the Spanish and mistakenly told her that it was for someone else, not her. After he stopped laughing, Remy offered to try and teach me how to ask a young lady to marry me in comprehensible Spanish. I immediately accepted his offer. He even agreed to be a best man at our wedding—if I succeeded.

On September 11, 1958, Leda and I were married in the Managua home of her Aunt Bruni and Uncle Jack, although that might be hard to prove since the official record of our marriage was destroyed in the 1972 Managua earthquake. And since her Uncle Jack forgot to put film in his camera, there's no photographic evidence either. But we do have a Consular Certificate of Witness to Marriage, four kids, eight grandkids, and, as of today, four great-grandkids and counting, so that may be proof enough.

Our wedding day was a bit unusual. The night before it was scheduled to take place Leda's Aunt Bruni called me to say that Leda was having an appendicitis attack and the wedding would have to be postponed. Bummer! Then Bruni called again. A doctor had examined Leda and pronounced her ready to marry. Great! But, he'd added, she'd have to spend our wedding night being attended by a nurse. But if I wanted to be close to my bride after we were married, it would be OK for me to sleep on the living room couch. Double bummer! And so began our marriage.

author's collection

Managua, Nicaragua, 1958: Jack and Bruni Starbird, Leda's aunt and uncle and the godparents of our marriage and our first born, Barbara.

The morning after we exchanged vows, with Leda sedated, we flew to San José, where her parents, Don Joaquin and Doña Maria, threw a second wedding party for us that evening. The party went so well that Leda didn't mention until it was almost over that her pains had returned. As soon as she did, off we went to the emergency room of San Juan de Diós Hospital, where her father, two uncles, and an aunt worked. After a quick examination, the doctor on duty decided she was having an appendicitis attack and sent her straight to surgery where he removed her appendix. Once she recovered consciousness, he came to see her and told her, "Sorry, I was wrong. Your appendix was perfectly normal. But I'm afraid that you will never be able to have children." The bummers were piling up fast.

At least the hospital let me spend as much time as I wanted at my one-day bride's bedside while she recuperated, although, since she was in an open ward with a dozen other patients, we had to stay absolutely still and be very, very quiet. Leda stayed in the hospital for the three days I had remaining for annual leave: So much for our honeymoon. My leave ended before Leda was able to travel, so I went back alone to Managua to return to my duties. A couple of weeks later, she was finally recuperated enough to join me.

In those days, when a Marine Embassy Guard married a foreign national, he was almost immediately transferred out of the program. (Unlike today, in the 1960s all MSG's were male Marines.) But, when the detachment's Gunny, Sergeant Whitman, the tall, good looking Marine standing to my right in the photo below, was killed in a tragic automobile accident I was kept at post until a replacement for him could arrive. I'd found and rented for us what I thought was a small room in a private home. But, my Spanish being less fluent than I thought, what I'd actually rented was a large, and largely unfurnished apartment. The refrigerator was barely able to keep a bottle of milk from souring overnight, our dining-room table was the top of an old sewing machine, our stove was a single burner electric portable, and Leda had to do the laundry the old fashioned way, by hand. Still, we were finally together, and that was enough.

author's collection

Managua, Nicaragua, 1958. By November 11, in time for the Marine Corps Birthday Ball, Leda was able to join me. I'm the Sergeant in the center, standing behind Leda, my bride of two months. Gunnery Sergeant Ralph Whitman, a decorated veteran of the Korean War, standing at the left of the photograph, was killed in an accident a few weeks later, and I became detachment NCOIC for the rest of my tour.

author's collection

Managua, Nicaragua, 1958. During our last months in Managua, we rented an apartment in La Casa Roa, an old Spanish colonial house, destroyed in 1972 by the great Managua earthquake. It came with this "washing machine."

In all the excitement, a number of things that would be important decades later failed to register. Among them was the presence at our wedding party of Leda's next door neighbors, Abdenago "Nago" and "Chelita" Hernández, their then fourteen-year-old son, Plutarco, and one of their nephews, Eduardo. I discovered decades later that Don Nago and Doña Chelita were key figures on the Costa Rican revolutionary left and played important roles in Nicaragua's original Sandinista revolution. Plutarco, who was to become one of my best friends many years later, after I had retired from the Foreign Service, went on to found Costa Rica's Communist Youth League and become one of the top figures in Nicaragua's original Sandinista Revolution, while their nephew Eduardo, using *Fermán Cienfuegos* as his *nom de guerre*, was to be the military commander of El Salvador's Farabundo Martí National Liberation Front (FMLN). When Plutarco's organizational activities came to the attention of the local KGB station chief, he was invited to attend a Youth Festival in Havana, where he was recruited by Soviet intelligence. From Havana they sent him to Lumumba University in Moscow on a full "scholarship." From Moscow, he was sent to Campamento Cerro just east of Havana, Cuba's main guerrilla warfare training center for Latin Americans. There he trained for a year as a guerrilla unit commander and did so well that he was then sent to North Korea for an additional six months advanced training in subversive operations under the personal tutelage of Kim Il. He later served as a National Director of Nicaragua's pre-1979 Sandinista Front.

author's collection

Caracas, Venezuela—Leda's neighbor, Plutarco Hernández, in Caracas at an international solidarity conference on July 19, 1979, the day the Nicaraguan Sandinista Front took power. A National Director of the Front, he rushed to Managua only to find he'd been stripped of his directorship. A nephew of Costa Rican President, Calderón Guardia and first cousin of a later President, Calderón Fournier, years later Plutarco would be Costa Rica's Ambassador to Russia and Dean of Moscow's Latin American Diplomatic Corps (Hoover Instution Archives).

author's collection

Reno, Nevada, 1959. The newlyweds.

Four months after we were married, my assignment in Managua came to an end, and Leda left with me for a foreign country she didn't know to join a family she'd never met that spoke a language she didn't understand, ate unfamiliar food, and worshiped the same God but in a very different way. We arrived in Reno in the dead of winter on a Greyhound bus from Los Angeles. My mother was there to greet us, take us to her home on a treeless hill overlooking the Truckee Meadows and help us settle into an unheated attic bedroom.

Even for me, the cold felt bone-chilling. For Leda, it was ten times worse. She could hardly breathe, shivered constantly and couldn't get warm no matter how many blankets were piled on the bed. But, slowly, her shock gave way to new adventures—seeing her first snow and catching snowflakes in her hands and on her tongue, watching wild horses race by just outside the front door, hearing the howl of coyotes from the hills behind the house, finding rabbit tracks in the snow, feeding the quail that came into the front yard looking for food, getting angry when one of my high-school sweethearts appeared down the hill, and hanging laundry on the clothes-line only to have it freeze solid and break into pieces when she tried to bring it in.

Then, just as Leda adjusted to the freezing Reno weather, I took her with me to my next duty station in a frying-pan-hot corner of California, Marine Corps Base Twentynine Palms. By then Leda was expecting our first child. But, despite the searing heat and the dryness of the California desert, she did her best to adapt, until she began having premature contractions and needed to be close to a major hospital. So I took her to live with some of my cousins in Long Beach, commuting when I could to visit her, as the doctors desperately tried to avoid a premature birth. When the baby was sufficiently mature to survive, she promptly stopped having contractions. Shortly after, I was discharged from the Marines and we moved back to Reno where I planned to enroll at UNR. A few weeks later, just late enough for us to lose our medical coverage, Leda gave birth to our first-born, Barbara, and became so homesick that I bought her and the baby airline tickets from Los Angeles to San José and sent her home. I then jumped into what we laughingly called our limousine, an aging clunker on its last legs, and headed down the Pan-American Highway to join them.

The drive through Mexico was relatively straightforward up to Mexico City, with regularly spaced gas stations, acceptable motels, and edible food. But as I continued south, travel became more challenging. Gas stations became increasingly scarce as did the availability of trustworthy places to stay or eat. Eventually I discovered that in almost every village, I could find someone with a few fifty-five gallon drums of gasoline in their backyard and a hand pump. I also discovered that the best food could be obtained simply by stopping where I saw a woman making tortillas, because they would always offer me some to eat, but never let me pay for my meal.

Well before arriving at the Guatemala-Mexico border, the paved portion of the highway ended. I could take the car to a railroad station and pay to have it carried by rail to Tapachula on the Mexico-Guatemala border at a price I couldn't afford. Or I could backtrack to another highway that would take me through the mountains of Chiapas. I chose the highway. When I backtracked, I found that the road as far as San Cristóbal de Las Casas was fairly good. But after I left Las Casas and headed south toward Guatemala, the road began to peter out, unless cow pastures can be considered parts of a highway. I remember one place where the road consisted of a long, low dam about three hundred yards across with a foot of water flowing over it. Luckily, it wasn't rainy season, so I wasn't washed away. But, all too soon, the highway turned to dirt, and the dirt turned to mud. I'll never know how I managed to slip-slide through mud so deep that even eighteen-wheelers and tractors found it all but impassable. But I did.

Finally, I arrived at the Guatemala-Mexico border crossing point. But after I cleared Mexican customs and immigration, my car wouldn't start. Thankfully, some helpful local folks, a couple of truck drivers, and even a policeman cheerfully gave me a push. I was able to start the car as I rolled downhill toward the bridge that connected the two countries. I made it up the other side to Guatemalan customs and immigration and stopped. At that point the car died again. The Guatemalans were clearly a bit suspicious of the Spanish-speaking Gringo with the five-day beard who hadn't bathed for at least a week. But they reluctantly stamped my passport, leaving me in a dilemma. To start the car again I'd have to coast back down the hill toward the border bridge. But once it started there would be no place to turn around until I got back to Mexico. Still, there didn't seem to be much choice. So, in for a penny in for a pound, I released the brakes, headed down the hill, started the car, and raced back into Mexico, flipped a U-turn, waved to the nice authorities there, and raced back to Guatemala. Luckily they didn't try to stop me, but simply waved back, though that wasn't the end of the fun and games.

Once in Guatemala, I found myself in a mountainous region with a war going on. The guerrillas, the government, or both had removed all the road signs. So there I was, trying to navigate a maze of narrow donkey trails with just enough asphalt to be called roads, without a map. I struggled to find my way from the middle of nowhere to the middle of somewhere, racing the clock lest the sun go down and I find myself in a war zone where both sides would mistrust me—the Marxists because I was a Gringo, the Guatemalan Army because I was dirty and bearded. Many years later I discovered that my odyssey through the mountains of southern Chiapas and northern Guatemala had been shared with "Pepe" Puente, the Marxist revolutionary that would become my friend much later. Thankfully, I made it to Guatemala City before the sun set. Two countries down, three to go.

My next stop was San Salvador, where I found what seemed to be a reasonably safe place to stay, mostly because it had a guarded garage, rented a room, got a good night's sleep for a change, got up early, and headed out. About two hours down the road toward the Honduran border one of my tires blew out. This was not an insurmountable problem since I had a spare. Then, about ten miles further down the road, a second tire blew. Two blown tires? At that point, I became suspicious. I took a careful look at both blown tires and discovered that they'd been slashed inside by a professional, or at least an expert, in such a way that I was able to drive an hour or two before they blew. When I looked even more closely, I saw that all four tires had been slashed, putting me in a real bind. Thankfully, a passing American missionary came to my rescue, took me to where he lived, and generously gave me four used tires. Once more, I headed out, entered Honduras without a problem and continued driving toward Nicaragua. But my sense of confidence was premature.

By the time I arrived at the Nicaraguan border, I looked like crap. I had a week's growth of chin whiskers and had been wearing the same clothes for several days. Still, since I'd lived in Nicaragua for two-plus years and had friends there, I didn't expect any trouble. So I stopped my car in front of the entry post, walked into customs, handed over my passport, smiled, and then waited—and waited, and waited, and waited. Finally, I turned to check on my car, only to find it swarming with customs officers. I had a fair load of personal junk in the back (mostly clothes, a few books), so I could understood why they'd chosen to go through my car carefully. But several of the officers had wrenches in their hands and it looked like they were about to take its fenders off. For all I knew they might be preparing to take the motor out too, which seemed a bit excessive. Still, having experienced my bureaucratic baptism in Managua earlier on, I knew that it would probably be counterproductive to throw a hissy fit. So I just smiled, walked over, and asked if I could help.

The senior customs officer responded with a reasonably friendly look on his face. "We're going to have to check your car over very carefully," he said. I took that to mean, "give me money, or we'll tear your car apart." The trouble was, I didn't have any money to spare. So I told him I understood that he was only doing his job. But I was going to be late for a lunch appointment in Managua if it took much longer, so I asked him if there was a telephone I could use to call my lunch host to let him know I'd be late. He said he was very sorry, but only officials could use the phone in his office, and regrettably there was no public telephone. So I then asked him if he might make the call for me and let my host know I was being detained at the border and wouldn't arrive as planned. He was clearly reluctant, until I handed over the name and private telephone number of my host, Don Pablo Rener, President of the National Legislature. At that point, an immigration officer joined us and, when the customs chief handed him my note, went straight to his office. He came back about three minutes later, apologized, and gave orders to have my car put back together. Then he explained. Just the day before, they'd caught a young man that looked a bit like me trying to enter with several automatic weapons and ammunition hidden in his car destined for a guerrilla band in the nearby mountains. So I fit their profile. Having dropped Don Pablo Rener's name, I thought the least I could do was go see his son Remy when I got to Managua to tell him what I'd done. This gave both of them a good laugh. They even gave me a late lunch.

After a night's sleep, I headed for Costa Rica, where I crossed the border with no additional excitement. Once in San José, I began looking for a job, only to find there were none available for people without proper paperwork, something illegal immigrants still find to be a problem. After several months, I swallowed my pride, told Leda I simply had to go back to the United States to find work, called my mother for money to buy an airline ticket, and flew to Miami. When I arrived, almost flat broke, I rented an upper bunk at the YMCA and went job hunting. I spoke both dominant languages, but Miami proved no more welcoming to jobless Americans than to illegals. As the days dragged on, I took to walking around downtown just to keep from dying of boredom. I had barely enough money to buy a loaf of old bread for one meal a day. When even that became difficult to pay for, I was forced to choose between bed and bread, checked out of the YMCA and began sleeping under the stars.

One afternoon, while I was sitting in a park fighting with pigeons for bread, a man walked up to me, said he'd seen me several times wandering the streets, and wondered how I was doing. After I explained my situation, he said he knew people that might be interested in a Spanish-speaking former Marine Sergeant and suggested I go to a particular bar where there was someone who could probably find work for me. Intrigued, I did just that. In the bar I found someone who looked like the person he'd described, and I mentioned I was looking for a job. He said he needed someone with precisely my skills to join an organization being put together for use in Cuba. I didn't immediately say no but, putting two and two together, concluded it probably wasn't the sort of thing I had in mind. Still, I asked a few questions. Finally, he said, "We'll even make you a platoon leader." At that I turned and ran. I was out of work, not out of my mind.

To this day I'm not absolutely certain. But the timing suggests that had I accepted the job, my next visit to Cuba would have taken place at Playa Jirón, better known as the Bay of Pigs. Given how that turned out, I made the right decision. Since then, I've visited Playa Jirón several times and, as a former Marine, each time I shuddered at the thought of trying to make an amphibious landing there, since it's probably the worst place in Cuba to make one. A better name for it would be Suicide Swamp. Still, my job search was becoming desperate and, having been reminded that I did have some skills, I went to the nearest Marine recruiting station and reenlisted. Since I'd been out more than three months, I was reduced in rank from Sergeant to Lance Corporal and sent on a train to Camp Pendleton, California. There I found out that, had I'd reenlisted immediately, I would have kept my three Sergeant's stripes, been promoted to Staff Sergeant, and received a reenlistment bonus. Even so, at least I had a job, and I was soon able to send for Leda and Barbara, find housing, and begin doing one of the world's most boring jobs—running a message center.

NINE

THAILAND — INTO THE REALM OF COIN

While in high school I'd worked as a telegram delivery boy, so my new career felt a bit like being back with Western Union, only without the tips. After a few months of casting about for something a bit more exciting than being a glorified messenger boy, I applied for Arabic language training. Naturally, in the middle of my first vacation in years, I received urgent orders to report to the Army Language School on the Presidio of Monterey to study Thai. Whoever cut the orders at Headquarters Marine Corps (HQMC) probably didn't think it made much difference, since Thai and Arabic are so similar. That same someone must also have assumed that it would be a snap to move my family from Southern to Northern California in a single weekend.

Not that the move went smoothly. It didn't. Even though Leda was expecting again, she pitched in once again like the trooper she was. We located a moving company that was willing to do a Saturday pack out, helped them cram our meager belongings into their van and headed for Monterey that same night, even though we were down to our last dollar, had only a half watermelon to feed the kids, and wouldn't have anywhere to sleep once we arrived. Thankfully, at the time my father was pastoring a small church in nearby Watsonville, and a member of his congregation owned an unoccupied upper story apartment in Pacific Grove and let us move into it without paying the usual month's rent in advance or making a deposit, and I managed to report in on time

The apartment hadn't been cleaned in months, the heat was turned off, the stove caked with old grease, and the refrigerator sported a layer of green mold. Adding to the fun, Barbara was deathly ill, Leda was suffering from morning sickness, and I had to report in the very next morning for duty. But, once again, Leda rose to the challenge and transformed it from a tenant's worse nightmare into a surprisingly snug nest for our growing family.

Our year in Monterey was to be one of the most enjoyable of our lives. Thanks to my newly discovered faculty with languages, Thai came surprisingly easily. The days were short, the weather nearly perfect, Monterey fascinating, and the arrival of our second daughter, Rebecca, free of the excessive complications that attended the arrival of our first. With only six hours of class each day, we were able to relax and, for the first time, enjoy ourselves as a family. I was even able to take my first college course. After Monterey, things returned to normal—as in all screwed up.

From the Presidio, I was sent to the Army Intelligence School at Fort Holabird in Baltimore, Maryland, to learn some intelligence skills. Because it was an unaccompanied training assignment, Leda took our burgeoning brood back to Nevada to wait. I turned out to be both the only Marine and the only NCO in the course, which put me in charge of an entire platoon of Ivy League privates fresh out of the Army's summer camp version of boot camp. The idea seemed to be that,

Monterey, California, 1960. While in Monterey, we spent many afternoons enjoying the ocean. Here, Leda is holding our first daughter, Barbara, while expecting Rebecca, born just weeks later.

because they were all Ivy Leaguers, they were extra smart, so they were able to take the intelligence course, go from there to hard language training Urdu, Swahili, French, etc., and then return to their reserve units to wait for a war. To me, the very notion that smart people never forget a language once they've learned it was pretty dumb. But, I supposed, it was no dumber than many other schemes. As the only NCO in my class my job was to treat these Privates like real soldiers, and I tried. Really! But, given that I was just a dumb ass Marine while they were all Ivy League college grads—my right guide was a graduate of Harvard Law, for heaven's sake—a number of them became quite patronizing. And most of them, who couldn't march a lick anyway, took to bitching about the stupidity of all things military, especially walking in formations. Finally, I got fed up. So one morning, instead of trying to form them up as a platoon and march them to class, I walked up to where they were milling about, said that since they'd been bitching so much they could damn well find their own way to the classroom, and walked off, monitoring their reactions with my ears. What ensued was near total chaos. Not one of them knew how to march in a formation, half of them hadn't a clue where to go, and the few that did couldn't figure out how to get there. Eventually, a couple of them remembered that if they arrived at class late they'd lose their weekend passes, yelled at their buddies and started running toward what they assumed was the classroom. Thanks to the instructors, with whom I was in cahoots, the classroom location had been moved, and most of them arrived late or not at all. As a result, the instructors ran out of extra duty chits and the whole platoon lost their weekend passes. It didn't help that when weekly grades were posted I was at the top of the class.

Interestingly, since they were stuck on base for the weekend, after they put two and two together they asked me to join them at a Saturday morning bull session. And since I wasn't going anywhere anyhow, I did. As it turned out they were curious about a few things, like why on earth armies march around in formations and make soldiers cut their hair short and keep their toilets clean. Apparently Ivy League colleges don't stress orderly conduct or even cleanliness.

I explained that when large numbers of people are together in very close quarters, things like dirty toilets breed diseases, long unkempt hair becomes a home for lice, and unorganized mobs can get lost on their way to battle or, as they had just learned, on their way to a training class. It was fascinating to watch face after face light up with understanding. Maybe Marine Corporals weren't totally stupid after all. And then, to my utter amazement, they began begging me to teach them to march like Marines. Biting my tongue, I said to myself, "Fat chance!" But to them I said, as sweetly as a Marine can, "Sure, I'd love to," which is how I wound up spending several afternoons counting cadence Marine-style and trying to teach basic close-order drill to a motley platoon of college-grad Privates. And I do mean basic. It took about five seconds for me to realize that I'd have to begin by teaching them how to tell their left foot from their right, another skill apparently not taught at Harvard. It was one of life's stranger moments, but a fun one.

My next assignment was to a then classified unit, the Marine Corps' 1st Interrogator-Translator Team (ITT), being formed at Fleet Marine Force, Pacific (FMFPAC) headquarters in Hawaii. So I headed west to pick up Leda and the kids to take them with me. Now eight-months pregnant with our third daughter, Tamara, according to the regulations Leda shouldn't have been allowed to board the MATS (Military Air Transport Service) flight to Hawaii. But it's sometimes hard to tell eight months from seven, so we kept our mouths shut and climbed aboard. All was going well until, just past the half-way point of no return, she looked out the window and noticed that one of the plane's engines was on fire. We made the rest of our flight on one engine with an escort of military jets, although what they could have done if we had crashed was hard to imagine. But we made it.

It was to be my year for bizarre military units. The 1st ITT consisted of the oddest collection of active-duty Marines yet, including every Far Eastern language speaker the Corps could scrape up, from Mandarin and Cantonese Chinese to Vietnamese, Indonesian, Japanese, Farsi, Russian, Ukrainian, and, in my case, Thai and Spanish. Though it wasn't yet front page news, the United States already had Marines on the ground in Vietnam, and our presence there was growing rapidly, so the Vietnamese sub-team was by far the busiest of the bunch.

Lance Corporal Ron Sawin, a PK preacher's kid like me, had been first to report in. Born and raised in Hanoi by American missionary parents, he spoke North Vietnamese without an accent and had spent part of his youth hiking up and down parts of the Ho Chi Minh Trail with high-school buddies. He also took his vacations in Saigon, much to the chagrin of the headquarters company Gunny, who barely spoke English, much less any other language. But, rather than just lazing around for the rest of us to appear, Sawin had taken the initiative and, by the time anyone else arrived, had the Team's offices fully equipped and ready to roll. The other members were equally interesting. The First Sergeant spoke Farsi, and we had a Ukrainian refugee Sergeant who also spoke Russian, several Vietnamese interpreters and, as I recall, two or three Malay linguists. Captain Don Cook, the Team's commander, was a Cantonese Chinese linguist. Later, after he left the ITT, he was captured by the North Vietnamese and taken to a prison camp inside that country. He received a posthumous Congressional Medal of Honor for valor for his conduct as a prisoner of war.

For some unfathomable reason, the name of the unit, the 1st ITT, was classified. Given the curiosity and irreverence of the average Marine, this led to speculation concerning the true meaning of its name. Guesses ranged from the 1st Italian Tetrazzini Testers to the 1st Interplanetary Transportation Team. The idea that we were all spooks gained considerable credence when three of us, Sergeants Jones, Smith, and Corporal Brown (me) took to marching in and out of the team's front vault door carrying identical briefcases.

While with the 1st ITT, my life among the more restless natives of this planet really began to roll. There were interesting wars underway all over the region, some of which the media knew about. When those in Vietnam, Laos, and Malaya vied in the press for "Best War of the Year" honors, Vietnam won. But there were a dozen others from which to choose. Among the more public conflicts, the Khmer Rouge in Cambodia were just beginning their efforts to best Nazi Germany at genocide, while in the Philippines the Huks were doing their best to take power. Other conflicts less likely to make the headlines, but just as deadly, were raging in the Assam hills of India and Shan States in Burma. There were also efforts underway to subvert Indonesia via its large ethnic Chinese population. And there were bubbling confrontations elsewhere, including Thailand, where I would spend more than half of the next four years doing both Southeast Asia intelligence analysis and hands-on intelligence collection, much of it at the village level.

In my copious spare time, with a great deal of pushing by Leda and the help of the Marine Corps, I would also manage to finish two and a half years of college at the University of

Hawaii's night school, pass the FSO written and oral exams, and write my first book, *A Guide to Thailand*, a pocket guide to that country's history, customs, traditions, and rules of behavior intended to keep my fellow Marines from sticking their feet in their mouths too often. And somehow Leda managed for us to have a family life.

I was the senior NCO of the ITT's tiny Thai sub-team, a marvel in and of itself. The sub-team's commander, Lt. Leon Cohan, was a mustang up from the ranks that had been given just six weeks Thai language training, and it showed. My deputy, Ming Kai Chang, who looked like he was about twelve years old, was a former Sergeant Major in the Chinese Nationalist Army. Chang didn't speak any Thai at all, but he did speak Cantonese and Mandarin Chinese, Japanese, and even some Russian and German. He loved to call himself "Corporal Ming Kai Chang, United States Marine Corps, by golly." A native of Beijing, one of Chang's brothers was a Major in the Chinese Army and Chang himself was a physical wreck, so I was surprised he was even in the Marines, much less as a member of a classified unit. But there he was. During World War II, he'd lived in the international community in Shanghai and had been recruited by Chiang Kai-shek's forces as an intelligence runner. He'd been captured by the Japanese and badly tortured. His toenails had been crushed with a hammer, most of his fingernails pulled out and he'd been partially blinded. As a result, he couldn't hold a rifle or stand in formation for more than a few minutes and had to use a magnifying glass to read. But as a native speaker of Mandarin he was

author's collection

FMFPAC, Hawaii, 1963. Some members of the 1st ITT. Staff Sergeant Pentony is standing at the far left with First Sergeant Bowen peeking over his shoulder. I'm next, while Corporal Chang is just in front of me. I don't remember the name of the Sergeant behind Chang. Sergeant Smith and the 1st ITT's second Commanding Officer, Captain Biel are on the far right.

very valuable to the Marine Corps, so they weren't about to discharge him. He was also the most squared away Marine I ever knew. Chang could go on a three-day patrol and come back with the creases still in his uniform. He also had a terrible temper and flew into a rage whenever he saw another Marine less than perfectly turned out, giving the lie to the myth that the Chinese are inscrutable.

WAIKIKI

Honolulu, Hawaii, 1963. During our rare opportunities to enjoy the delights of living in paradise, Leda and I loved to stroll through Waikiki.

While there were Several other insurgencies underway in the region, my own primary focus was on Thailand. By 1961, the situation in Southeast Asia was becoming more and more challenging, and the media had begun to concentrate primarily on the war in Vietnam, even though there were common threads that tied the various conflicts together, such as their shared ideologies and the external support they were receiving, especially from China.

I was particularly interested in the role being played by expatriate Chinese communities throughout the region. The main challenges to American interests immediately after World War II involved the former colonies of our European allies, the French in Indochina, the Dutch in Indonesia, the British in the former Raj and Hong Kong. But the region's strategic Gold Ring then, as it still is today, was the Strait of Malacca, possibly the world's most important maritime choke point, or SLOC (Strategic Line of Communications), through which almost all seaborne trade between the Persian Gulf and the Pacific passes, especially oil. That made Indonesia, Singapore, and Malaysia the most important countries to the United States, not Vietnam, Laos, or Cambodia. Not that a mere Marine NCO, barely out of his teens, had much of a role in strategic planning. Mine was just a bit part, albeit a very tasty one.

During those years I also became an amateur anthropologist. In my copious spare time, and to escape my sub-team commander, I took to disappearing from the office for days on end to "work on essential, job-related research" at the University of Hawaii and Bishop Museum in Honolulu. At first simply a way to get away from the office, my initiative slowly developed from an escape device into an extensive study of the various tribes and cultural groups in Southeast Asia from China, Burma and Thailand's large overseas Chinese communities.

In an effort to sensitize the FMF staff to the ethnic complexities of the region into which we were sticking our noses and other more delicate body parts, I wrote a series of short studies of various Thai hill tribes including the Shan, Meo, and Thai Dam. Trying to figure out which tribe was which turned out to be more difficult than I'd expected. The names of the various tribes differed from researcher to researcher. And even those that appeared to be the same were often spelled differently. In self-defense and, I must admit, to confuse my sub-team commander, I also developed something I called a Polylingual Ethnic Nomer Index. As suspected, when I tried to explain it to him he really didn't understand it. But his *amour propre* kept him from asking what the hell I was talking about. Instead, he smiled sagely and left me alone, which was exactly the result I'd hoped for. All in all, it was a busy few years.

During one of my very first missions in Thailand, euphemistically labeled "forward area language training," I received my baptism into the realm of counterinsurgency operations (or COIN). With a hot war being fought in Laos just across the Mekong River, Thailand's Lao-speaking North East was to be my primary region of interest. The Thai were planning to build a series of dams to provide the region with better controlled irrigation water and electricity. Since the reservoirs behind the dams would flood the farmlands of dozens of peasant villages, the villagers were to be fully compensated and resettled to other farming areas—at least theoretically. But the money allotted to do so wasn't trickling down. Instead corrupt local officials were siphoning it off. Understandably, this was generating a great deal of anger among the peasants, making the region ripe for exploitation. The Pathet Lao, taking advantage of the situation, were sending in agitprop

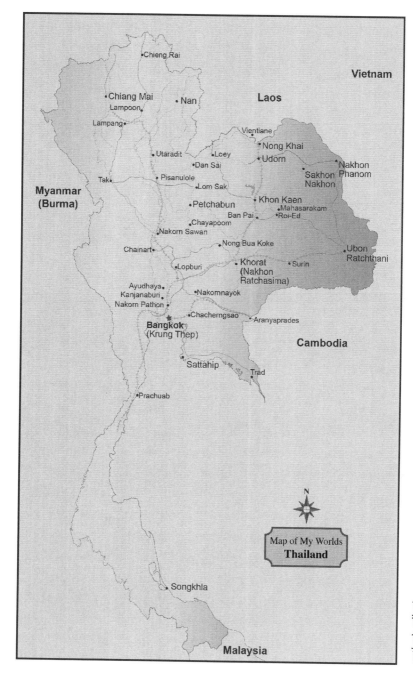

(agitation and propaganda) teams to exploit the unrest in the rice villages between the region's capital, Udorn, Nakhon Phanom, and around Sakon Nakhon. This created a golden opportunity for me to explore a classic pre-insurgency situation.

I vividly remember arriving at one village where entire families were moving slowly through the paddies, knee-deep in the water, feet in the mud, planting rice shoots one by one in lines as orderly as Marines in a parade formation. The villagers carried themselves with natural grace, even though the work was no doubt backbreaking.

During the planting season, the landscape was dominated by paddies full of newly planted rice shoots so painfully green that they seemed to glow in the tropic sunlight. Still, they took the time to look up, smile, and wave hello to the young, blue-eyed Caucasian strolling along the paddy walls watching them work. An elderly gentleman came over to greet me, the curiosity in his eyes turning to wonder when I greeted him in Thai and told him I'd worked on farms in the United States cutting grapes at harvest time, but never planted rice. When I asked him to teach me how, he immediately agreed. To the amusement of the villagers, he handed me a few rice shoots, explaining that they'd been germinated in a different paddy and uprooted when they'd grown big enough to be transplanted. He carefully explained the process - move slowly through the water, reach beneath into the mud, make a hole with your finger, and carefully place the shoot so its roots are firmly planted while its leaves remain exposed to the sunlight. I left my flip-flops on the bank of the paddy and waded in barefoot. He then put one of the shoots in my hand and explained that I had to submerge it straight down to avoid damaging it. The shoots felt surprisingly fragile and, needless to say, my first several tries went badly, and the ones I tried to plant floated quickly to the surface.

With the patience that peasant farmers always seem to have for the young and ignorant, he repeatedly guided my hand down to demonstrate how the tender shoots should be planted. Time after time, he plucked my failures out of the water and handed them back to me, until I finally got it right. The work was nowhere near as easy as it looked. While the villagers made it seem so easy as they cheerfully planted shoots by the dozen in a minute's time, for me it was a real struggle. Eventually I more or less got the hang of it, although I suspect they went back later and straightened my crooked line of plants. My adventure in rice farming, joining the peasants in their labor, even for just an hour, gave me a deep respect for them. By rich world standards, the rice farmer's world involved an incredible amount of effort for very little gain. But the dignity with which they did their work was admirable. What looked to me like poverty they viewed as wealth, enough for them to cheerfully offer to share some of it with me, a wandering stranger.

After my adventure, the gentleman that had been teaching me invited me to go with him to his village. As we walking along dirt paths they themselves had built, the elderly man that had been so patient with me revealed himself to be the village chief. He proudly led me to his home, a surprisingly spacious wooden house standing on stilts, with chickens, pigs, children, and the occasional duck wandering about below. After introducing me to his wife, and who knows how many children and relatives, he offered me what must've been for them a luxury, a bottle of beer. I drank it graciously, even though I hate the taste of the stuff.

At first, as we sat quietly on the porch, our conversation was innocuous—the weather and the possibility of a good harvest. But as the day wore on, I slowly nudged the conversation toward more serious subjects and was soon able to confirm what I'd suspected. The chief knew his seemingly pastoral life wouldn't last much longer because his village was one that would be flooded behind the new Nam Phung irrigation dam and our talk became increasingly sober until finally he told me that there was growing unrest among the villagers. They had been promised compensation and equally rich land on which to build new farms. But those promises weren't being kept and the villagers were beginning to believe that regional officials, rather than providing the assistance promised, were siphoning off that money into their own pockets. To lose their ancestral homes would be bad enough, but to lose their way of life would be much worse. Outsiders had begun to drift through the area, condemning the government's failure to make good on its promises, to exploit the discontent. This was the topic of greatest interest to me. Just who were these strangers, and what were they up to?

Realizing that I had a very real interest, the village chief began to explain what was actually happening. Small teams of Pathet Lao agitators from north of the Mekong River were traveling from village to village condemning the government for the exploitation. They were also carefully identifying the least happy villagers and recruiting them into networks of malcontents. He had been to several meetings in Sakon Nakhon to discuss this with regional officials, including the governor and senior police officers. As a result of these and similar meetings elsewhere, news of the growing unrest had reached Bangkok and the King. In response, His Majesty had put out a call to the country's university students, especially the children of the elite, asking them to help him demonstrate His concern. In response, small groups of student volunteers began arriving in nearby villages to do just that.

The village chief said he'd assumed my appearance was related to the growing unrest, an assumption I confirmed. He also said that the Pathet Lao agitation teams were no doubt aware of my presence. As the day was growing late, he suggested that, for my safety's sake, I sleep in the village temple that night because no one would dare touch me while I was there, since, like Renaissance churches in medieval Europe, Buddhist temples were inviolate, even for the Pathet Lao. He also offered to go with me to a nearby village the following day to meet a team of university students working there in response to the King's call, and invited me to dinner. His wife cooked an exceptional dinner for me of small fish from the rice paddies; pork marinated in chili juice then covered with yet more chili, and one of my favorite dishes to put out the flames, smoked sticky rice prepared in woven bamboo baskets over an open fire. After dinner, the village chief walked me to the temple and introduced me to the priest, who promptly invited me in and assigned me a piece of bamboo floor where I could sleep, which I did after doing some homework.

In the morning the village chief and I headed for the next village. It was much like the one I'd just left, wooden homes built on stilts with *nipa* roofs of palm fronds, with pigs, chickens and children running around below. Each house had its own small shrine in a corner of its front yard, most often a beautifully made miniature Buddhist temple, where they burned incense and placed small offerings in appreciation of what they had or in supplication for what they needed. When we arrived, the leader of the Thai team was waiting for us. But rather than taking me directly to the village temple, he led us to a small schoolhouse where the rest of the team was already assembled. They were young and very different from the villagers—taller, more filled out, less burnt by the sun. From upper-class families from the Bangkok area, they were all university students or recent graduates. Responding to the King's call, they were engaged in efforts to blunt the actions of the Pathet Lao agitprop teams circulating among the villagers. For the next several hours they explained to me why they had volunteered to answer the King's call and become members of a Rural Development Team.

author's collection

Near Sakon Nakhon, Thailand, 1962. I often slept in village temples for security reasons. I also usually carried college text books with me. Here I'm doing homework as Buddhist temple boys watch.

As the weeks and months wore on, it became increasingly clear to them that the Pathet Lao were having some success in their efforts to organize clandestine support networks in preparation for launching a guerrilla war. One especially convincing experience had come when visiting government officials were met with organized protests, the sort of confrontation that's rare, if not completely absent, from village life. While there had not yet been any violent incidents, they were beginning to see small groups of armed men moving quietly between the villages, a development that convinced them that the Pathet Lao were on the verge of launching their insurgency.

Although no guerrilla attacks on US forces in Northeast Thailand took place until late 1964, after my last deployment to the region, not long after my return to Hawaii I began seeing reports that small guerrilla units had begun launching probing attacks on Thai targets, indicating it was getting underway.

Prior to this deployment, Thailand's counterinsurgency effort to blunt Pathet Lao efforts to stir up an insurgency in Northeast Thailand using Rural Development Team, RTDs, hadn't been mentioned in any of the intelligence that crossed my desk back in Hawaii, even though the RTDs were the cutting edge of their efforts. The arrival of upper-class, well-educated young Thai in a village, willing to plant rice alongside them, help them with small irrigation projects, maintain their roads, and live among them was, in the end, to prove a somewhat effective antidote to the Pathet Lao's efforts.

What I had seen was the public face of Thailand's efforts to blunt the efforts of the Pathet Lao. But the RTDs also worked hard to identify the villagers who'd become members of the clandestine networks they were organizing. When they were able to identify someone that had been recruited, they would try to convince them to abandon their efforts, using persuasion not coercion, because coercion could simply deepen their discontent.

The Thai RTDs gave me my first hands-on experience with counter-insurgency. In fact, they were to be my one and only experience with a successful preemptive COIN effort. Unlike my later experiences in the Philippines, Nicaragua, and elsewhere, the Thai program was initiated early enough to nip an insurgency effort in the bud before it could take root, a rare if not unique example of why an ounce of prevention is always worth more than a pound of bullets. While the outside world never gave them the credit they deserved, Thailand's RTD program was to serve as the template for our own CORDS (Civil Operations and Development) counterinsurgency program in Vietnam and CORDS, in turn, was to be the template for our more recent embedded Provincial Reconstruction Team (ePRT) program in Iraq. I myself later commanded a CORDS Team in Vietnam and forty years later, during the famous Petreus Surge, my son commanded the 1st ePRT (embedded Provincial Reconstruction Team) in Baghdad.

But we never seem to learn. The Thai RTD program met with success in large part because of two things. The threat was detected early enough for them to nip in the bud the creation by the Pathet Lao of the single most important part of any insurgency, clandestine support networks. And the RTDs were manned by Thai, not, as CORDs and ePRTs teams, by transitory foreigners on short assignments to countries where they neither spoke the language nor fully understood the culture.

T E N

COLONEL CLUELESS

Just weeks after I returned to Hawaii from this first mission in Thailand, and before I could do much more than say hello to Leda and the kids, off I went once more, this time on the USS Point Defiance, a landing ship dock (LSD), to the Philippines to hunt Huks. Not that that was what I'd expected to do. That was just what I wound up doing. This time the trip took nineteen days versus two, but at least my accommodations were better, thanks to my sub-team commander's efforts to screw me. For those not familiar with Navy boats (excuse me—ships), an LSD is essentially a giant floating hole in the water kept dry by walls containing berths for troops on either side of a vast, open well deck where amphibious landing craft or other heavy equipment can be carried.

There were three of us from the 1st ITT on board - our sub--team commander, Lieutenant Cohan, Corporal Chang, and me. The moment we drove up to the ship, Chang turned pale and rushed to the wharf side to throw up, which seemed a rather exaggerated way of announcing our arrival. It turned out that Chang got seasick just looking at seawater, something he proved to my entire satisfaction by spending the next nineteen days tossing his cookies overboard. I was sometimes tempted to do the same, since the *Point Defiance* was essentially a flat-bottomed barge and bounced constantly as it boinged from wave to wave across the whole damned Pacific Ocean. And that sometimes got a bit tiring. And, as if that weren't bad enough, our Navy hosts hot bunked us and fed us poorly. Conditions were especially miserable in the troop decks, where hundreds of Marines huddled together with nothing more than narrow bunks stacked seven high to call home.

A few days after our odyssey began, when I mentioned to Lieutenant Cohan that I was getting bored, he smiled an evil grin and said he might be able to find a little job to keep me busy. Apparently our hosts were looking for a sucker to take charge of the ship's library, and I could read. Cohan led me to the office of the ship's recreation officer and told him (without asking me) that I'd volunteered to be the ship's library clerk, then quickly disappeared to resume his own arduous duties elsewhere, although heaven knows what they were. The squid JG (slang for a Junior Ensign, the lowest rank of a Navy officer) in charge of fun and games told me to follow him, led me to the library, handed me the keys, for which I was now solely responsible, and left, never to be seen again. Presumably, he too had other arduous duties to perform elsewhere, like counting ping pong balls, marking decks of cards, or cheating at chess. Anyhow, abandoned by my superiors, I took a quick look around the library and confirmed that it did, indeed, contain books. It even housed some magazines and furniture. From that moment on I spent all day every day buried in the library waiting for my first customer, who never came.

For all I could tell, Cohan may have been right when he said I might be the only one on the ship that knew how to read, although presumably at least the ship's Captain had to be literate, and every time I saw Cohan I bitterly bitched and whined about the boredom brought on by my arduous job.

This seemed to warm the cockles of his heart. Unfortunately, since neither he nor my titular Navy supervisor ever visited the library, I never found it necessary to describe to them my real situation. Unlike any other cabin aboard the ship (with the possible exception of the Captain's suite) the library was spacious, fully carpeted, well above the water line, and had portholes with windows that opened, so anyone in the library - meaning, in this case, just me - could access fresh air free of engine oil and see the water, waves, and clouds outside. There was also a large, overstuffed leather easy chair and ottoman that, when pushed together, served as my six foot long bunk for the rest of the trip. Other than visits to the chow hall, the well deck to watch a movie, or to check on Chang (who was not doing very well, I might add), I spent almost every waking moment and every night protecting my new territory. I had far and away the best quarters of any Marine aboard. But, discretion being the better part of whining, I never complained about these positives to the man that found me the job.

Once we arrived at the island of Mindoro, we joined up with some other Marines that were already there, as well as with a small unit of Filipino Rangers, better known as Black Pyjamas, for an extended counterinsurgency exercise made especially realistic by some Huk guerrillas lurking in the nearby jungles. Shortly after we arrived, a messenger came huffing up to my new quarters and said that the commanding Colonel needed an interpreter "immediately." Given Chang's heavy Chinese accent and the Lieutenant's lack of languages, I was chosen to do the honors. I faithfully followed the Colonel's lackey through the camp to his boss, who stood on a ledge overlooking a small, peaceful ravine that "We, the Few, the Proud, the Marines" were busily filling up with garbage.

Obviously distraught, or at least pissed off, the Colonel turned to me, pointed at the garbage heap, and asked, "Do you see what those @#*ing people are doing down there? They're digging in our garbage!"

"Yes, sir, they are," I said.

"Well, tell them to stop it, dammit! It's unsanitary."

Frankly, having been in the boondocks (Marine-ese for the backside of beyond) in developing countries from Nicaragua to Thailand, it looked to me like they were simply proto-environmentalists that were ahead of the times, recycling things the Marines had thrown away, tin cans they could make into lanterns, cardboard they could use to keep rain out of their huts, and all sorts of other goodies. In fact, they were doing exactly what twenty-odd years later environmental greens began demanding everyone do. But the Colonel was apparently not an environmentalist.

So, when I hesitated, his face started turning red, "Dammit, Marine. I just gave you a direct, @#*ing order. Tell those gook sons of bitches to get the @#* out of our garbage!"

I responded in as non-mutinous a voice as I could muster, "Yes, sir. Right away, sir!"

Stepping to the ledge alongside the Colonel, I looked down at "the gooks," cupped my hands over my mouth, and yelled as loudly as I could, "The Colonel says for you to get out of our @#*ing garbage and stay out."

The Colonel turned and looked at me in total disbelief, "Tell them in their own @#*ing language, you idiot. You're an interpreter, aren't you?"

"Yes, sir. But I don't speak their language. They speak Tagalog, and I'm a Thai and Spanish interpreter. But I do have a phrase book. Let's see if I can figure out how to say 'stop digging in our @#*ing garbage' in Tagalog."

Actually they probably spoke one of the other one hundred and eighty or so languages spoken in the Philippines. But the Colonel didn't seem especially interested in cross-cultural confusions in the tropics, or anywhere else for that matter. So I kept my mouth shut. After a few seconds, he just shook his head and stomped away.

At that point a light bulb went off in my head. The Colonel had requested a team of interpreters without specifying which language. His cultural insensitivity to the fact that different people in different countries speak different languages was about to cost me three months of my life. So there I was, five thousand miles and nineteen days from home, sitting in the middle of an island in the Philippines, deep inside an area teeming with Huk guerrillas, with little to do but pout. I didn't even have Cohan handy, since, realizing that he was at least partially at fault for accepting the assignment without getting the necessary details, he was making himself scarce.

ELEVEN

THE LOST PATROL

Thankfully, the unit's Counterintelligence (CI) Officer came to my rescue by asking me to help him devise a discreet way to stay in close contact with the Filipino Rangers that had begun to fan out into the jungles around the operations area to try to keep the Huks off our backs. After thinking it over for several long seconds, I suggested putting a network of Marines in the hamlets and villages via which the Filipino Rangers could contact us without compromising their security. He responded that, while it seemed like a good idea, he didn't have anyone willing to do that sort of a job. At that point I committed a venial sin by volunteering to take on the task. I spent the next day racially profiling my fellow Marines looking for brown, or at least well-toasted, Marines that might be able to live in a Filipino rice village without sticking out like a sore thumb. They also needed to have enough common sense not to get too drunk or horny.

I still have the field notebook in which I wrote their names, from Chang, Chung, and Chicovega to Velasco, Tumbaga, and Davenport. They were mostly Hispanics, Mexicans, Puerto Ricans, second-generation American Filipinos, or Chinese, including Chang. A couple of them were Recon Marines, and all of them were volunteers. Being the palest face among them, I started to spend every possible moment in the sun trying to get a dark tan. But since there wasn't much I could do about my eyes, I also disguised myself as the "Sunglasses Kid." When I got back home, Leda looked at me and said she didn't know she'd married an Indian.

My motley crew of volunteers was enthusiastic about doing something entirely different, even after I explained that it would involve their living on their own among a local population that included girls. After giving them a quick briefing, I met with the Ranger commander and the Marine CI officer to discuss the project and to select the villages where my men would be both relatively safe and available should the need arise to make contact.

Before deploying them to their new homes, I thought it would be useful to build some unit cohesion, so I scheduled a helicopter flight to an open field behind a nearby hill from which we could leisurely stroll back to our base camp. Yeah, right! The air wing came up with a helicopter big enough to transport us all, I picked a landing zone (LZ) well within our defensive perimeter and nowhere near any reported Huk activities, ran my choice by our intelligence office, and then carefully marked the spot for the pilot and copilot on their terrain map. Since it was supposed to be just a short hike in friendly territory, we didn't draw ammunition or rations.

When the pilot announced that we'd landed on the designated LZ, my men quickly jumped out of the helicopter. After all the others had exited, I jumped out, and the chopper took off like a bat out of hell. Slowly picking myself up, I looked around to see if anyone else had made a hard landing. It turned out that the pilot hadn't landed at all, but had simply hovered over a field of saw grass. The good news was that only three of us had made a hard enough landing to damage anything.

author's collection

Mindoro, Philippines, 1962. The hut from which I ran the ad-hoc CI network. The village housed six families of refugees from other islands, each of which spoke a different language.

The bad news was that one was my radio man who'd landed on his radio and smashed it. I was another, with a finger sliced open by the saw grass. That wouldn't have been a problem, if the third man who'd sustained serious equipment damage hadn't been our medic. Still, I wasn't too worried since we'd be back at camp within an hour where I could have the doctor at the clinic put a bandage on it.

So I pulled out a small scale terrain map and began trying to orient us with the hill overlooking our base camp. The hill behind which we'd been dropped was much steeper and higher than any of those on the map, and I couldn't find it or the jungle opening where we were standing anywhere on it.

So I pulled out a larger scale map I'd brought with me and, sure enough, instead of dropping us at the designated LZ, the pilot had flown an extra six or seven miles and dumped us behind the wrong hill right in the middle of a red zone of recent Huk operations. So there I was, leading a patrol of Marines in combat uniforms with no rations, a limited water supply, a broken radio, no medical supplies, and ammo-less weapons.

Mindoro, Philippines, 1962. Handwritten roster of my "actors," the fruits of my ethnic profiling. Most were Latinos, Pacific Islanders, or Chinese. Even then, Marines were an eclectic lot.

As soon as I realized what had happened, I made a snap command decision to get the hell out of Dodge as fast as we could. After hastily briefing my Marines on our situation, I told them it was forced march time, because we had to get back to base camp before dark adding that, given the terrain and distance, our only option was to climb straight up the mountain in front of us and straight down the other side as fast as we could. Had it not been for having to keep our eyes out for Huks and local headhunters, it would have been a great hike. Even so, it turned out to be one of my most memorable experiences in Southeast Asia.

Sending one of my recon Marines forward as a scout, we began marching as quickly as we could up the mountain, mostly following what looked like game trails. Unfortunately, we had very little time to stop and admire the flora of what appeared to be a climax rain forest. After about an hour we began to see trails and smell smoke. We continued upward until we came to a small clearing that appeared to be the home of several families of natives. Thankfully, the only firearms they had were a couple of very old flintlocks they probably used for hunting, hopefully meaning they weren't Huk sympathizers. Pulling out my trusty Tagalog phrase book, I asked in my best Gringo accent if they could kindly point the way to the nearest road. They just stared at me in bewilderment. When I asked again and was met with more blank stares, I realized that they probably spoke a different language. So, using one of the few phrases I'd carefully practiced with the Filipino Rangers, I asked if anyone understood Tagalog. In response, one of the children ran off to a hut that stood slightly apart from the others and came back with a village elder who turned out to be the only person in the village who spoke it.

Finally, I was able to get directions to the nearest road, or so I assumed, when he gestured forcefully up the mountain and said with unusual urgency something that sounded like, "Get the hell out of here, fast. There are Huks around here!" It seemed like good advice.

As we continued up the mountain, the trails became scarcer and scarcer until we came to another web of trails that led to a second village, this one consisting of primitive lean-tos. Once again, none of the villagers seemed to speak Tagalog or to understand my questions. So I began making hand signals, imitating someone driving a car and making noises like a motor, while pointing and then shrugging. Once again a village elder came to our rescue, pointed up the mountain and began making gestures that indicated some not very nice people with guns were in the area, and so we might want to get the hell out of there as fast as we could. As a parting gesture, they also offered us water. But since it probably hadn't been treated for *e coli,* we politely declined.

As we clambered further up the mountain we saw the occasional faint trail. But we didn't run into another web of trails until we started down the other side of the mountain. There we ran into a third group of natives that weren't wearing anything at all, except for the men, who were wearing penis shields. They seemed even more anxious than the other groups to help us move on, lest our presence cause them problems. My Tagalog phrase book was even less useful with this group, until one of the young men offered, as best I could tell, to lead us down the mountain, which he did.

By then it was late afternoon, we'd almost run out of water and even the Recon Marines were begging for a break since we'd been force marching for more than five hours. But I wasn't about to take more than five-minute breaks until we could get ourselves out of the mess the pilots had put us in. Even with a guide it took us another two hours to get off the mountain and another hour or so to reach the nearest road. Only then did I decide it was safe enough to take a longer rest. After we all caught our breath and managed to cadge some cool drinks from a passing truck, we headed for our base camp at a fairly leisurely pace, finally arriving just as the sun set. When I told the CI officer what had happened, he blanched. But since we'd returned safe and sound, he opted not to file an official complaint against the pilots, deciding to talk to them at the Officer's Club over the few beers they'd owe him for keeping his mouth shut. Since, as a mere NCO, I wasn't allowed in the O'Club, I went back to my tent and collapsed.

Safely back from "solidifying unit cohesion," just as the *Guidebook for Marines* recommended, I began putting my little network in place. Two men would be in each village identified by the Filipino Rangers so that if one of them needed to run a message there would still be one to cover the village. They clearly enjoyed pretending to be spooks, although being required to wear combat boots at all times made it difficult for them to blend in with the barefoot natives. This came into play especially once the training exercise began and the main unit started sending out patrols to sweep the villages. Within days, several of my men had been detained as suspected insurgents, put into POW camps and interrogated, all good, clean Marine fun until, suddenly, our mission went from training to real.

The Rangers contacted one of my outposts to report that a patrol of ten to twelve armed Huks had been spotted moving toward our main base. Just as we'd practiced, a courier came to me to report the information. The minute he delivered his message, I sent a FLASH ACTUAL message by runner

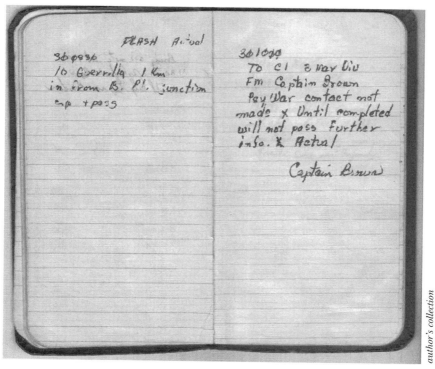

Mindoro, Philippines, 1962. The draft of my FLASH ACTUAL message reporting the sudden appearance of a Huk patrol moving toward our positions.

indicating that a patrol of real live Huks was moving toward our base camp. Not that a small squad of Huks was likely to attack a battalion of Marines. The concern was that they might steal weapons from us which, I found out later, they did anyway—a couple of rifles and a machine gun. I now realize that we'd created a covert support network that would have made the Huk's guerrilla warfare instructors proud. After a couple of months of such nonsense, I was anxious to get back home. Instead I received orders to fly to Bangkok on a Military Air

Transport Service (MATS) flight by way of Saigon, where I found myself on yet another COIN mission in the boondocks.

But one thing about my "lost patrol" experience kept bothering me. On our way up the mountain, we'd passed through three different tribal villages, each more primitive that the last. When I got back to Hawaii, I called my University of Hawaii anthropology professor, and described what I'd seen. He responded that it was a classic settlement pattern that repeated itself throughout much of Southeast Asia. When a wave of newcomers arrives, they'd usually be more technologically advanced than the people already living on the land, and force the earlier settlers to retreat. When a still more advanced group moves into the area this pattern repeats itself. This process slowly pushes the more primitive groups up the mountain. It seemed like a good explanation, except for one thing. What happens when they reach the top? Solheim had no answer.

TWELVE

3 MEB—3rd Marine Expeditionary Brigade

Several months after I returned to Hawaii, the phone rang. It was the kind of call I'd come to expect and Leda had come to dread.

"A jeep is on its way to pick you up. You're leaving on an assignment."

"For how long?" I asked.

"We don't know."

"Where to?"

"I can't tell you."

"Can you give me an address so my wife can stay in touch?"

"No. No address. No phone. No direct contact. She'll have to communicate through us."

Less than an hour later I was holding a sealed set of then Secret/Eyes Only orders that read (and I'm not making this up), "You are hereby directed to report immediately by first available transportation to the Commanding General, JTF116, wherever he may be." Who and where he was no one seemed to know, not even CINCPAC's Movement Reports Center, the one place that was supposed to know the location of all American military forces between California and the Mediterranean. When I asked my then commanding officer, Captain Cook, he didn't know either. He simply told me, "Comply with your orders." So I winged it.

Actually, it wasn't all that hard to guess where I was supposed to go, even if I didn't know what I was supposed to do or who I was supposed to do it for once I got there. But I knew from intelligence reports that had crossed my desk that Pathet Lao units were moving toward the Thai border. I also knew I was a Thai interpreter. Putting two and two together, I packed my gear, went to Naval Air Station Barbers Point and said I wanted to go to Thailand. That was the start of one of my most surreal experiences.

"Why do you want to go to Thailand?"

"I can't tell you."

"Where are your orders?"

"Here," I said, patting the envelope. "But I can't show them to you. They're Secret Eyes-Only."

"What unit are you from?"

"That's classified."

Finally, a decision: "Oh, what the hell. We have a flight leaving for the Philippines in about thirty minutes. Do you want to get on it?"

"Sure, why not? That's the right direction."

Within hours of receiving my super-secret orders, I found myself on a Marine cargo plane sleeping on the hood of a jeep all the way to Clark Air Base in the Philippines. When I arrived there I went directly to the movements control office and said, "I want to go to Thailand," and I found myself reliving my earlier conversation at Barber's Point.

"You can't go to Thailand unless you show me your orders."

"I can't show them to you, dammit."

"Then you can't go, dammit!"

And so it went for about an hour until I finally said, "I want to speak to your commanding officer."

Big mistake. His commanding officer turned out to be a 2nd Lieutenant who had neither common sense nor the authority to make decisions. So, I asked to speak with his commanding officer's commanding officer, who turned out to be a Captain with a bit more authority but only slightly more common sense. The whole thing was becoming ridiculous. But, since I wasn't about to stay in the Philippines in violation of my orders, I asked to speak to the Sergeant's commanding officer's commanding officer's commanding officer, who was a Major getting ready to go home, or maybe to one of the more colorful sporting houses in Olongapo, the lively services village just outside the gates of Clark Air Base, who seemed to be in a hurry and said, "Oh, @#* it. You can go any damn place you want."

Eventually I reached the Royal Thai Air Force Base in Khorat, Thailand. It proved to be extremely busy with dozens of aircraft and thousands of American troops frantically coming and going. Much to my surprise and relief, it was the headquarters of "Two-Gun" Peers, the newly arrived Commanding General of Joint Task Force 116 (JTF 116). When, in accordance with my orders, I went looking for its Commanding General to report in, his Command Sergeant Major looked at my two stripes in bewilderment and asked to see my orders.

"Here, Sergeant Major. But they're classified Secret. But what the hell, I'm sure I'm in the right place. So open the damn things."

After a quick look, he said, "Right country, wrong place. Go over to the flight line, jump on that Marine plane sitting there ready to take off for Udorn. That's where the Marines are."

And that's how, a mere cross-Pacific odyssey later, I found myself reporting in to General Ormund R. Simpson, the Commanding General of the 3rd Marine Expeditionary Brigade (3rd MEB), as his personal interpreter.

author's collection

Udorn, Thailand, 1962. Some months after the 3rd MEB left Thailand, I received this photo from Brigadier General, later Lieutenant General Ormond R. Simpson for my work as his personal interpreter and primary liaison with Thai officialdom.

General Simpson was a true gentleman of the old school. The first time I went with him as his interpreter was to a meeting with the Thai Police Commanding General for Northeast Thailand, both generals seemed especially appreciative of my ability to do simultaneous interpreting because it made the meeting go smoothly. While I was technically assigned to the Brigade's counterintelligence office, I bunked near the General's office so I'd be available to him at a moment's notice. When it became apparent that General Simpson would only need me once in a while, he began loaning me out to the medical staff, the military police, subunit commanders, and so forth. He also assigned me as escort-interpreter for VIP visitors, including journalists, congressmen, and the American Ambassador to Thailand, Kenneth Todd Young. I even interpreted for the King when he visited the Brigade, which is how I came to be watching when "We the Few, the Proud, the Marines" almost killed His Majesty—twice.

GUIDE TO THAILAND

**HEADQUARTERS
FLEET MARINE FORCE, PACIFIC
C/O FLEET POST OFFICE, SAN FRANCISCO**

author's collection

FMFPAC, 1962. After my first experiences in Thailand, I realized that my fellow Marines needed a bit of "Miss Manners" style guidance to help them avoid excessively annoying the natives in Thailand. So I wrote and produced my first book, a guide to local customs and traditions. FMFPAC ordered that every Marine assigned to Thailand be given a copy, beginning with the 3rd MEB. Whether or not they read it was another story.

THIRTEEN

To Kill a King - Twice, Almost

Now, as you can imagine, kings rather like to know what's going on inside their kingdoms, and the King of Thailand, Phumiphon Adunyadet, was no exception. So not too long after the MEB arrived, His Majesty decided to formally welcome the new arrivals to his realm. To ensure that his visit went smoothly, General Simpson took personal charge of preparations and assigned me, among other duties, to assist the Thai authorities in any way that I could. Needless to say, I found the prospect exciting—up to the point when the Royal Governor of Northeast Thailand, a member of the royal family, asked me to interpret His Majesty's speech to the Brigade. But since the King might give his speech in royal court language I didn't speak, like a good Marine I didn't just adapt and improvise, I also cheated.

Thankfully, among the Thai officers I'd come to know during my short time in Udorn was a dashing young Air Force Captain who'd been an aide to the King while he was Crown Prince. He understood court language and became enthusiastically helpful once I let him know that I had some dirt on him. He was married to the owner of a local Chinese restaurant but was secretly sleeping with her gorgeous young daughter, so I offered him a deal he couldn't refuse. In return for my not ratting him out, he agreed to obtain an advanced copy of the King's speech and to translate it into conversational Thai in time for me to translate it from Thai into English.

When the great day arrived, General Simpson was on the flight line, a flight of Marine jets was circling above the airfield preparing to put on a demonstration, and His Majesty's aircraft was on final approach and feathering down, when all hell broke loose. The emergency radio channel of the Marine Forward Air Controller (FAC) crackled to life. One of the Marine jets had a cockpit fire and needed to make an emergency landing, but couldn't because the King's aircraft was in the way. The King's pilot immediately powered up and started to go around so the Marine jet could land. But once a piston engine has been feathered down, suddenly pushing it back to max power creates a real strain on its engines and the King's aircraft lost one.

Now, while I don't know how long humans can hold their breath, I can guarantee that most of those assembled, from General Simpson down, stopped breathing as the King's pilot managed to complete his climb, circle around, and land safely. Compared to that feat, the rest of the ceremony seemed anticlimactic. But it did go well enough that the King and the Crown Prince, who was accompanying him, despite our nearly killing both of them, were quite pleased. But as the cliché goes, all's well that ends well. So, resplendent in a newly ironed utility uniform, to the utter amazement of the Thai officers that were present, I successfully interpreted the King's speech into English.

author's collection

Udorn, Thailand, 1962. I snapped this picture of King Phumiphon Adunyadet of Thailand as he arrived to welcome the 3rd Marine Expeditionary Brigade.

After the close call, the King watched the mock air strike with even greater interest, did a ceremonial review of the honor guard, accepted refreshments, and flew away. But we weren't finished. His second flight gave us a second shot at him, one no less accidental than the first, but potentially just as deadly. From Udorn, His Majesty took off in one of his Alouette helicopters to visit nearby villages. As an aside, I heard later that His Majesty had been especially impressed when several villagers told him that all the Marine pilots were Buddhist priests. I thought that decidedly strange until one of my Thai friends explained that Buddhist priests and Marine flyers both dress in saffron - Buddhist priests in saffron robes,

Marine air crews in saffron flight uniforms. Putting two and two together, the villagers concluded that we were the most pious country on earth since we only let priests fly our war planes.

With the King's visit over, or so I thought, I was just beginning to relax, when the Thai Air Force FAC raced up to me in a panic and said, "We've lost contact with the King's helicopter, and I'm afraid it may have crashed! Do you have it on radar?" We didn't, but the Marine FAC controlling our fighters chimed in and offered to ask their pilots to look around for it. I said, "Do it, now!" (Even NCOs have to make command decisions sometimes.) He immediately radioed to those nearest to the King's supposed location. Initially, they reported that they'd not seen the King's or any other helicopters in the vicinity. Needless to say, that made us nervous, until, almost immediately, they radioed back in somewhat unorthodox language, "Holy shit! There's this really big helicopter right between us! I hope to @#* it's not his, because we just damn near made it crash!" (For those not accustomed to flitting around in helicopters, they become extremely unstable when "fast movers" zip by at a couple hundred miles an hour, generating severe air turbulence.) The pilot of the Alouette later commented to my Thai buddy in equally colorful language, "Do you have any idea how close those @#*ing Marine jets came to causing us to crash?"

Kenneth Todd Young, at the time the American Ambassador to Thailand, also came to visit a couple of times, always accompanied by a horde of photographers and hangers-on. As part of each trip, he would meet with local officials and visit nearby villages, taking me with him as his interpreter. I remember one incident during one of his visit especially well. A village elder asked him a seemingly obvious

question, "So why are the American Marines in Thailand?"
But, rather than answering it himself, the Ambassador turned
to me and said, "Tell him."

Udorn, Thailand, 1962. I'm in the foreground with General
Simpson to my left and Ambassador Young between us. The
Ambassador's aircraft is in the background.

I was a mere Corporal, so no one had told me why we
were there. But I swallowed hard and winged it in front of
a gaggle of cameras and microphones. When I finished, the
Ambassador smiled and said, "I hope you got it right, because
what you said is going out over the Voice of America in about
an hour as a statement on American foreign policy." It was

my first real foray into foreign policy making, and the experience convinced me that I was in the wrong line of work, since the senior Embassy officer with him, who should have been doing all the interpreting, just stood there and let me do the work.

author's collection

Udorn, Thailand, 1962. I'm on the far left interpreting for Ambassador Young as he speaks with the Thai Police General, center as the Lord Mayor, far right, looks on.

FOURTEEN

WHORE HOUSES, LABOR RELATIONS, AND COCA COLA

Once he'd gained sufficient confidence in me, General Simpson made me his official liaison with the Thais on almost everything. Since he didn't have a Civil Affairs Officer, to my amazement and the Sergeant Major's shock, he also asked me to sit in on General Staff meetings as his de facto G-5. This made for some decidedly odd staff meetings involving one General, four Colonels, and a Corporal. Also, in addition to being his key contact with the Thai military and police on base-security matters, he also made me Brigade VD (venereal disease) Control Officer [today they're called STDs, sexually transmitted diseases.] The job mostly involved working with the Brigade's medical staff and Thai public health officers to determine which local whorehouses seemed to be giving the most Marines the clap (gonorrhea) or, worse, elephantiasis of the gonads.

Since the entire industry was controlled by the Thai Army, getting information was easier than you might think. Soon after I began doing that job, the regional Thai Army General asked me to distribute a map to the Marines showing which whorehouses were for enlisted, which were for NCOs, and which were for officers, as well as how much each house charged for its services. He also asked me to do what I could to see that no one overpaid, since that would push prices up for everyone.

Most Americans may be shocked by such a businesslike approach to prostitution, especially those from states where it's illegal, unlike my home state of Nevada. But the French would find it very familiar, since their Army routinely deploys mobile field brothels alongside their troops, arguing that the practice improves security, reduces the risk of disease, and gives them a cadre of practical nurses when necessary. The Thai approach allowed them to keep close tabs on the "working girls", something that worked to our advantage.

At one point, according to the chief medical officer, about 10 percent of the Brigade's enlisted but, surprisingly, not a single officer, had gonorrhea. Although, he added, 10 percent of its officers but none of its enlisted had nonspecific urethritis. This made me wonder whether enlisted men and officers might be genetically different, until he explained. It was the Marine Corps' regulations that were different, not the men. If an enlisted Marine contracted VD, it was just another medical problem, and treated as such. But if an officer contracted it, he was subject to disciplinary action, ergo the difference.

One day, while waiting with General Simpson for a visiting journalist, I casually mentioned that my family was pro-organized labor. My father was a Retail Clerks International Union retiree, my mother an officer in the Nevada chapter of the Association of Former Government Employees (AFGE), and my stepfather was on Nevada's AFL/CIO Committee on Political Education (COPE). Simpson made me Brigade Labor Officer on the spot and gave me responsibility for dealing with locally hired workers as well. As a bonus, he also made me the Brigade's main purchaser of goods from local businesses.

Labor relations were pretty straightforward, since jobs with the Marines were in great demand and we treated our workers quite well. But purchasing taught me lessons in cross-cultural relations I've never forgotten. One was the importance that others assign to the cultural link between Americans and Coca-Cola. Whenever I entered a Thai business, the merchant would invariably hand me a Coke - sometimes cold, sometimes warm, but always a bottle of what the French call *champagne Americaine*. We'd chat a while about the weather, current events, or why the Marines were in Udorn, until finally I would tell them what we might like to buy. At that point, they'd hand me another Coke. They'd then give me their high-ball opening price, and we'd talk for a while about tomorrow's weather, yesterday's events, and why the Marines were still in Udorn, at which point I'd give them a low-ball offer. And so it would go—Coke, chat, price, Coke, chat, counter-price—until we reached an agreement. It didn't take too long or too many trips to the head to realize that the more time I spent in conversation, the lower the price. In fact, if I spent enough time, the price might drop to the item's actual cost. On a couple of occasions, it even fell below cost because time was more valuable to them than the money, up to a point. Plus, as the "American's preferred supplier," they could jack up the price for everyone else.

One thing I quickly learned in Udorn was that, in Thailand, an interpreter is not just someone who interprets. An interpreter is treated as if they hold the same rank as their principal, a perception based on how interpreters for the King or other high ranking officials are to be treated. So to the Thai, when I was carrying out Simpson's instructions, I wasn't Corporal Brown, I was surrogate Brigadier General Brown. This made for some very interesting relationships, not to mention a vast divide between how I was treated by the Thai and how I was treated by some Marine officers. On more than one occasion this also made me a curiosity to my fellow Marines.

Among my closest Thai contacts were the Police Commanding General, the manager of the local bank that handled foreign exchange for the MEB, and the Lord Mayor of Udorn, who was an official of the Royal Court and the *de facto* if not *de jure* Governor of Northeast Thailand. The Police General got me in the most trouble, the bank manager caused the most raised eyebrows, and the Lord Mayor taught me the most valuable lessons.

In Thailand, at least in those days, a man never held hands with a woman in public. But men did hold hands with each other as a sign of trust. After every meeting, the bank manager would invite me out for lunch and we'd walk hand in hand from his office to a restaurant, while the occasional passing Marine would look at us in total disbelief and call the MPs. The General found that strange but, after I explained the custom to him, just shook his head, so it never caused me a problem. But the way the Thai Police General treated me did occasionally cause one. Once, when the Police General asked me to go see him, I arrived at his office at the same time as the Lieutenant Colonel commanding the Brigade's infantry battalion, and the General asked the Colonel to wait outside while he spoke with me in private. The Colonel was incensed. How dare a mere Corporal upstage him! And no matter how hard I tried to explain, he was never able to accept my admittedly bizarre position. But then I don't believe he ever made General either. As for the Lord Mayor, my dealings with him over a road roller taught me the most.

When our engineers realized that they needed a road roller to compact several roads in the base area before the monsoon arrived, they were faced with a choice—fly one in from Okinawa or find one locally. Flying one in would require a special transport mission and the only one available locally belonged to the Mayor. If we'd been in the United States or Latin America, I would have simply asked the Lord Mayor to loan it to us for a while. But this was Thailand, and there was an elaborate protocol for making such requests. When I explained to the General what needed to be done, he looked a bit perplexed but agreed to follow my recommendation.

My first step was to call the Mayor's office and make an appointment to have afternoon tea with him. At first we chatted, and he told me fascinating stories about his experiences during the Japanese occupation of Thailand in World War II, a time when he played a double role. Overtly, he was the key Thai liaison with the Japanese occupiers. But covertly, he was the King's regional intelligence officer. He regaled me with stories for about a half an hour as we sipped tea and nibbled on delicacies. When I left, the Mayor insisted on accompanying me. I demurred, thanking him for the offer but insisting that wasn't necessary. He insisted, and once again I demurred, until we'd gone through this obligatory courtesy three times. At that point I surrendered and said I'd be honored to have him walk out with me, which he did, accompanying me all the way to the gate of his compound, a route that took us by his motor pool. As we walked by, I admired his fire truck, his dump truck, his tractor, and especially his magnificent road roller.

I then went back to camp and recommended to General Simpson that he make an appointment for the next day to have tea with the Lord Mayor and listen to his war stories. On our way, I briefed the General on how to proceed. Thankfully, he wasn't a Lieutenant, so he was willing to follow my suggestions, though he found them a bit excessive. When we arrived at the palace, the Lord Mayor met us at the door and escorted us to his office, where we sipped tea while the General listened to his war stories. About half an hour later, the General began to take his leave, and the Lord Mayor offered to walk out with us. General Simpson demurred the customary three times and then accepted his kind offer. Once again he walked us out past his motor pool, where the General admired his fire truck, his dump truck, his tractor, then stopped and expressed a great deal of admiration for his beautiful road roller.

At that point, the Mayor said, "Yes, it is a rather nice road roller, isn't it. By the way, I've noticed that you might be able to use one on your new roads. Would you like to borrow it?"

The General responded, "I wouldn't dream of taking your road roller from you. It's so beautiful!"

"No, I insist," said the Lord Mayor. "I'd be honored if you would allow me to lend it to you for a few days. I'll even throw in the driver, although I hope you don't pay him more than we do, since I wouldn't want him to come back and ask for a raise."

Once again, the General said no, the Lord Mayor insisted, the General said no less emphatically, the Lord Mayor insisted a bit more forcefully, and finally the General agreed, but only because that would make the Mayor happy.

When we got to his jeep, General Simpson looked at me and asked, "What in the world was that all about?"

I explained, "Had you simply asked the Mayor if we could borrow his road roller without going through the rituals of Thai courtesy, he would have immediately lent it to us, even if he'd needed it desperately to save his daughter's virtue. The ritual avoided your directly asking him for a favor because, if you had, he would have been obligated to grant it immediately regardless, because refusing your request would have caused you—not him—to lose face. And, in Thailand, causing another person to lose face is to be avoided if at all possible. During my earlier visit I set the stage for your visit by making a special point of admiring his road roller. More than likely he'd immediately sent someone to investigate and was told that we could use one. So when you came to call on him, he was already prepared to loan it to you. That's the way it works in Thailand."

One incident while I was serving as General Simpson's surrogate still gives me nightmares. It began when the Thai Police General asked me to come see him because he needed help with a problem being caused by our men. There were a dozen or more crippled child beggars scattered throughout a neighborhood liberally salted with restaurants, bars, and whorehouses. The area was frequented by off-duty Marines looking for a good time. The problem was that the Marines were giving the children money. At first I didn't understand. Marines giving money to crippled kids hardly seemed like something to criticize. The Thai General explained, "Some of them weren't crippled until you arrived. Let me show you something."

He took me to a neighborhood of small warehouses on the outskirts of town. When we stopped in front of one, the General led me inside. Four or five children, the oldest about the age of my oldest daughter, were lying on mats lined up against the walls. When I took a closer look, I saw several with broken legs and backs, all of them bound with ropes in positions that guaranteed they would be crippled permanently. He then explained. A criminal gang had been buying, or simply kidnapping, small children from poor villages, bringing them in and deliberately crippling them to make then look as pathetic as possible. They then placed them on street corners in the neighborhood the Marines were visiting to beg for money. The more pathetic they were the more the Marines would give them. They then took most of the money away from the children and kept it for themselves. If a cripple wasn't collecting enough to make them worth exploiting, the criminals would simply kill them and go back to the villages for replacements. It was as coldblooded a racket as I could imagine. The police were trying to stop them. But with the amount of money the Marines were giving the beggars, when they rolled up one gang, another would take its place. So they needed our help.

Back at the Brigade, after I stopped shaking, I told General Simpson what was happening. He immediately called in his Chief of Staff and told him to launch a campaign to keep the troops from giving money to any of the beggar children, because it was just attracting more to the region.

A few weeks later, when the Lord Mayor threw a ball in honor of General Simpson, I learned the rest of the story. A traditional Thai orchestra and troop of temple dancers were providing the entertainment; the Lord Mayor and General Simpson were seated at the head table; and I had positioned myself between, but slightly behind them so they could maintain eye contact without being distracted by me. Halfway through the festivities a pretty young Thai girl, impeccably dressed in a traditional sarong of handmade silk, approached the Lord Mayor on her knees, bowed low, and began speaking to him. When I didn't immediately interpret what she was saying, the General looked at me and asked me what was happening. I promised to explain as soon as she finished, but wanted to listen in on their conversation closely to be sure

I got it right. When she finished, the Mayor gave her some instructions and returned to watching the dancers, and I turned to the General to explain. The "young girl" was an undercover police officer reporting the arrest of the criminals running the networks of crippled child beggars. The Mayor's orders had been simple and to the point, "Execute them." I suppose one could argue that they didn't get proper trials. But I couldn't feel much sympathy for them. And, given the admittedly draconian executions, the crippled children, and hence the racket that was leading to their being crippled, did largely disappear.

A few months later, when the Brigade began to withdraw from Thailand, I received orders to return to Hawaii. But they were immediately countermanded by a second set of orders instructing me to travel wherever necessary in support of its withdrawal. And then, as soon as the Brigade had completed its withdrawal, those orders were countermanded by yet a third set, ordering me to report to the J2, Assistant Chief of Staff for Intelligence of the Joint US Military Advisory Group in Bangkok, for assignment to yet a different mission. That mission took me to two places. The first was a then-secret remote installation. The second was Nakhon Phanom, a small town on the Mekong River in Northeast Thailand where I was asked to collect intelligence on possible security threats to American military installations that were to be built nearby. It was not until several weeks later that I was finally able to return to my family in Hawaii. Leda tells me that, to this day, I still occasionally scream in Thai in my sleep.

FIFTEEN

DON'T ASK, DON'T TELL. DON'T EVEN KNOW?

1ST INTERROGATION-TRANSLATION TEAM
HEADQUARTERS
FLEET MARINE FORCE, PACIFIC
C/O FPO, SAN FRANCISCO, CALIFORNIA 96601

LC:ghm
5062
11 March 1963

From: Team Commander
To: Sgt T. C. BROWN

Subj: Report of status, lack thereof

1. You are directed to immediately submit a report of your whereabouts, expected time of return, and present duties. If for some reason you are not permitted to divulge this information, then a report to this effect will be sufficient.

L. COHAN, Jr.
Acting

While I was on another mission, this March 1963 memo from my sub-team commander, Lieutenant Cohan, reached me via Air America's covert post office inside the Udorn Royal Thai Air Force Base. It was so bizarre, and because it was unclassified, I couldn't resist keeping a copy.

author's collection

Near Sakon Nakhon, Thailand, 1963. Author while serving as interpreter for a survey archeology team headed by Dr. Solheim of the University of Hawaii that was making an inventory of sites to be flooded behind new dams. Left to right: Chet Gorman, then a doctoral student, the author, wearing a turban, and Dr. Solheim (photo repaired by Gabrielle Peterson Newman).

At the time, I was moving in and out of the Udorn base in civilian clothes, not always via the main gate, investigating the situation in some rural villages in nearby parts of Northeast Thailand where Pathet Lao agitprop teams were said to be active. As strange as Cohan's memo was, my response was even stranger. "Sorry, sir, you don't have a need to know." I was under instructions from the G-2, the Assistant Chief of Staff for Intelligence, FMFPAC, Cohan's boss's boss. And if his boss's boss hadn't told him where I was, what I was doing, or when I might return, I wasn't going tell him, either. The Colonel had verbally told me what he wanted, but hadn't given me written instructions on how I should go about collecting it. I had a suspicion that his sending me to collect intelligence was more than a bit to the left of kosher, since it was the sort of information the Office of Naval Intelligence (ONI) was supposed to collect, but apparently wasn't. It was the sort of nitty-gritty, low-level information a Marine infantry unit would need were it deployed to a given location—black, white, and grey lists identifying who was a friend and who was a foe in a given area, road trafficability, that sort of thing. But orders were orders, so of course I complied.

I also suspected that Cohan might not have approved of how I was going about collecting it, especially the fun stuff, like joining an archeological expedition, going into hill-tribe country with Thai Border Patrol Police (BPP) on counter-narcotics patrols, or simply wandering from village to village sleeping in Buddhist temples, ingesting and then extruding some of the world's hottest chili, taking the political temperature of the villagers.

It wasn't the only time I worked out of an Air America facility. There had been others and there would be more. In this instance, I'd volunteered to join an archeological expedition led by Dr. Solheim. The expedition itself was a joint Thai-American effort to survey archeological sites that would be flooded behind several new dams, precisely the areas where the Pathet Lao were reportedly were active. The archeology taught me a great deal about the history of the region, while the opportunity to revisit some of the region's troubled rice villages gave me an opportunity to take the temperature of the villagers. And accompanying it and other opportunities such as accompanying BPP (Border Patrol Police) patrols into the tribal highlands gave me an opportunity to investigate other problems, especially the opium trade and elephant smuggling. The Colonel had also asked me to investigate the condition of several long-abandoned airstrips built by the Japanese occupation forces during World War II. I was able to obtain a list of about thirty of them from a local contact and went to look at several. Over the years they'd been slowly buried by drifting soil, and now they simply looked like open fields. But the runways were still there underneath and, as far as I could see, still in reasonably good condition. So with minimal effort they might quickly be made usable. Scrape off the dirt, patch a few cracks, and, voilà, you'd have an airfield!

As for his request that I assess road traffickability and indigenous transport capabilities in the region, this mostly involved my riding oxcarts along the region's secondary dirt roads and measuring the depth and stickiness of the mud during the rainy season, when they became impassable to anything other than large-wheeled oxcarts and elephants. So the question was, how many oxcarts and elephants were there in the region, and how many would it take to move a Marine battalion ten miles in the mud? After riding oxcarts and counting elephants for a couple of weeks, I had my answer. I estimated that, by using every oxcart and elephant in the region, you might be able to move a Marine battalion ten miles in ten days. In the meantime, a guerrilla force like the Pathet Lao, moving on foot, could probably run six or seven laps a day around it, much as the Plains Indians had done to slow-moving caravans of settlers many years earlier.

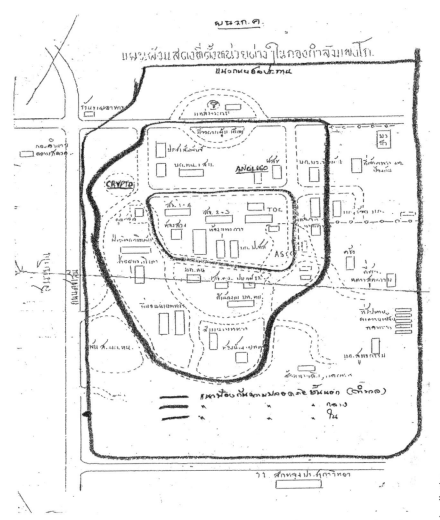

Petchabun, Thailand, 1964: Thai Army sketch-map of Tango Remote Site.

Note USMC ANGLICO detachment, crypto center and three defensive perimeters

author's collection

Phetchabun Mountains, Thailand, 1964. At the request of a senior Thai Army officer, I was sent to Remote Site Tango to help survey its three ring perimeter security system and interpret during a visit by the King. They gave me this map as a souvenir (partial translation by Watchara Ruaisanthiah Lizama).

Toward the end of this rather long deployment, I was sent to the Thai Navy's airfield at Sattahip on the Gulf of Thailand to help an engineering team survey it for use during planned future US military operations. The team's main concerns were housing and base security, which was fairly straightforward and only took up part of my time. So, while I was there I also helped the Thai Marines upgrade their English-language school. Then one day, I suddenly received yet another set of orders directing me to return immediately to Bangkok for another assignment. The King was planning to visit another remote installation in the mountains near the capital of Phetchabun Province and a senior Thai Army officer I'd dealt with earlier in Udorn had asked for my help while they prepared for it. It turned out to be a remote site called, rather unimaginatively, Remote Site Tango, housing a Marine Air and Naval Gunfire Liaison (ANGLICO) detachment being protected by a Thai Army unit. Once at Tango Site I was asked by the Thai security team to accompany them to inspect its defensive perimeters. (I learned just recently that they were probably using Agent Orange precursors to keep the site's perimeter free of undergrowth.)

Back in Hawaii, I wrote a trip report, sent it to the G-2, and forgot about it, until the ITT's new commanding officer, Captain Biel, dropped by my cubicle to say that FMFPAC Commanding General Krulak wanted to chat with me. I quickly put down my coffee cup, brushed the cookie crumbs off my uniform, buffed my shoes on the back of my trousers, and trotted up to his office to see what he had in mind. He seemed mostly interested in some of the raw intelligence information I'd brought back concerning the regions fronting Laos. Apparently, a contingency plan his staff had prepared in case Marines were deployed to Thailand again, had concluded that there was nothing to worry about. There was a really big river between Laos and Thailand, the Mekong. So the Pathet Lao shouldn't be a concern, since they probably didn't know how to swim. Or at least that's what I surmised it said when the General asked if I thought the Mekong River would stop an attempt by the Pathet Lao to invade Thailand. I replied that the Mekong and the region's miserable roads might be seen as barriers by us, but they probably wouldn't even slow down the Pathet Lao. They'd just use canoes. At that point, the General stopped asking questions and I wandered back to my cubicle, finished my coffee, and went back to my office to study for night school.

One of my last deployments was especially sensitive. I was tasked with being cultural advisor and interpreter for a team assigned to prepare the Royal Lao Air Force for future operations. Since I spoke neither Lao nor French, (the Lao's second language), I had to improvise. French? No problem. Spanish is close enough, so I'd use it. Lao? It's no further from Thai than Italian is from Portuguese, so it would do. Within days, off I went on yet another C-130. (Marines called them GV-1s.) After quick stops at Kadena Air Base in Okinawa and Tan Son Nhut, Vietnam, I found myself back at the supposedly ultra-secret Air America base in Udorn. Its parking aprons were covered with weird, unmarked airplanes being flown by temporarily defrocked Marine pilots into a country we weren't allowed to mention, making for some very strange conversations between the pilots that were already there and those I was working with.

"Hey, Abbot, what the @#* are you doing here in civvies?"

"Shit, man, I've been a civilian since Tuesday. Now I'm an Air America pilot flying a Porter STOL (short take-off and landing aircraft) north. Won't get back to the Corps for another month or two, maybe more. Man, that thing can land on a dime. Good thing, too. Some places I land are about fifty yards long, a @#*ing mountain at one end and trees at the other."

"Where's that?"

"Can't tell you. It's Top Secret."

"What kind of bullshit is that? There ain't nothin' north of here but Laos!" And off they'd go to the slop chute to get wasted.

As for my own work, I found myself involved in what Clint Eastwood once delicately described as a "cluster @#*." The Lao Air Force officers we were training would listen carefully to detailed explanations of complex systems by well-qualified American Marines. I would promptly interpret their explanations into both Spanish and Thai. Then one of the Lao would interpret my interpretation into Lao. After a few weeks of this, the Lao left for the country with no name.

Actually, the Lao were great guys, smart and, despite us, dedicated to absorbing everything they could. While our next stop was likely be Hong Kong for some R&R (rest and recuperation), theirs would more likely be some God forsaken clearing in the Plaines des Jarres (PDJ) or isolated patch of jungle surrounded by enemies hell-bent on killing them. I've often wondered what happened to them, at least those whose names didn't cross my desk on a KIA, killed-in-action, list. I even burned a couple of candles for them, and I'm not even a Catholic. I've since also often wondered if well-intentioned but half-baked efforts like this one aren't why we keep losing wars.

But at least my work with the Marine training team, along with some related activities, earned me a highly classified Letter of Commendation from the American Ambassador to

Laos, although it took a while to catch up with me—fifty years to be exact. Only recently declassified, the Ambassador's commendation confirmed that I had been one of many in the American military deeply involved in operations in and out of "the country with no name." Those missions also convinced me that, while I loved being a Marine NCO, that wasn't how I wanted to spend the rest of my professional life. And I certainly didn't want to put Leda and our growing brood through another Hawaii.

SIXTEEN

DIFFERENT CORPS, SAME FOREIGN POLICIES

Ever since the day in Managua in 1957 when I overheard Ambassador Whelan tell President Somoza of Nicaragua to shove it, I'd been dreaming of becoming an FSO so that I could one day do the same. It seemed a pretty lofty dream for a career Marine Sergeant with only a high-school diploma. But when I learned the FSO written entrance exam was to be given in Honolulu, I decided take a shot. Despite the distractions of my Marine job, Leda was pushing me to get a college degree and, in my copious spare time, I'd managed to finish more than two years of college courses at the University of Hawaii's night school. So I said to myself, "What the hell. Why not give it a try?" The exam was free, I could take it again if I didn't pass the first time and, just maybe, lighting would strike. I signed up and began to prepare by burying myself in the base library.

Thankfully, when the day came to take the exam I wasn't on another deployment. It was by far the hardest test I'd ever taken and I wasn't at all confident that I'd passed, although I did have an unexpected advantage. Part of the exam required writing an essay on a topic selected from a list they provided, and one of them was "The Overseas Chinese in Asia." I had a great deal of knowledge about precisely that subject, since I'd just completed an all-sources classified report on it because of threats to Indonesia emanating from within its Chinese colony. But I had two problems. One was how to keep my essay within the exam's limits, because I knew too much about the subject. The other was to avoid including classified information. To my amazement, I passed.

The next steps included an oral exam, a security background investigation, and, if those went well, a medical checkup. The security and health parts didn't worry me. I'd had a Top Secret Specat (special category) clearance since Managua. And, despite brushes with diseases like cholera, malaria, and various and sundries tropical parasites, I was in reasonably good health. The problem turned out to be that, as the only available strategic level Thai interpreter in the Pacific theatre, I was subject to deployment at a moment's notice. The first several times the State Department scheduled me for my oral exam, I was deployed. The first time, I was deep inside the Thai boondocks. The second time I was working what were delicately called "remote sites." The third time, I was on yet another mission. After that one, the State Department Board of Examiners told me it wouldn't be given again in Honolulu for more than a year, but I could schedule to take it in San Francisco, if I was willing to fly there to take I, which I was. But when the day came, once again I was back in Southeast Asia.

The Board finally gave up trying to schedule it anywhere convenient and told me that, with three weeks' notice, if I was willing to go to DC they would arrange for me to take it there. Some weeks later I was in Udorn helping to open a new Consulate, when a window of opportunity appeared. So the second message sent from the Consulate was from me to the State Department asking them to schedule my exam in DC the next month. I had to fly from Thailand to Washington space available on military aircraft to take it, which I did. I showed up at the State Department in uniform, complete with the three stripes of a buck Sergeant, two hash marks for having been a Marine for more than eight years, and three rows of ribbons, including a Good Conduct medal with two stars that confirmed that I'd never been caught doing anything naughty.

The exam took about an hour, during which five examiners asked me questions designed not so much to test my knowledge as my reactions. One I'll never forget. I was asked to list the ten busiest seaports in the United States by gross tonnage forward, for heaven's sake. I doubt the Commandant of the Coast Guard could have recited that off the top of his head. But they didn't expect me to know the answer. They just wanted to see how I handled the impossible. My answer was short and sweet: "I have no idea. But if you want me to, I'll guess." They told me later that I missed nine out of ten.

Near the end, the examiners threw me what I assumed they thought was another curveball. "You're an officer in the American Embassy in a country of your choice, and you've just been assigned as its Desk Officer back in Washington, DC. You've been granted a fifteen-minute interview with the Foreign Minister of that country. Take a couple of minutes to make your choice and to prepare your questions."

When I said I was ready, they asked which country I'd chosen. It was interesting to watch the examiners exchange glances when I said Burma (today's Myanmar), since, as I suspected, few if any of them knew much about that country. As for my questions, they concerned specific issues: Burmese

Army operations in the tribal areas, the illegal traffic in emeralds, relations between Burma and China, the problems in the Ten Thousand Rice Fields. The tactic could have backfired. But thankfully, it didn't. Instead, the examiners seemed to enjoy having a candidate who could help them with the answers.

Then they threw me what they no doubt considered yet another curve ball, "Now you're back at the Embassy. Dictate a reporting cable to the State Department on your interview." Since I was a trained interrogator and intelligence analyst, and accustomed to drafting reports on conversations, I was able to respond without hesitation. I was also prepared for their next approach, a Mutt-and-Jeff routine in which one of them pretended to be hostile, while the others remained neutral. I'd been trained in the use of this good guy/bad guy approach and using it myself for years, so I knew better than to let them rattle me.

When the exam ended, they asked me to wait outside. Within fifteen minutes, an examiner came out to congratulate me on passing, but asked me to come back into the exam room because there was a problem. They'd never had an enlisted Marine show up in uniform, much less an area specialist who spoke an Asian language at the simultaneous interpreter level, were very interested in my candidacy and were prepared to offer me a commission on the spot. But that would make me the only officer in the Foreign Service without a college degree. So they wanted to know what I was planning to do if I hadn't passed. I said I intended to leave the Marines and go to college to complete my degree. I don't know if similar deals were ever offered to other candidates, but the one they offered me was magnanimous, to say the least. Even though I had three children and a fourth on the way, they recommended that I give college a try. But they would guarantee me immediate entry into the Foreign Service with the very next class if it became too much.

With my next career largely set, I trotted back to Hawaii. Shortly after I arrived, my battalion commander, Colonel Antink, called me into his office to discuss my future. He explained that the Marines were losing far too many linguists, so HQMC would give me a direct commission as a Warrant Officer or Limited Duty Officer if I stayed in the Corps. He suggested that I take my time, since an immediate decision wasn't necessary.

author's collection

Reno, Nevada, 1964. "The house at the bottom of the hill" where we lived during my year at the University of Nevada, Reno. Note the elaborate landscaping.

I answered, "I'm very proud to be a Marine, sir. But I'm going to take the Foreign Service commission."

The Colonel looked at me, smiled, and said, "I told them you weren't stupid!"

I was and still am proud to be a Marine, although leaving the Corps for the Foreign Service is a decision I've never regretted. A few weeks later, I shipped out to Mare Island in San Francisco for an early discharge so I could start classes at the University of Nevada on time.

During my year in college, we lived just down the hill from my mother's house in a small house that Leda somehow managed to furnish for just one hundred dollars. My first move was to meet with my faculty advisor, Dr. Larry Pippin, who's still a personal friend, and ask him what I would need to do to graduate in two semesters. After some back and forth with the university's administrators, he told me they would give me credits for my military service. But I would still need fifty-eight more credits, making it almost impossible for me to graduate in one year. Almost: But not quite. My first step was to convince the Registrar to give me twelve credits for my Thai, even though the university didn't teach it. I also successfully challenged two Spanish courses, earning six more credits. That still left me forty-one credits short, so I would have to take nineteen semester hours the first semester and twenty-one the second if I wanted to graduate in two semesters. And despite that heavy load, I would still have to feed my family.

To support my family, I took a job as a waiter in the Golden Rooster Room of John Ascuaga's Nugget Hotel-Casino in Sparks, a haven Ascuaga reserved for college students. Since tips were our main source of income, Ascuaga put our personal stories on our tables in hopes our guests would tip even more generously than usual. For the next ten months, we lived off those tips.

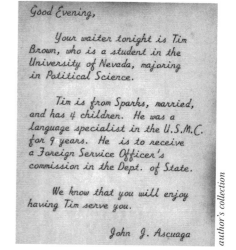

Sparks, Nevada, 1964. The card I placed on my tables while waiting tables in the Golden Rooster Room of John Ascuaga's Nugget Casino Hotel.

In June of 1965, when I received my Bachelor of Arts in Political Science, the State Department made good on its word and offered me entry in July. So we began preparing for the trip to Washington. My last three days as a waiter brought me the fewest tips of the year, so we would barely be able to pay the costs of the trip. But I had my BA and was on my way to beginning a second career. The packers arrived and packed up our Salvation Army furniture, meager household effects, and the kid's toys for shipment to Washington. Then all six of us crammed ourselves into a Nash Metropolitan on its last legs and headed east. Ten days later, the Nash wheezing on three cylinders, we limped into DC, found the only apartment in Northern, Virginia, willing to take four kids, and parked it out front, where it promptly died, never to move again. But we had arrived safely, and were very happy. Next stop, the Foreign Service Institute (FSI), then in Rosslyn, Virginia.

Dressed in my best shopping-mall suit, a survivor from my Marine Security Guard days, I reported in, almost saluted, and promptly went into culture shock when I found myself surrounded almost exclusively by civilians. The course turned out to be mostly a series of familiarization lectures by escapees from Foggy Bottom regarding the disorganization of the State Department and how to fill out a travel voucher.

Having handled highly classified documents for years, I was amazed by how little time was spent on security. I'd worked with Marine officers who spent four years at Annapolis plus months in combat and specialized training just to become platoon leaders. And we were spending mere weeks learning how to man America's first line of defense. Not that it wasn't enjoyable, it was. But for officers that were expected to spend much of their lives as diplomats, a profession in which every act and word has the potential to reflect well or poorly on the entire United States, the course seemed, to say the least, cursory.

The entry course was followed by a short class on consular affairs, visas, passports, adjudicating citizenship, and protecting Americans abroad. It also involved introductory visits to other federal agencies, including the Departments of Commerce and the Interior, and the CIA. Privately, I was shocked by just how superficial it all was, given the deadly serious nature of the jobs. I kept repeating to myself softly enough so that no one could hear me, "Holy shit! Is this how we prepare diplomats to man America's first line of defense?" My classmates, clearly some of the best and brightest America had to offer, were being launched into a global shark tank with less training than the average high-school ROTC cadet. But there I was. And I wasn't about to bitch, not with a regular paycheck coming in and a future in air-conditioned offices and foreign ministries, instead of pup tents and Buddhist temples. Toward the end of the Foreign Service entry course, the moderators began to hype the State Department's marvelous personnel system, assuring us that our onward assignments would be selected with the utmost care, taking into full consideration our particular skills and interests. They even handed out a form for us to complete, apparently intended to capture our notion of a dream assignment.

At last the great day arrived. The course coordinator, Alex Davit, who would later be my boss during one of my overseas assignments, after repeatedly assuring us that the State Department had meticulously considered our preferences and abilities when making our assignments, stood in front of the class and began reading the list to us. The very first one was of a devout Jewish officer to the Embassy in Cairo. Needless to say, this caused quite a stir, so much so that he stopped reading. After a whispered conference with his colleagues and one or two of us, Davit announced that, on second thought, they would take another look at that assignment. He then continued. One of the next assignments he announced was that of a Dutch-speaking officer to Curaçao, which seemed much better—until she went into culture shock (or at least successfully faked doing so). But real or faked, her reaction resulted in to her reassignment to a slightly more cosmopolitan place called Paris.

In my case, since I spoke Spanish and Thai, they came up with a compromise, Tel Aviv. It would have been nice to go someplace where we could immediately fit in. But the Holy Land wasn't bad. To assure that I would feel right at home, the Department decided not to teach me Hebrew. Instead, it sent me to its Middle East Studies course, a series of fascinating lectures on the history and customs of Saudi Arabia, Libya, Morocco, Turkey, Iran, North Africa, and on and on, presented by the best experts available. The only country not covered, or even seriously mentioned, was Israel, the key to the region's most difficult and intractable problem. Armed with new knowledge of countries I wasn't going to, my family and I packed up our household effects again, and off we went to Israel. Thanks to my father and my Pentecostal upbringing, I took with me a fairly solid knowledge of the region's geography, although it was, admittedly, almost two millennia out of date. Regardless, Tel Aviv would be the beginning of an eye-opening new career during which I would be reasonably well-paid for a change.

SEVENTEEN

IN THE HOLY LAND

I learned my first lesson about foreign affairs as actually practiced even before arriving in Tel Aviv: While Marines and diplomats may see exactly the same things, they see them through very different eyes. A Marine tends to see the world through the sights of a rifle, in black and white, and always potentially lethal. A diplomat tends to see the same world through a multi-faceted prism and in a rainbow of colors. This became clear to me when I went to the State Department to be briefed by the Israel Desk Officer who explained that his job was just to manage the paper flow. United States-Israel relations were too politically important to be run out of the State Department. In light of the deep commitments of America's Jewish and evangelical constituencies to Israel, the White House considered US-Israel relations to be exceptionally sensitive and micromanaged almost everything. It was a perspective I'd never encountered while I was a Marine. But it made sense. I learned later that the White House micromanages relations with the Vatican for much the same reasons.

While I considered the political side of the Embassy's work the most interesting, I also figured that, as the most junior officer in Tel Aviv, I wouldn't be dealing with "important affairs of state." And I was right—almost. I soon learned that no matter how junior, a diplomat is subject to scrutiny by everyone he meets and a few he may never meet, including the local spooks who keep diplomats under surveillance. Neither he nor his family can lead truly private lives abroad, because everything they say or don't say, do or don't do, can have consequences. It's a lot like living in a fishbowl surrounded by hungry cats. After a while it becomes second nature to think of your-self as potential dinner for one of them, and act accordingly.

Thanks to my experiences as a Marine, especially during my second enlistment, I'd already picked up most of the habits necessary for someone who is "a person of interest." And Tel Aviv proved to be an especially good place to relearn them, since it was then, as it still is today, a nation that must be "eternally vigilant." It made for a good place for Leda and our children to begin to adapt to the same sort of life.

Our arrival in Israel was much nicer than our earlier arrivals to Marine bases. The Embassy Administrative Officer, Tom Solitario, and his wife, Helen, who was originally from Mexico and especially interested to meet Leda, a fellow Latina, were standing planeside to greet us as we debarked. They immediately took us under their wing, whisked us off to a fully furnished temporary house already stocked with necessities and more than a few luxuries, and made us feel right at home—sort of. The Shin Bet (Israeli domestic intelligence) Colonel who lived next door appeared soon after we unpacked our bags to meet the newest American Embassy officer and his family. He must have been impressed (or maybe unimpressed), since we were later shadowed far less than many of the other Embassy officers. The Solitarios apparently thought more of us than he did, since they later became the godparents of our two youngest, Tamara and Tim.

The next morning, a car full of future ambassadors showed up at our door, and off I went with them to my new digs. Anyone familiar with today's Inman fortress embassies would have been appalled by the openness and lack of security. The Marine Security Guards stood post much as I had in Managua, at a front desk open to everyone who came in, not as they do today, inside a bulletproof glass vault full of security devices. Today, moving from floor to floor in an Embassy requires a special ID card. But then, even to visit the Ambassador's office simply required strolling down the hall and taking the elevator. In short, it was 1957 Guatemala before the Dragunov, not one of the armor-plated diplo-fortresses inside which today's American diplomats spend most of their time.

Since in Washington, I'd finally begun to receive a regular paycheck, we'd graduated from Salvation Army to Sears Roebuck and purchased a few upscale pieces of furniture. And not long after we arrived, it caught up with us. So, within weeks, we were able to move into a rather nice three-bedroom house in Kfar Shmaryahu, a suburb of Tel Aviv near the International School, where we enrolled our two older daughters, Barbara and Rebecca. The younger ones, Tamara and Tim, stayed at home. An English, country-style cottage in a farming area, the house was an idyllic setting precisely halfway between the Jordanian artillery batteries and the main north-south highway linking Tel Aviv to Haifa, making our neighborhood strategically important in the event hostilities broke out. With a steady job, regular income, and a nice home in a pleasant neighborhood, life in Tel Aviv was vastly different from the one we'd led during the first years of our marriage.

Although I wasn't directly involved in the political activities of the Embassy, I was able to keep abreast of events in the region thanks to my carpool mates, staff meetings, and a sanitized collection of cables I read regularly. The Jordanian artillery batteries were to come alive during the first phases of the 1967 Arab-Israeli war, but by then we'd left Tel Aviv for my next assignment in Madrid. Still, it was fun to be able to watch reports of the artillery duel Israel and Jordan fought over the roof of our former home—from a distance.

While we were in Israel, on the surface all appeared peaceful. But there were clearly dangerous currents running just beneath. The Israelis were warm and hospitable toward Americans, and we made a number of friends among the community. But I could see some ambiguity toward us as well, based on their unspoken but very real fears for the futures of both Israel and US-Israeli relations. One particular reality quickly stood out. While Israel and the United States were friends and allies, the relationship was asymmetrical. Israel was more dependent on us than we were on them, and many FSOs, academics, and political analysts believed our unusually strong support for Israel was contrary to the best interests of the United States. But to the American Jewish community, Israel was the realization of the Jew's millenarian yearning to return to the ancient homeland from which they'd been exiled by the Romans almost two thousand years before. The establishment of Israel marked the fulfillment of the haunting words spoken at the end of every Seder, "Next year, Jerusalem." And to evangelical Christians like me, it was the fulfillment of the words of Jesus Christ as foretold in Luke 21–24 that, in the last days, the Jews would return to Jerusalem.

author's collection

Kfar Shmaryahu, Israel, 1966. Dressed for Sunday church, Leda and I are standing in front of the trees in our front yard behind Barbara, Tim, Tamara, and Rebecca.

And yet, while in Israel I also became better able to see the other side of the Arab-Israeli conundrum, the one seen by so many specialists in Middle East affairs. My first brush with this came in a strawberry field next to our home when I noticed that almost all of the workers picking strawberries were school-age Palestinian children. When I asked the Israeli supervising them why they weren't in school, he responded matter-of-factly, "Arabs don't need educations." Leda had a similar experience when she invited our next door neighbor, Zipphora, a Sephardic Jew, to lunch at a nearby café, but its owner, an Ashkenazi, refused to serve Zipphora because she was "the wrong kind of Jew."

Another took place when, in my role as an American Consul, I went to help a young American woman who had married a Palestinian and had a child by him. Because its mother was an American citizen so was the baby, and her mother had obtained a Consular Report of Birth Abroad and American passport for the baby confirming this. But when her marriage hit a rough patch and she decided to return home to the United States, she discovered that she needed the father's consent to take the baby with her. When her husband refused to give his permission, she was stuck. Either she could leave without the baby or stay against her will. Thanks to these and other experiences, I developed parallel sympathy for the Palestinians and considerable sensitivity for the difficult relations between them and the Israelis. Perhaps more importantly, I came to better understand the answer of renowned cross-cultural psychologist B. F. Skinner to a question he was asked during a lecture, "You're an expert on the Middle East, Dr. Skinner. So tell me. Between the Jews and the Arabs, which side is right?"

Dr. Skinner replied, "Both sides are right. And if you can't understand that, you don't understand the essence of a real tragedy."

But our daily life in Israel didn't revolve around such age-old problems. After all, we were living in the Holy Land, had a steady income and a car that actually ran, and that we could use it to visit dozens of places we'd only read about and were well worth exploring—The Sea of Galilee, Capernaum, Bethlehem, Haifa, and Solomon's Stables, among others.

The 1967 Arab-Israel War was yet to be fought, and Jerusalem was near enough to visit, providing that the Jordanians who controlled one side of the Mandelbaum Gate were willing to let us in without stamping our passports. The process was simple: Fill out an application for Jordanian permission, send it by diplomatic pouch to the American Consulate General in Jerusalem, drive to the Mandelbaum Gate, park the car on the Israeli side, pick up your luggage, walk past the Israeli soldiers with weapons at the ready, weave through the concrete, dragon-tooth antitank obstacles as Jordanian soldiers tracked you with machine guns, go to the Jordanian control point, and pray that permits were there. If they were, everything went smoothly, providing the Jordanians agreed not to place an entry stamp in your passport, because that would make it invalid for visiting any other Arab countries. And if your permit wasn't there, you had to walk back to the Israeli side of the Gate hoping that no one would wonder why you'd been rejected and take a shot at you.

We must have made for quite a sight, mom, dad, and four little tykes, each carrying a suitcase, zigzagging around antitank obstacles through a free-fire zone. But Jerusalem and Jordan were more than worth it, from the Via Crucis, Nazareth, and the Mount of Olives, to the ancient marketplaces. Once, when we were driving to the Jordanian side of the Dead Sea in a rental car, we stopped near a horse-mounted Jordan Legion patrol, and its commander insisted that our three-year-old son, Tim mount his horse so we could take a picture - but not his three older sisters, since "only males ride horses." The girls are still a little miffed. But traditions are traditions.

Today, almost fifty years later, the tragedy of the Holy Land continues and has become even more dangerous than it was then. But even while we were in Israel, we were reminded many times of just how tense the situation was. When we went to the Sea of Galilee on picnics with the children, as we often did, it became almost second nature to park our car behind, rather than in front of, the antitank traps while visiting sniper-proof observation points that looked down on the Jordan River. We even learned to relax and enjoy the Saint Peter's fish at one of the best fish restaurants in Israel that was located on a kibbutz on the southeast shore of the Galilee and became accustomed to obeying the signs lining the road from the highway to the kibbutz that read "vary your speed." The first time we went, it seemed a rather strange admonition—until we saw the machine gun emplacements on either side of the road and caught glimpses of several fully armored tractors working in the fields.

We tried to always take a table right next to the water so the kids could toss pieces of bread in and watch the fish swarm to the surface. On our first visit, there was a cool breeze blowing, a rare treat in Israel, the service was good and the fish tasted delicious, so we were halfway through lunch before I noticed that, while the dining room was open on three sides giving us extraordinary views of the Galilee, it had a steel-reinforced concrete roof more than a foot thick. When I asked our waiter about it, he casually answered, "We put that on after losing two customers to sniper fire from the Golan Heights, so people would feel safe during lunch."

Of course, life was not all picnics and excursions. Before going to Israel, I'd also been given a course in consular affairs.

Not that I had any interest in making them my career. I didn't. But the initiation of an FSO into the profession almost invariably requires their doing consular work during their first tour abroad—stamping visas on passports (or not), supporting the day-to-day affairs of other federal agencies, providing protection to Americans, processing passports. In a normal Embassy, doing this sort of work is usually boring. But in Israel, even consular work could be exciting.

When I arrived I was assigned to citizenship work, a job that turned out to be far more difficult in Israel than in most places. Many Israelis, including especially those of American origin, had dual or even multiple nationalities. But both their dual nationalities and their status as residents of Israel put them at risk of losing their American citizenship if engaged in what was known as "an expatriative act" such as voting in a local election or volunteering for military service. It was my legal responsibility to look for evidence they had done this and, if they had, to take their American citizenship away from them. I also was obligated to determine whether or not the child of an American citizen whose spouse was not also an American citizen had acquired US citizenship at birth.

At most Consulates, questions concerning citizenship rarely arise. But in Tel Aviv they were a daily occurrence. So there I was on my first tour, making life-shattering, semi-judicial decisions every day. Over the course of my first year in the Foreign Service I had to determine dozens of times every month whether or not a US citizen had committed an expatriative act, because if they had, they'd lost their US citizenship and therefor weren't eligible for American passports. Needless to say, when informed that they'd committed an expatriative act they often became understandably outrage.

Some cases were particularly bizarre. I still remember one in particular. Since Israel has universal military conscription for both men and women, at her parent's insistence, the Israel-born teen-age daughter of two American citizens applied for a tourist visa to visit relatives in the United States before going into the Israeli Army. When the visa officer reviewed her application, he noticed that both her parents were born in the United States and sent her case to me because, when both parents are American citizens their children automatically acquire US citizenship at birth, and a visa cannot legally be issued to an American citizen. After reviewing her visa application I told her I needed to speak with her parents and that they should bring their identity documents with them. Their documents showed that both of them had voted in Israeli elections. By the end of the day I'd cancelled the American citizenship of both of her parents and forced their daughter to accept an American passport against her will, making me depressed and everyone else screaming mad.

Working in the Embassy in Tel Aviv did have its good points, however, many of which could be seen sunbathing on the nearby beach. Now, as every office worker knows, the ritual of the coffee break is a tradition deeply embedded in American workers and strongly supported by their bosses, mostly because caffeine acts as a stimulant and can keep them awake. But there's more than one kind of stimulant. And, in Tel Aviv, we took bikini breaks. Rather than going down to our grungy Embassy cafeteria for a cup of tepid liquid pretending to be coffee, most members of the Embassy's male cohort, took walks along the beach that stimulated us more than caffeine. Once, when I mentioned this to an officer of the French Embassy, he commented that, while they often did the same thing, he wasn't entirely happy about it, because no matter how hard he tried he simply couldn't get the Israeli lasses to buy French bikinis, because they covered too many places they wanted to tan. Being an experienced intelligence analyst, during my first visit to his digs, I noticed that the Ambassador had a very large telescope in his office aimed down the beach. When he noticed my interest, he quickly explained that he used it simply to watch ships entering the port of Haifa twenty or so miles to the north. My own assumption was that it was his way of joining us on our bikini breaks. But that was only part of the job.

EIGHTEEN

THE PROPHET AND THE STRIPPER

While passports and citizenship took up most of my time, I was also responsible for the protection and welfare of local American citizens, including a tribe of hippies. The Dean of the Tel Aviv tribe was a former math professor from an Ivy League university who had dropped out, adopted the vagabond lifestyle of a Prophet, settled in Tel Aviv to practice his new profession, and appointed himself the tribe's guru and go-between with them and the Embassy. Whenever a member of the tribe got into trouble they would talk with him, and he'd come to my office as their advocate. The first time he came in to see me, I asked to look at his passport. His name on his passport was Hallelujah. Seeing my surprise, he gave me a lesson in consular regulations they hadn't taught in Washington. As a professional, he could use his professional pseudonym on his passport, instead of his birth name. And, since he was a Prophet by profession and went by the name of Hallelujah, that was the name on his passport. It sounded strange to me, but when I checked the regulations, sure enough, he was right.

Hallelujah lived with part of his tribe in an abandoned house he'd commandeered. To help feed them he traveled a regular restaurant-to-restaurant route every day to collect food.

His live-in girlfriend, Carolyn, also an American, worked as a stripper in a bar just down the street from the Embassy. Since she didn't always get along well with her boss, on a couple of occasions she came to my office in tears asking for protection. To prove he had mistreated her, she insisted on pulling up her skirt and pulling down her blouse to show me the bruises. I remember asking Hallelujah during one of his visits, a bit playfully, if he didn't think it was improper for a prophet to be living with a stripper. "Not at all," he responded. "God sent me to help sinners, and she's the biggest sinner I know." I had to admit that his logic was impeccable. But then, he'd been a math professor.

One afternoon my usually unflappable senior consular assistant burst into my office out of breath from having run several blocks, "It's Miss Carolyn," he said. "She's outside the bar down the street demonstrating."

My rather obvious first question was, "Really? What's she demonstrating?" When he told me, I ran down to the scene of the action to see for myself. And sure enough, there she was, wearing pasties that barely covered her nipples and a G-string that didn't cover much of anything at all, doing bumps and grinds while holding above her head a sign that read, "Bar Owner Unfair to Strippers." Needless to say, Carolyn had collected quite a crowd of sympathizers, many of them also amateur photographers. There was even a TV camera crew busily filming her performance.

I'd met her boss while looking into one of her earlier complaints. So when he came over to me I congratulated him on all the free publicity. But he was not amused. "This just isn't right, so I called the cops. But look at them. They aren't doing anything!" That wasn't exactly true. They were watching her as carefully as everyone else.

author's collection

Tel Aviv, Israel, 1967. When Hallelujah found out I was leaving Israel for my next post in Madrid, he gave me this self-portrait as a going-away present.

Always the peacemaker, I walked over to the officer in charge and asked him what his men were going to do. "This kind of problem isn't within our jurisdiction. So we're just keeping things orderly until the right people get here. And here they are now."

Sure enough, when I looked around I saw a group of middle-aged men accompanied by a camera crew that quickly set up its equipment and began filming Carolyn's gyrations. When she saw the second camera, she began grinding harder than ever. It turned out that they were from the Ministry of Labor and, I must say, they were going about their job meticulously, filming her from all sorts of angles, interviewing witnesses, taking a statement from the bar owner, who by then was so mad he was practically foaming at the mouth. Then, as the sun began to sink slowly into the nearby Mediterranean, they huddled together to discuss the problem before issuing their edict, "Miss Carolyn's engaged in a legal labor demonstration - on with the show!"

NINETEEN

ESSENCE OF A
THOUSAND ARMPITS

Another of my more colorful protection and welfare clients, John of the Armpits (not, obviously, his real name), smelled pretty much like anyone would if they'd been sweating profusely for months without taking a bath or changing clothes. The redolence of John's magnificent residential address, Number Two Herbert Samuel Esplanade, belied its amenities. His home was actually a storeroom beneath the boardwalk where Tel Aviv's beach entrepreneurs stored their rental chairs and parasols at night. In daylight, it had a marvelous view of the bikini-clad lasses of intra-war Israel. What it didn't have was a shower, or even a toilet. In short, Number Two smelled like its address.

John was a man with a checkered past. I first met him in my capacity as consular wailing-wall for indigent or disgruntled Americans when he came to the Embassy to report he'd "lost" his passport. But, as is often the case in consular work, his real problem turned out to be quite different. I learned later that during a visit to Cyprus, John had somehow managed to push the enormously tolerant British authorities there into tossing him off the island when, one afternoon, he cornered the British

High Commissioner in a local bar and berated him loudly for Britain's alleged preference for Greeks over Turks. But that wasn't his problem. His problem was that he'd been unfairly deported from the UK and the British wouldn't give him permission to visit his fiancée at her current abode, a home for the mentally bewildered just north of London. And if they continued to refuse, he was going to swim from Cyprus to England and sneak ashore to see his beloved. Instead the Brits put John on the next boat leaving Cyprus and he found himself, backpack, greasy shorts, slimy hair, and all, on his way to Israel.

Unfortunately for John, personal problems often get their wires crossed with foreign policy problems. And his was a case in point. His foreign policy problem was the Arab embargo on trading with Israel. Because John claimed to be Jewish, the British couldn't send him to an Arab county, they'd put him on the only ship that sailed back and forth between Cyprus and Israel. But when he arrived in Haifa the Israelis refused to admit him, probably because stamps in is passport indicated he could become a problem. So he had to stay on board the ship and sail back to Cyprus. Seven or eight round trips later, John seemed well on his way to becoming a modern man-without-a-country until finally, one night, he managed to sneak down the gangway in Haifa, losing his heavily annotated passport as he did so by flipping it overboard. He then managed to stay ashore until the ship sailed without him. This created a problem for the Israelis, because John claimed to be Jewish based on the religion of a mother whose name he said he couldn't remember and who, in any case, had borne him out of wedlock. But, as a self-proclaimed Jew being persecuted for his Jewishness, they had little choice but to admit him to Israel. And once John was solidly on Israeli soil, my own fun began.

Within hours, John made his way to Tel Aviv to ask for a replacement passport. At first I delayed issuing him a replacement passport, partly because he was simply bizarre. But more importantly, because his "lost" passport had already been found by our Consular Agent in Haifa, Jacob Sassower, and was en route to me even as we spoke. So I asked John to come back later. When he returned, to his dubious joy, I handed him back his waterlogged passport, having first photocopied all its pages, taking special care to copy the pages holding an impressive collection of annotations and stamps confirming that he'd been expelled from more countries than I'd ever visited. Busy man, John. I might as well not have bothered. He "lost" it again within days.

Now under the gun, I sent a quick cable to the Department of State asking whether he should be issued yet another replacement passport. Consular Services shot back a biting bureaucratic retort I can still remember verbatim:

"Department authorizes issuance replacement passport. Please advise John [----] Department views loss twenty-two passports serious."

That afternoon I issued John his twenty-third passport and passed along to him, for what it was worth, the Department's stirring admonition. I must say he held up rather nicely. A weaker person might have felt the overwhelming shame implicit in such a resounding verbal admonishment. But then John was a former Marine living off a disability pension. I should have known.

For some bizarre reason, John took a liking to me and began to appear in my office several mornings a week, inflicting with each visit an increasing level of pain, rather like a persistent and growing hemorrhoid. I could always tell by the smell that he'd come calling well before I reached my office. A few weeks' worth of encrusted dirt, especially when baked on with copious perspiration and uncut by soap or water, does tend to enhance one's natural body odors, and John was the quintessential example of this fundamental principal of hygiene. Not that he was entirely unaware of the concept of bathing. He wasn't. But even when he tried to do the right thing, the less tolerant often balked. I tried to convince my professional colleagues, several of whom went on to become Ambassadors that, in John's case, any engagement in a bathing ritual, no matter how strange, was better than none. But they felt that washing his armpits in the Embassy water fountain on his way to my office was a bit too much. Besides, one argued, the water was icy and he might catch a cold.

A few months and a dozen alarums and excursions later, I was finally able to convince John that he'd earned a rest from his arduous travels and really should take a break from them and go home to America. Unfortunately, by the time I did, he was broke and had lost his twenty-third passport. I assured him that such problems were solvable. In the first place, I'd located his long-lost "Jewish" mother, and she'd sent him a first-class airline ticket home. She'd also sent him some pocket change, although I strongly suggested he save all of it to cover his travel incidentals. As for paying the fee for a new passport, I magnanimously arranged for him to borrow a little US government money to pay for his twenty-fourth. Of course, since the regulations at the time required that I limit its validity to use for one-way travel home because he now owed the government money, I had to limit its validity exclusively to travel to the United States.

On his first try, John of the Armpits appeared at Lod International Airport clad in his traditional tribal

dress—greasy shorts, dirt-caked shirt, sandals on his cal-
lous-encrusted feet, and a delightfully colorful robin-red
beret atop his dangling, mid-back-length tresses. Ever the
diplomat, and acutely mindful of Miss Manners guidance,
I politely introduced John to the airline's Station Manager,
who promptly began to gag. At first my erstwhile Station
Manager friend offered to help me find John another way
home. But, when I demurred, he threatened to have the pilot
invoke his authority to deny passage to anyone who appears
mentally disturbed. But the certificate I produced signed by
his airline's very own psychiatrist trumped this ploy. We
finally reached a compromised that made even John smile
a silly grin, presumably of happiness, although the psychiatrist's generous use of a needle a half hour before may
have had something to do with his being in a mellow mood.
Still, in a spirit of compromise, before boarding his plane
John agreed to take a shower—with soap and water. Then,
dressed in a clean shirt and trousers, gifts from Leda that she
assured me she never wanted to see – or smell – again, he
joined his fellow to First Class passengers aboard his plane.

Being the less-than-trusting type, the minute John's
flight was wheels-up I sent Flash cables to the embassies in
Athens and Rome where his flight was scheduled to land en
route to New York. Noting that John had been deported earlier from both Greece and Italy, I suggested that they might
want to watch over him during his stopovers lest he accidentally wander back onto their territory. And it worked.
Embassy Athens sent me a thank-you cable saying that two
nice Greek policemen met John as he tried to debark and
took him into protective custody lest he get lost in the crowd
and miss his flight. Embassy Rome chimed in to report that
the Italians had been even nicer. Two handsomely dressed

Carabinieri with submachine guns had stood quietly by protecting John during his entire short stay in their country. John never returned to Israel, at least not on my watch, and I've often wondered how he's doing now. After all, Marines do look after their own.

TWENTY

GENERALISIMO FRANCO'S SPAIN

Halfway through my "posting" in Israel, as FSOs pompously call their assignments abroad, I had the bright idea to begin angling for my next assignment. I wrote to my Career Destruction Officer, or CDO (also known as a Career Development Officer), to tell him that I was having a great time, but would like an even plusher post next time, either in Europe or a Spanish-speaking country. How was I to know that on the very day my note landed on his desk at State, an officer in Europe had been honey-trapped by unfriendlies on behalf of its government, the wife of a junior officer at a second post had been compromised (yes, Virginia, even diplomats have libidos), and a wave of red-lined Cuban refugees had begun washing up on European shores. In any case, the Department of State saw my innocent request as a heaven-sent way to solve all of these problems at once by playing a game of "Ring Around the Med," and my family and I soon found ourselves on a slow boat to Madrid.

It was a transfer trip to remember. A little known sub-clause in an obscure travel regulation authorized travel by ship if anyone in the family was unable or unwilling to fly, while another equally obscure clause allowed travel on a non-US flag vessel if no US ship was available. And, since there were no US flag ships going our way and one of our kids was not willing to travel by plane, that left the *SS Renaissance*, an all-first-class French cruise liner, on which Washington authorized us to travel on as far as Naples. And since taking our car with us would cost the government less than shipping it separately, we were also authorized to take it with us.

So, after a delightful week at sea punctuated by stops in Turkey and Greece, we arrived in Naples, disembarked our car, and took the weekend off. Since we arrived on a Friday and weren't required to travel on what turned out to be a four day holiday weekend, we were forced to spent all of it in Naples, including a day trip to Capri, before driving to Rome. And since it was the holiday season by the time we got the to Rome and Italy was launched into its annual Christmas to New Year holiday week, we had to take that off as well. Properly rested from our arduous journey, we then headed to Madrid via Pisa, Monaco, the French Riviera, and Barcelona, making sure not to drive more than the authorized 250 miles per a day, just as the regulations said. Eventually we managed to reach Madrid.

Spain under Franco, the next bump on my slide through diplo-life, may not have been everyone's idea of a fun place. But it was certainly different from the Holy Land, and so was my job. When I arrived in my new office, it took me about fifteen seconds to realize why I'd been yanked out of Tel Aviv so quickly. My cubicle was just behind the visa section's front counter, where our Spanish employees were being besieged by hordes of Cubans fleeing Castro's paradise. Now, any conversation between more than two Cubans can make a room seem jam-packed. But in this case, there were twenty or more at a time, not just two, all of them even more animated than usual, because their natural high spirits had been replaced by fear. Their presence in Madrid was the result of what was known as the Varadero process. For some years, the legal exit of Cubans from their homeland had been blocked by both the Cuban and American governments. But recently the two governments had reached an agreement. The first step that had to be taken by anyone wanting to leave the country was to obtain an exit permit from Cuba. Only then could then apply to the US Interests Section (USINT) in Havana for authorization to board a Varadero refugee flight directly to the United States. But the process was neither as simple, nor as magnanimous as it sounds.

To obtain an exit permit, they first had to quit their jobs, abandon all of their property, and obtain Cuban passports without knowing whether or not they would be authorized to join the Varadero exodus to the United States or even allowed to enter a third country. In most cases, they were able to fly directly to the United States. Most, but not all, because we were rejecting hundreds of their applicants because we had derogatory information about them. When this happened they had few options. They no longer had a job, a ration card, or permission to stay in Cuba, and they'd been labeled counterrevolutionary *gusanos* (worms) and enemies of the state by the Castro regime. That left them with but one alternative. Find a third country that was willing to accept them.

When the Varadero process began, those we refused to authorize travel to the US on a Varadero flight were able to get entry permits from other counties, most notably Mexico, and hundreds, then thousands, of Cuban refugees began to land on its doorstep. At first the Mexicans assumed that the Cubans were simply in transit to the United States. But we were denying the visas of hundreds of them, mostly persons with criminal records, personal histories of serving as

Cuban intelligence agents, or other problems that disqualified them. The most difficult were what we called "red-line" cases, meaning we had potentially derogatory classified information about them. In effect, we were skimming the cream but leaving the rest. It didn't take Mexico long to realize what was happening and close its doors to them.

That left Spain as their only out. In Madrid, I became a member of a vastly overloaded consular team trying to process hundreds of Cuban refugees, all of them clamoring for immediate attention, including many who weren't eligible for approval. The pressure was intense. The Cubans wanted admission documents and wanted them right now! And their families were flooding Congress with letters, phone calls, telegrams, and Lord knows what else, demanding instant approval for family members. The pressure for prompt action and the volume of paperwork was such that we'd begun accepting applications prepared by local nongovernmental organizations (NGOs), which took some of the pressure off us by putting them under the gun. Still, while I was under pressure to over perform every work day, we were living in Spain, my evenings and weekends were free, and we had a car, although I did manage to hit an occasional non-Cuban bump as well, as happened one morning.

TWENTY-ONE

WHO THE HELL IS PAUL LAXALT?

One morning, the instant I arrived at the office, the Consular Administrative Assistant told me to go straight in to see Consul General Margaret Hussman, who was waiting for me. The moment I walked into her office, she said in a rather ominous voice, "Ambassador Duke wants to see you—now! Go straight to his office."

"Yes, ma'am," I said. "I'm on my way, ma'am," executed a smart about-face and headed for his office.

Needless to say, I was a bit nervous, especially since I had no idea what it was all about, but assumed it wasn't something good. I'd met the Ambassador briefly at a couple of social occasions, but we were hardly bosom buddies. After all, I was just a recently defrocked Marine Sergeant while Ambassador Angier Biddle Duke, was the wealthy scion of the Reynolds tobacco family. So there was certain social distance between us.

When I arrived at his office, his secretary (excuse me, Senior Administrative Affairs Manager) looked at me without smiling and said, "Go straight in. The Ambassador has been waiting for you."

Ambassador Duke was standing behind his desk about twenty yards away, so I dutifully plowed my way through the deep-pile rug covering his office floor and braced myself in front of him. Looking at me without smiling, the Ambassador asked me bluntly, "Who the hell is Paul Laxalt?"

His question caught me completely off guard. Of course, I did know who Laxalt was. As Nevada's first FSO, I'd made a courtesy call on him in his gubernatorial office in Carson City before heading for Washington, so I answered, "He's the Governor of Nevada, sir."

"Do you have any idea what that son-of-a-bitch just did?"

"No sir, Mr. Ambassador, sir." One thing I learned in the Marines was that, when "it's" hitting the fan, it's best to say as little as possible. At that point, Ambassador Duke's angry face changed into a broad grin. It turned out that he'd received a telephone call early that morning from none other than Generalisimo Francisco Franco himself, who had given him a dressing-down about something Laxalt had done just the day before.

Governor, later Senator, Laxalt was the son of a French Basque sheepherder and Basque mother who ran a boarding house for sheepherders in Carson City. As a first-generation French Basque who'd done exceptionally well in the United States, he was a hero to Basques in both France and Spain, and his family's ancestral hometown in the French Basque region invited him yearly to be the guest of honor at their annual festival. That year they'd also taken him to visit "some friends" on the Spanish side of the border who, being members of ETA, a Basque separatist group known for its bomb making talents, were mortal enemies of Franco. By the time the Spanish police found out what had happened and their report reached Madrid, Laxalt was already back in France, so there was nothing Franco could do about it but "bitch." So he'd called the American Ambassador and chewed him out, albeit probably in his own inimitable Galician manner, not the expletive rich style Ambassador Whelan had used a decade before in Nicaragua. And, since I was the only Nevadan on his staff, Ambassador Duke was, in turn, passing Franco's demarche on to me because, as he delicately put it, "It flows downhill. And you're at the bottom of my hill."

author's collection

Washington, DC. As the first graduate of the University of Nevada, Reno to enter the career Foreign Service, I always made an effort to make myself available to all of my congressional representatives regardless of party, including Senator Laxalt, who later appointed our oldest daughter Barbara to West Point.

I was Consular Duty Officer one weekend a month or so later and decided to return Ambassador Duke's favor, or so I thought, when on Sunday morning, a rather bizarre incident in the Canary Islands gave me an excuse to use a key the duty officer always had on hand. It opened a little used back door that connected the Embassy chancery to the Ambassador's residence to be used only as a last resort, so I decided to use it. I should have known better. When I walked in Ambassador Duke was in his underwear, standing next to his dining room's sideboard, pouring himself a cup of coffee. But far from being embarrassed, he simply turned, smiled, and said, "Good morning, Tim. Would you like some?" He wasn't the one that was embarrassed. I was. A year later, I had better luck with Laxalt.

One afternoon, when we were back in Nevada on home leave, we were driving through Carson City and decided to have lunch at the coffee shop of Laxalt's Ormsby House Hotel. At the time he was no longer Governor, but not yet a Senator, and when I asked if he was around, he dropped by our table. After introducing Leda and the children to him, I told him what had happened in Madrid. It gave him a good chuckle and earned us a complimentary lunch. Later, while he was a Senator, I made it a habit to call on him whenever I was in Washington, a gesture of simple courtesy that was to have unexpected consequences, not the least of which was his appointment of our oldest daughter, Barbara, to West Point.

As I've mentioned before, my day job in Madrid was strictly consular. But from time to time, I was able to find opportunities to dabble in what really interested me, politics and economics. Early in my tour I met two men that were members of circles surprisingly close to Franco. One was the Honorary Consul of Israel, Hans Meyer Morgenthau. The other was the brother of Manuel Fraga Iribarne, President of the Falange, Franco's political party.

My friendship with Meyer Morgenthau developed from a courtesy call I made on him shortly after arriving in Spain to introduce myself to him as an American Embassy officer recently arrived from Tel Aviv. As a young man before and during World War II, Meyer Morgenthau had been part of a group that convinced Franco to issue Spanish passports or other identity documents to Jews in Germany, because any formal document linking them to Spain would allow them to exit Nazi controlled territory. The Nazis usually knew full well they were Jews. But, because of the relatively friendly relations between Franco's Spain and Hitler's Germany, the German authorities were under orders to allow anyone bearing Spanish identity documents to leave the country. According to Meyer Morgenthau, Franco had used his alliance with Nazi Germany to save hundreds of Jews from the Holocaust. It was a story I'd never heard before and one I've almost never heard since. He also took me to visit a synagogue that he said had survived the 1492 Spanish Expulsion of Jews, despite the Inquisition and the still virulent anti-Semitism of the Spanish Catholic Church and much of the country's oligarchy and gave me the names of a number of very close advisers to Franco that he said were Jews.

Soon after we arrived in Madrid, we hired a young girl from the Spanish province of Extremadura to help with the house and children and, the first time Meyer Morgenthau came to our home for dinner, she served the meal. An old-fashioned Spanish gentleman, as he left he gave her a tip and, while we were cleaning up, she was bubbling over about how nice our guest was. So I told her that he was the Honorary Consul of Israel. My explanation meant nothing to her, since she had no idea what either an Israeli or a Consul was, so I tried to elaborate. I told her he was a Jew and represented the Jewish people in Spain.

She looked me straight in the eye and said emphatically, "No, he's not. He can't be. He doesn't have horns."

Rather startled by her comment, I responded, "Jews don't have horns. Where in the world did you get that idea?"

"The village priest told me in catechism class at church, that's who!"

To prove her point, she went to her room, brought back her catechism text, and showed me several pictures depicting Jews with horns. "But maybe his horns are very short and covered up by his hair," and that was as much as she would concede.

It wouldn't be the only time I was to hear medieval opinions while we were in Spain. Another instance involved a movie. While we were there the Concordat (treaty) between Spain and the Vatican made the Spanish Catholic Church the official guardian of the country's national morality, and some time earlier the Church had exercised that authority to ban the Academy Award-winning movie *Gentleman's Agreement* from being shown there. When, during our stay in Spain, the public uproar this caused became especially loud, the Cardinal Primate of Spain, Cardinal Pla y Deniel, finally made a public statement explaining the Church's decision. The Catholic Church had an obligation to protect the public against false doctrines and *Gentlemen's Agreement* was heretical because it was about brotherly love between a Christian and a Jew, but the doctrine of brotherly love does not extend to Jews.

As for Fraga Iribarne, I met him for the first time when, one sunny Sunday afternoon, the owners of our apartment invited us to their weekend country house in the hills above Madrid. There were only a few other guests, one of them being a gentleman standing next to an outdoor grill. Once the kids had gone off to play and Leda and our hostess had retreated inside, I grabbed a cold drink and went over to say hello. As we chatted, I watched him cook the best paella I ever ate. It wasn't until later that my hosts told me he was the brother of Manuel Fraga Iribarne, the President of Franco's Falange political party.

author's collection

Madrid, Spain, 1967. Enjoying the day while waiting for Fraga Iribarne's paella.

Now, when a diplomat gets a chance like that, he jumps, especially when it's been deliberately set up, as it was in this case. A few weeks later we invited Fraga over for supper. While I was fixing him a drink, he began looking through our collection of phonograph records, came across a Smithsonian recording of Spanish Civil War songs, and asked if he could put it on. While his request made me a bit nervous, I said "of course." As soon as the music started, he began singing along. It turned out that, while I knew the words of a few of the songs, Fraga knew almost all of them by heart, and I soon found myself singing Communist marching songs, among them *Los Cuatro Generales,* and *Jarama Valley,* the anthem of the American-led Abraham Lincoln Brigade that fought against Franco—with the brother of one of Franco's top officials. He even knew the ones in German, like *Das Thaelmen Brigaden.* When I looked surprised, he laughed and said that he'd learned them as a child because his family used to sing them. The bizarre image of the Fraga Iribarne family standing around a campfire singing Spanish Civil War marching songs is still seared into my mind.

Not that Spain was my first exposure to a dictatorship. It wasn't. That had been Somoza's Nicaragua. But a couple of incidents while we were in Spain taught me just how ubiquitous an efficient dictatorship can be, while others reminded me that prejudice obeys no boundaries. One involved *une femme d'un certain age* that came to the Embassy to renew her American passport. While she waited for it to be processed, when I asked how her visit to Spain was going she told me a story. She was staying in a small *pensión* (the Spanish version of a B&B) in a quiet neighborhood some distance from the center of Madrid. Very much a creature of habit, every morning after breakfast she would visit one of the city's many museums or art galleries, returning well before supper was served. One evening when she returned several hours later than usual, she was greeted with obvious relief by the manager of the *pensión.* "You gave us quite a scare! It's great to see you back safe and sound," he said. Surprised, she assured him that she was just fine.

When she asked him why he was so worried, he explained. At around six, an hour after she normally returned, the neighborhood Guardia Civil patrolman had come to the *pensión* to ask if the American woman had checked out, since he hadn't been informed. When they told him no he left, but came back about an hour later to ask again. When they told him once more that the American woman hadn't checked out, the Guardia asked to use the telephone. He called Guardia Civil headquarters and reported that the American woman was still registered at the *pensión* but hadn't returned at her usual time. About thirty minutes later, two Guardia Civil walked up to her several miles away in another part of the city and asked if she needed any help, which she did because she was lost. After confirming her name and the name of the *pensión* where she was staying, they politely took her to a bus stop and told the driver her destination. She arrived back less than an hour later, after changing buses twice under the watchful eyes of their drivers.

So what's my point? If she'd been visiting San Francisco or Chicago, both about the size of Madrid, would the local police have been able to find her in just thirty minutes? And even if they had, would they have taken the trouble to make sure she got back to her hotel safely? And how did the Guardia officer know that she was missing in the first place? If you've traveled in Europe, you probably remember being asked for your passport every time you checked in to a hotel or even a campground. But did you know why? It's because, in Europe, hotels, B&Bs, and campgrounds are required to promptly report the arrival and departure of each guest to the authorities. That's simply a part of everyday life on the Continent. The police in Europe keep a discrete, but fairly close eye on the comings and goings of not just tourists but their own citizens.

In almost every European, and many other countries around the globe, the level of surveillance of people is, by American standards, extraordinary. If the authorities in America were to try to do the same, the members of the American Civil Liberties Union would probably have a collective heart attack. It was a lesson I was to relearn many times during my decades abroad, and not just in dictatorships. A level of surveillance that would not be tolerated in the United States is just a normal part of daily life in most other parts of the world.

A second example: As I mentioned earlier, during our trip from Tel Aviv to Madrid, we drove much of the way, stopping wherever evening found us. It was a great trip, and we enjoyed every minute. But in the context of this story, the stop that best illustrates my point came in Monaco. We arrived late one evening, tired and hungry, checked into the first hotel we came to, left our passports at the desk, and walked across the street to get some sandwiches. That probably took us all of fifteen minutes. The moment we got back to the hotel, the desk clerk called me over to tell me that the protocol office of the Palace had just called and wanted to offer us a personally guided tour the next day. Fifteen minutes in Monaco, the country of Prince Rainier III and Princess Grace (Kelly), and the authorities already had us in their sights.

A third example from my later years as Consul General in Martinique. One afternoon, I received a frantic call from a distraught American father whose wife had suddenly taken deathly ill. He was desperately trying to locate their daughter, who was traveling with her boyfriend somewhere in the Caribbean. He didn't know where she was. But before leaving home, she'd mentioned that they would be island hopping and that one of the islands might be French. By then

I'd learned the drill, and I immediately called Gendarme headquarters in Martinique. Within fifteen minutes, the Gendarmes called back to say they'd located her on the beach near the campground where she was staying with her boyfriend and told her that her father needed to talk with her urgently. They asked me to inform her father that she was getting dressed and would be calling home in a few minutes, and assured me they would keep an eye on her to be sure she did just that. Try that in Miami. The daughter thought she'd been traveling incognito, but she wasn't, at least not in France.

I could give another dozen examples without breaking a sweat. But my point has been made. What Americans would see as a totally unacceptable violation of their privacy practiced only by totalitarian dictatorships is, in fact, the norm in most of the world, including in countries that are undeniably democracies, like Monaco, France, and the Netherlands. The difference is not in the method, but in what the authorities do with the information they collect. A dictatorship uses it to control its citizens: A democracy uses it to protect them.

Another difference between the United States and every other country in which I served involved racial prejudices. One of the heaviest crosses American diplomats abroad must bear is the United States' reputation as a racist country. I can't remember how many times I was cornered at a cocktail party or dinner by someone who ranted on about this. Yes, there's an element of racial prejudice in everyday America. But there's racial prejudice everywhere. In fact, in my own personal experience, in every country in which I served racism was far more prevalent that it is here. In Thailand the targets of racial disaffection were numerous, Chinese, Cambodians, Muslim Malays, hill tribesmen,

Japanese. In the Philippines, my deputy, Corporal Chang's head was shaved by a barber because he thought Chang was Japanese when, in fact, he was Chinese. In Mexico the racial targets were *indios*, Native Americans, and, to an extent, Central Americans. In Nicaragua it was also *indios*, plus the Segovian peasants that comprise more than 40% of the country's entire population. (I've written a whole book about that one!) In Argentina, Paraguayans and Blacks were targets. In Peru it was Bolivians and Ecuadorans; in Chile, Peruvians. In many of the countries that claimed most loudly not to be racist, including in Europe, racism was just as bad, or worse, than in the United States. In Germany it was against Turks. In France it was against Haitians, North Africans, and Muslims. In the Netherlands it was against Surinamers. Even in Israel, a country whose people have suffered intensely from anti-Semitism for centuries, prejudice was rampant. Ashkenazi Jews looked down on Sephardic Jews; orthodox Jews looked down on the secular, and vice versa. And almost all of the Jews looked down on Palestinians even as the Palestinians looked down on them.

In short, prejudice existed everywhere I went. But in my personal experience in eighteen very different countries, there's less of it in the United States than in any of them. Don't hold your breath for a Black to be elected President in France, a Muslim Prime Minister to take office in Germany, or a Protestant to be named Prime Minister in Italy. As for Spain, the objects of racial prejudices were pretty much spread across the entire spectrum: Gypsies, Basques, Jews, Muslims, Blacks, Protestants, you name it.

I recall one particularly noxious instance in Spain when I was cornered at a cocktail party by a Spaniard berating me for America's horrific race problem until finally, fed up, I asked him a simple question, "What about Gypsies?" His answer was a classic case of denial of the truth. "Gypsies don't count because they're not civilized people. They're barbarians." I just shook my head and walked away.

TWENTY-TWO

VIETNAM: MY FIRST DIPLO-WAR

As some of my older readers may recall, the Vietnam War era overflowed with political passions, the embers of which continue to smolder to this day. Certainly my own memories of that era remain vivid. During my second Marine enlistment, the Vietnam War was going on, but it was not yet a dominant political issue and I concentrated mostly on Thailand. I also spent some of my time doing Southeast Asia regional intelligence analysis from my perch at FMFPAC and followed Vietnam War-related political developments in the United States, Europe, and Latin America. And, as early as it may sound, by 1963 I'd reached three sobering conclusions. First, that for both ideological and strategic reasons, the United States was right to try to defend South Vietnam; second that we were going to lose the Vietnam War, not on the battlefield, but on the streets and on college campuses at home; and third, that the American people simply do not have the will to fight prolonged hot wars anywhere. The third was not limited to Vietnam and, as far as I can tell, remains applicable pretty much any war anywhere, regardless, Iraq and Afghanistan being the most recent examples of this. So all our enemies have to do is keep a war going long enough and, sooner or later, we'll discover or invent a rationale that allows us to cut and run while convincing ourselves that we've done otherwise. When I left the Corps, I took these conclusions with me.

During my tours in Tel Aviv and Madrid, the streets of America were slowly becoming more and more convulsed with anti-Vietnam War sentiments. But with ten years of Marine service under my belt, four small children and a new career, I kept telling myself that I had ample reason to sit it out. The trouble was that I also had a conscience. So in 1968, when a cable from the State Department crossed my desk asking for volunteers to go to Vietnam to work with the Civil Operations and Rural Development Support program (CORDS), I talked it over with my long-suffering bride, she gave me her blessing, and I tossed my name in the hopper. It didn't take long for orders to arrive.

Since Vietnam was to be an unaccompanied tour, my orders authorized families to go to safe havens in Taiwan, Thailand or a place of our choice at government expense. My repeated absences during my years flitting in and out of Thailand had caused enough of a strain on Leda. So I asked for and received permission for them to go to Costa Rica, where she would have the support of her family, took them there, found a small house for them to live in and enrolled the kids in a bilingual school.

A few months later, after a cursory orientation course and a couple of weeks of Vietnamese language training, I landed once more at Tan Son Nhut Air Base in Saigon and was motored to US military headquarters. Given my Marine and Southeast Asia intelligence experience, I was offered the District Advisor position of my choice, an exercise in "Petreaus Surge"- type tactics decades before the Petreus Doctrine came into vogue.

DATs, or District Advisory Teams, were military advisory units, so assigning a civilian to command a DAT was, to me, an exercise in desperation. I was given a choice of several and sent on my way to visit them, which is how I wound up trying to sleep through a firefight on my very first night up-country. I crashed at about ten that night, while a Nung bodyguard cradling a submachine gun stood watch at the foot of my bed only to be jolted awake when, around midnight, a sharp firefight started nearby. The rattle of machine guns, grenade explosions, and occasional whump of an incoming mortar round kept me awake most of the rest of the night, until the shooting ended just before dawn.

The next morning, the Vietnamese District Chief, an Army officer, took me to see where the fighting had taken place, no more than five hundred yards from where I'd been trying to sleep. The "Charlies", our affectionate name for the Viet Cong (VC), had attacked and captured a major two-span bridge on the main north-south coastal highway and held it for most of the night before fading back into the local civilian population just before sunup. But before they'd withdrawn, they'd blown up one of the bridge's two spans, which seemed odd. Why blow up one and leave the other? When I asked the Vietnamese District Chief, he was surprised. To him the reason was obvious. The Viet Cong had to use the other span during the day just like everyone else. It was a lesson I've never forgotten and have tried my best to pass on to others, especially to my students. Never burn all your bridges. You may need one of them yourself some day.

I was now in-country. But I wasn't nuts. And trying to sleep in the middle of a firefight my very first night convinced me that, "Enough is enough, already!" In a war zone discretion really is the better part of valor. So I bid a mock-tearful farewell to serious Indian country and chose instead to go to Ninh Hòa, a relatively peaceful district just north of Cam

Ranh Bay that had largely been loyal to the French during the colonial period. I arrived soon after the 1968 Tet Offensive, a resounding military defeat of the VC that they and their sympathizers, with the enthusiastic help of the antiwar crowd abroad, had been able to transform into a political victory.

The Army Major I would replace was still high on the adrenaline the Tet offensive had generated. The goings-on in Ninh Hòa had been pretty hot, but even the VC sometimes made mistakes. In the case of Ninh Hòa, a VC unit that had entered the city to attack the main police station two blocks from the CORDS compound got lost when their commander misread his map and attacked the wrong objective, the building housing the DAT. When the team successfully resisted their first assault the VC climbed onto the roof in an effort to breach their defenses. That was their second, and most fatal, mistake. Once on the roof they were out in the open and made great targets for an AC-130 gunship, known affectionately in Vietnam as "Puff the Magic Dragon", lurking nearby just waiting for a target to appear. Within minutes, Puff hosed the Charlies off the roof with a deluge of 40mm cannon fire. Of course, that also reduced the roof and upper floor of the building to rubble. So I arrived to find a brand-new compound, complete with three shiny hedgerows of perimeter razor wire sown thickly with antipersonnel mines, covered six ways from Sunday with the crisscrossing firing lanes of as many machine guns as they could fit into their bunkers. It seemed an idyllic place from which to practice my new trade as a diplo-warrior in command of a non-diplo unit, smack dab in the middle of a diplo-war.

I quickly learned that my predecessor had been a security underachiever who kept his classified files under his bunk, which is where I found them when I finally got around to changing the sheets a few weeks after I arrived. I also learned that I was destined to inherit Vietnam's model District Intelligence and Operations Coordinating Center (DIOCC) that was one of Vietnam's most popular combat tourism attractions. A combined intelligence and operations center staffed theoretically by fully vetted Vietnamese intelligence officers who had proven their loyalty to the government, it drew a constant stream of VIP visitors, from Generals and headquarters pogs to the President of Vietnam.

One visitor who arrived unannounced in his very own helicopter was the CIA's own Bill Colby, of Phoenix Program fame, who kicked me out of my bed that night. That didn't bother me nearly as much as you might think since just a few days earlier my Vietnamese counterpart had shown me a drawing taken off a VC who'd been killed in an ambush. It was a hand-drawn diagram of my headquarters building, with each room labeled with the name of the person who slept in it. It even showed whether they slept with their head toward the door or toward the window. Objectively, it was a rather good example of brilliant intelligence work. But, subjectively, it scared the crap out of me. The handwriting belonged to a Vietnamese officer who worked in the DIOCC and was privy to virtually all of our intelligence and operational planning. He'd been a spy for several years and even had the *chutzpah* to run a telephone wire from his desk in the DIOCC to a VC commander in the nearby mountains so he could phone in reports. So, as long as Colby slept with his head to the door, he was welcome to stay, even though years later his Phoenix Program almost cost me my career.

TWENTY-THREE

TRADING WITH THE ENEMY

Ninh Hòa did have its attractions. Had it not been for the minor irritant of war, it could have been a tourist's paradise. The district's crown jewel was the most beautiful beach I'd ever seen. Almost three miles long and more than a hundred yards deep, it was made up of fine, white, ceramic-grade sand and extended along an azure-blue bay protected from the sea by several small barrier islands. On the beach's south end stood a hundred-year-old walled village, built by the French in their colonial heyday as a resort for troops and their families. At the other end was a mountainous, forested peninsula with beautiful waterfalls cascading down to its rocky shores. Cam Ranh Bay, on the other side of the peninsula, was filled with American cargo ships bringing in goodies like bullets, bandages, and prime steaks.

The end of the beach closest to the peninsula was the safest place in the area—if you were a Viet Cong guerrilla. The other end was equally safe for us, thanks to the Commanding General of the South Korean White Horse Division that was camping out just a mile or so away. He and the local VC commander had cut a deal to divide the beach between them, giving each a piece to call his own, on which they wouldn't bother one another. A low wooden barrier marked the property lines.

Those who haven't been in an insurgency combat zone may
find such a local truce incredible. In fact, it wasn't even all that
unusual.

author's collection

Ninh Hòa, South Vietnam, 1969. I spent more time in combat
as an FSO than as a Marine. Here I'm authorizing an artillery
fire mission.

During the day we could safely take a swim even though
we could see some VC just a few hundred yards away enjoying
their slice of the beach. And, for all of their Marxism, the VC
were even happy to engage in entrepreneurial behavior when
the chance arose. The seaward coastline of their peninsula

teemed with lobsters, since no one other than the VC dared fish there. But even proletarian guerrillas tire of lobster, so a brisk trade had sprung up. At dusk the Vietnamese Army, the Koreans, and, I must admit, we CORD-ites, would place offerings like beefsteaks, fresh vegetables, and eggs on the platform marking the beach's dividing line, rather like sacrifices on an altar. By morning, these would have been miraculously transformed into some of the sweetest live lobsters I'd ever tasted.

Of course, there was a war on. So every once in a while, some VC would come down from their hideouts to take a potshot at someone, and we'd respond with an artillery barrage or two. Once, when they'd been excessively obstreperous, I suggested to my Naval Gun Fire Officer, a Marine Colonel, that we arrange for an Arc Light B-52 strike. He pointed out that my idea had two drawbacks. The vibrations that would be caused by exploding five-hundred-pound-plus bombs would disturb the lobsters and might knock down most of the buildings in the White Horse Division's headquarters, and that would piss off the Korean Division's Commanding General. Besides, the peninsular VC weren't the problem. The problem was their colleagues in the mountains, who weren't nearly as nice as their peninsular brethren and sometimes insisted on actually fighting with us, which could be annoying. We'd respond with 280mm fire from our American artillery battalion, and their outgoing rounds would sail right over my head making noises as loud as those of a freight train and disturb my sleep. One night a premature burst almost knocked my building down.

author's collection

Vietnam, 1969. Here, I'm practicing a "New Diplomacy" skill—zeroing in a rifle. In Vietnam, I usually carried a .45 cal. pistol, adding a rifle or submachine gun when moving about in the countryside.

For a long time I thought that these fireworks would be the highlight of my tour, until the mountain Charlies became even more annoying. I suppose they assumed that we couldn't do anything about them since they were far from any place where we could land helicopters, and whenever we landed a few troops, the distance between our LZs (landing zones) and them always gave them time to prepare their defenses or to melt away before we could reach them. One day, when I casually mentioned this to my Naval Gun Fire Officer, a Marine Colonel, a fleeting smile crossed his face. But I didn't think much of his response at the time. Then, one warm and balmy night (of course, they were all warm and balmy), all hell broke loose when a series of the loudest explosions I'd ever heard shook the entire valley. I quickly rushed to the DIOCC to see if anyone knew what had happened and wondering if the VC had blown up the railroad or an ammo dump.

Instead, my deputy grinned, handed me our tactical radio, and said, "Guns on the line."

After a quick authentication to make sure I wasn't talking to Hanoi Hanna, I gingerly asked in my best diplomatic voice, "What the @#* just happened?"

"Oops. Sorry, sir. I forgot to tell you. When I heard the *New Jersey* was going to pass by last night, I asked for a favor. Those were sixteen-inch airbursts. If you send up a FAC [forward air controller] tomorrow, I think you'll find some new LZs."

Sure enough, since the *New Jersey* carried nine 16 inch guns capable of firing 2,700-pound shells twenty-six miles, and their bursting radius was about a hundred and fifty yards, we found several new clearings, each large enough to land a couple of troop-carrying helicopters.

Actually, the Koreans had already figured out how the war was going to end, so they saw no reason to be particularly aggressive. Why risk getting killed when the PX could be raided for goodies that could be sent home and sold to make you rich? Even better, since brass was especially valuable in Korea, why not fire about fifty times more artillery than necessary, pick up the brass casings, and send those home too? Double the brass, double the profit; and you didn't even have to go to the PX. Not only were the Koreans' reluctant to stick their necks out unnecessarily for a lost cause, they regularly beat everyone to the PX when a new shipment of stereos arrived. In truth, they were damn good fighters.

TWENTY-FOUR

MY VERY OWN KOREAN WAR

My primary mission in Ninh Hòa was to make sure that two strategic lines of communication, the north-south coastal railroad and the two highways running through it, remained open. The more vulnerable of the two highways was the one into the Central Highlands, which was used heavily by both American and Korean convoys taking supplies up into the Vietnamese highlands surrounding Ban Me Thuot, the region's main city. One day a Korean convoy heading east out of the highlands and an American convoy headed west into them got into a fender bender. In the normal world, this would not have caused a major problem. But nothing was normal in Vietnam. After both convoys stopped to take a look at the damage, the Americans decided it was no big deal and got back into their trucks. But the Koreans were under different orders. No vehicle was to be moved until the Korean MPs checked the damage and gave their approval. So the Korean commander went over to the American commander and told him that they were under strict orders to stay put until the MPs arrived. The problem was that the nearest Korean MPs were about twenty miles away, it was late afternoon and, once the sun went down, the Viet Cong pretty much owned the highway.

For a while, the Americans went along with the Koreans. But the later it got, the antsier they became. The last thing they wanted was to spend the night in Indian country without the cavalry. The more impatient the Americans became the more adamant the Koreans became, until finally, with no MPs in sight, the American commander ordered his drivers to start their engines and prepare to move out. Seeing this, the Korean convoy's commander objected as forcefully as he could, but the Americans continued preparations to move despite his concerns. So the Korean commander ordered one of his truck's shotgun riders to lock and load his machine gun and open fire on the first American truck that tried to move. The moment the lead American truck began to move, the Korean gunner did exactly that and fired a string of .30 caliber rounds into its radiator, which pretty much stopped it in its tracks. The instant the bullets began to fly, the Americans bailed out and set up defensive positions on one side of the highway, weapons aimed at the Koreans. The Koreans did the same on the other side, and both began frantically radioing for orders and help.

The developing potential for a major battle between the Koreans and the Americans began attracting a radio audience big enough to kick *Good Morning, Vietnam* into second place in the popularity polls. I learned later that even the VC had been listening and found the prospect of a firefight between their two archenemies priceless. So there we were with two large convoys of military trucks full of war materials stuck deep inside Indian country; the VC doing their damnedest to find a way to take advantage of the whole mess; and Korean and American machine gunners glaring at each other through their sights, rounds chambered and fingers on the triggers. Talk about friendly fire incidents! I couldn't imagine a bigger disaster—both militarily and politically—than a firefight between them, especially if it produced casualties.

Then, in the nick of time, just as the sun was setting in the west, the cavalry arrived. More precisely, the American Army Colonel who was senior advisor to the White Horse Division's General arrived with two American Huey helicopters. He was riding in his slick (passenger helicopter), closely followed by his gunship. The first thing he did was to catch the attention of the men on the ground on both sides of the confrontation by having his gunship make a live-fire pass just behind each of them. He then had his slick land in the middle of the highway between the two, jumped out in full combat uniform and, wearing a brace of .45 cal. pistols and using a bullhorn, ordered both commanding officers to report to him—immediately!

Shocked, awed, and also aware of what would happen if they blew away a full Colonel, both did so immediately. He ordered them, as he so delicately put it, to "knock this shit off and get the @#* out of here," his voice being broadcast in all its glory over our tactical radio net. His was the gutsiest performance I'd ever heard of. Thus ended my first personal Korean war, but not my Korean disasters.

A few weeks later, I had to make one of the hardest decisions I've ever made. The memory of the unnecessary deaths that resulted from it still makes me quiver. Not long after the Korean War that wasn't came the Korean War that was, one no Colonel, gutsy or otherwise, could fix. At least this time it wasn't friend-on-friend. One night a VC force slipped into Ninh Hòa and occupied the railroad station, effectively blocking both the railroad and the north-south highway. They took dozens of unarmed civilian hostages, put them in front of their defensive perimeter as human shields, and waited for our reaction.

For the Viet Cong it was a win-win tactic. Holding the railroad station cut our supply lines, giving them both a military and a propaganda victory. Since we couldn't just leave them there, we had only two alternatives — dig them out by hand-to-hand combat or blow them out with artillery. Either way, the VC couldn't lose. And we couldn't win. If we used artillery, we would suffer fewer casualties, but the cost in innocent lives among the human shields would be horrendous. If we dug them out hand-to-hand, we'd suffer more casualties but could minimize—but not eliminate—the loss of innocent lives. I ruled out artillery because that would cause many more innocent civilian casualties. And that would give the Viet Cong a greater propaganda victory since we would be accused of "committed a crime against humanity" that would be trumpeted worldwide as loudly as possible by the antiwar crowd. The best we could hope for was a resolution that minimized civilian casualties in hopes of softening the political consequences. Sadly, the only way to do that was to dig them out hand-to-hand and that would cost many more lives of our Korean allies.

My calculus, as simple as it was sickening, was purely political. The humanitarian sensitivity of the international human rights community to any loss of innocent lives at our hands (albeit not at the hands of the VC) had to be assuaged with the blood of others. So when the Korean General asked me for clearance to do the only militarily sensible thing— blow them out with artillery—I refused and instead ordered the use of the tactic most likely to minimize civilian casualties - dig them out hand-to-hand. He was shocked, as was his senior American military advisor because my decision was tantamount to signing the death warrants of many of his soldiers. Militarily, I agreed with them. But Vietnam wasn't a military war. Those are fought with guns between uniformed soldiers of national armies. It was a political war, and political wars are fought more with words than with bullets. So I had to make a political decision, not a military one. The attack cost more than a dozen Korean lives, including that of the General's personal aide, a brilliant young officer destined to become a General himself one day had he not been killed as a consequence of my decision. As if in atonement, this battle was soon followed by one of the most successful combat operations I ordered in Vietnam.

One day not long after, we received an unusually precise agent report that a company of mountain VC was scheduled to come together for a change of command ceremony. The report included the exact date, time and location, and I thought it was too good to be true, but figured, what the hell. Artillery scattered all around the district had been shooting at shadows for years. So, just in case our intell was right, why not fire a T.O.T. (time-on-target) barrage from several different types of artillery timed to hit a specific location at precisely the same instant. Among the tubes that could reach it were two battalions of 105mm Vietnamese Army guns, the Korean White Horse Division's 105s and 155s, my pet battalion of American 280s, and several platoons of Vietnamese 4.2-inch mortars. So I asked all of them to turn one small patch in a very big forest into living hell for a tenth of a second—which they did.

At first we didn't know if the T.O.T. had been a success, or just a nice exercise. But on the second day, we began seeing body parts floating in the stream that ran through the place where the formation was to have taken place, confirming that we'd given the mountain VC a very bad day. Admittedly, it was a bit sickening. But I would have felt worse if I hadn't seen what the VC had done to the baby of one of my village chiefs just a few days earlier.

I'd gone with my District Chief to see what they'd done to a village chief that had cooperated with us and his family. A Viet Cong squad had entered the village and forced all of the villagers to assemble in its small square. They'd then dragged the village chief, his pregnant wife, and their one year old baby girl into the square to deliver a diatribe against him as an "enemy of the people." To demonstrate what they did to "enemies of the people" (them), they tied up the village chief's wife. Then, as her husband and the villagers watched, they sliced open her abdomen, ripped the fetus out of her womb, and forced it into her mouth, holding it there while she struggled until she suffocated to death. Then they grabbed the village chief's baby girl, tied her to a pole, and roasted her alive over an open fire. As a finale, they spent about three hours slowing cutting off the village chief's appendages, beginning with his fingers and toes and working upward until he bled to death. Before they left, the VC warned the villagers that if they dared cooperate with us again, they and their families would suffer even worse deaths.

Personally, I view firing artillery at uniformed enemy troops as a far less serious violation of human rights than slaughtering babies. Still, I suppose that some of the antiwar protest groups demonstrating for the cameras on the streets of America would probably have disagreed. They probably would have viewed placing the bodies of VC on the field beside my compound so that their families could come claim them as more disgusting than the mere roasting alive of a baby or two by those same enemy soldiers. But then, you can't please everyone.

After this series of incidents, I began to wonder about the real-world cost of human rights. Not the ones so eloquently described in abstract, universal declarations or by participants in joyful street festivities on the safe streets of America and Europe, those that have real-world implications in terms of blood, guts, and tears. It's a quandary that still haunts my thoughts, especially when I think about the countries I worked in or on where the human rights of citizens were being systematically violated—Franco's Spain, Stroessner's Paraguay, Castro's Cuba—in addition to the less obvious but sometimes brutal one-party systems like the one in Mexico while I was there. I had no problem denouncing violations of human rights, and often did. But the more I dealt with some of the activists in the human rights establishment the more I began to wonder whether or not many of them were more motivated by ideological goals than humanitarian considerations. In Vietnam, men died to minimize casualties among innocent civilians that the VC were using as human shields, and yet there was no outcry from human rights activists or the mainstream media against the VC. They could torture, rape, and kill unarmed civilians almost at will, while we were forced to adopt rules of engagement that resulted in our suffering greater casualties. It was a war in which we tried to follow the rules of the Marquis of Queensbury, while the enemy was free to follow those of the Marquis de Sade. The real-world results of this were more casualties, not fewer, among both our military and innocent civilians, precisely the opposite of what the human rights establishment claimed to be its intent. Ideologically selective moral indignation isn't just immoral. It also gets people killed.

TWENTY-FIVE

PHOENIX

Other images from my tour in Vietnam also remain vivid in my mind; the portable crapper local officials mounted on the open bed of a three-quarter-ton truck for then President Ngo Dinh Diem's use during a visit to Ninth Hòa on the off chance he might want to drop his drawers and take a dump before the masses; the sheet of aluminum roofing that sliced a telephone pole in half just outside my window when the downdraft from a Chinook helicopter broke it loose from a package of pallets and sent it whizzing through the air like a crazed guillotine; the strings of lights that ran through Ninh Hòa at night lit by electricity being stolen from our generator; the water buffalo we turned into hamburger one night with an artillery barrage when it triggered our antipersonnel radar. But some of my most disturbing experiences while in Vietnam involved my own government's Phoenix program, the Vietnam War-era's version of drone attacks.

As I understood it, the idea behind Phoenix was to selectively "neutralize" individuals who, while not openly combatants, were vital to the guerrillas' ability to operate. But as far as I could tell, in practice the program not only re-outraged those already outraged by the war and made the stomachs of others, including me, queasy. It occasionally made the security situation worse, not better. I'm not an absolutist and don't consider targeted assassinations always anathema. I'm of the school that would rather have had someone assassinate Hitler before Kristallnacht than wait for him to die in his bunker after much of Western Europe had been reduced to rubble. But I did firmly believe then, as I do now in the Age of Drones, that they should be the absolute last resort.

I'm reluctant in part because, especially in the case of an asymmetrical counter-insurgency war, determining whether an unarmed civilian is an innocent or an essential part of the enemy's war-making capabilities is rarely cut and dried, despite what Hollywood, spy novels, and politically motivated rhetoric may lead you to believe. In guerrilla warfare, those who are unarmed and wearing civilian clothes may engage in innocent activities during the day and become armed enemy combatants when the sun goes down. The biggest challenge is to tell the difference between a nighttime enemy and a daytime innocent, and insurgents knowingly exploit the revulsion of the general public to the killing of unarmed civilians by hiding themselves and their organized support networks within the civilian population.

I've had the opportunity to study in some depth the organization of several insurgent movements; the Thai Seri/Pathet Lao efforts in northeast Thailand; the Viet Cong; Nicaragua's pre-1979 Sandinista Front; El Salvador's Faribundo Marti Front; and the Nicaraguan Contras. I've also personally interviewed more than a hundred former insurgents and reviewed tens of thousands of pages from the central archives of three of them, the Sandinistas, the Faribundo Marti and the Contras. And in all three cases the key element of each movement was its clandestine support networks not its armed combatants. Like the heads of a Hydra, it was their clandestine support net-work not their fighters that was the real key to their insurgency. Kill or capture an armed insurgent and the insurgency's clandestine support network, which was six or eight times larger than their armed branch, would just produce another one – or two. The only way to kill any of the movements I studied would have been to kill the Hydra itself. But I digress.

In the immediate case of Phoenix operations in my District, I was especially reluctant after my first experience with the program came when a Phoenix team entered my district without my knowledge and killed the wrong person. That error pushed the deceased man's family and his entire village into the hands of the VC. To compound the problem, the Phoenix team then blew its cover and had to call for help for extraction. Now, one of the most dangerous small unit combat operations is an unplanned movement at night in a lethally-charged environment full of ambushes. In Ninh Hòa, all the forces on our side—from the Koreans to local Regional and Popular Forces, or RFF/PFFs (pronounced Ruff-Puffs), set nightly ambushes. In theory they kept my operations center informed of their locations. But in practice, no one trusted anyone. So the ambush sites of local forces were often not known to the Koreans and vice versa. This could, and sometimes did, result in friend-on-friend incidents up to and including deaths by friendly fire.

So when the Phoenix squad radioed in to say that they were in trouble and needed help, responding created an exceedingly dangerous situation. To help them I had to put lives at risk. And that was just the first of several Phoenix screw-ups. After another such incident I began to insist that Phoenix operations obtain my clearance before being deployed in my district. With some reluctance, my bosses at provincial headquarters began to do so, until one night when, for whatever reason, they requested immediate clearance for a squad to execute an operation in a village that, according to my intelligence information, housed few if any enemy civilians. When I denied them clearance, the Army Colonel responsible for writing my performance report became enraged. I learned later that he'd secretly retaliated by putting a statement in my performance report claiming that on occasion I "refused to follow direct orders" without specifying what those orders were or even whether or not they were legitimate - more about that later.

On a broader scale, my wartime experiences in Vietnam reinforced the most valuable lesson I'd learned during my earlier counterinsurgency experiences as a Marine. Insurgencies are political conflicts, not military ones. In Thailand, the government had spotted the developing Pathet Lao threat in its pre-revolution clandestine network building phase. This is the phase during which subversives build the civilian support networks I discussed above, without which armed cadres cannot sustain an insurgency. The Thai government identified the problem early, reacted politically, and succeeded in nipping the Pathet Lao inspired Thai Seri (Free Thai) movement in the bud.

In Vietnam, by putting coercive force first and civil governance second, we not only entered the fray too late, we also misread the nature of the battlefield. We arrived decades after the VC had established covert, countrywide civilian support structures that consisted of networks of compartmentalized, clandestine cells untouchable by mere firepower and all but impermeable to outsiders. That they were made up of unarmed civilian supporters gave them undeserved but very effective protective cloaks of political untouchability. Inside these networks specialized clandestine cells of unarmed, but very much involved, civilian supporters provided the movement's armed cadre with food, housing, safe houses, safe storage of their weapons, intelligence, early warning systems, propaganda platforms, recruits, local guides, and so forth. Vietnam was to be just the second in a life-long series of experiences I was to have with such systems.

TWENTY-SIX

EXITING VIETNAM—LESSONS LEARNED

By the time I arrived on the scene, the Vietnam War was, in my view, unwinnable by arms alone, which was why the State Department had committed FSOs to join the fray. It had, by then, deteriorated into a rather desperate attempt to defeat an exceptionally well-entrenched insurgency with a hybrid or, more precisely, bastardized civilian and military mixture of guns, butter, and bullshit known as CORDS. Unlike the Thai approach on which I'd cut my counterinsurgency teeth just a few years earlier, the CORDS effort was both too little and too late. The message that CORDS was supposed to deliver had long since been drowned out by the bark of guns. Further, Vietnam had neither a revered King to rally around nor youths willing to compete with the Viet Cong in the country's rice villages.

Put simply, because we didn't understand the nature of the real battle, we were trying to defeat a deeply entrenched enemy with tactics that put bullets first and politics second. It was the same mistake we were to repeat in Iraq in the form of the Petraeus Surge—deploying mixed military-civilian forces in a combat zone with the military in charge when the civilian side of the battle was the more important. In both Iraq and Afghanistan we failed to treat insurgencies as political conflicts with military dimensions and instead chose guns before butter. As a consequence, thanks to our overwhelming firepower, we were able to win all the major battles. But, by putting guns first, we lost both wars.

In the case of Vietnam, it was made even worse by being essentially held captive by Secretary of Defense McNamara's mathematical approach to all things defense, an approach that made the civilian side of the struggle even more ineffectual. The most egregious example of this was a monstrosity called the Hamlet Evaluation System (HES), pronounced *hiss*. Under the HES system, a major part of my job as a DSA was to evaluate each and every hamlet in my District by grading dozens of variables on a numerical scale, an exercise based on three false premises. First, it was based on the assumption that we had near-perfect knowledge of what was happening in every hamlet, which we didn't. In my case alone, I was expected to keep close tabs on thousands of civilians that lived in 107 different hamlets. Lord knows how many we were supposed to keep track of throughout the entire country. Second, the HES approach assumed that politics is an exact science when, in the real world, it's an art, and often a rather arcane, sloppy one at that. And third, the HES approach assumed that statistics never lie when, in fact, they often do. It was an immensely time-consuming, labor-intensive exercise in futility that, as far as I could tell, had very little practical value. Compared to the Thai Regional Development Team's subtle approach, the HES was an exceptionally crude example of taking an ethnocentric, first-world approach to a third-world problem.

My main problem with the HES was that it was deflecting our attention away from the real problem into a world of ephemeral smoke and mirrors that was all but irrelevant to figuring out how to ferret out the village support networks that made it possible for the VC to operate. Without supporters to provide them with food, information, propaganda platforms, recruiting help, and so forth, they would have been far less effective. But knowledge of such networks had to be collected at the local level by people that spoke the language, understood the culture, and were able to gain the trust of villagers, something swarms of foreign "birds of passage" like me simply couldn't do during short stays in a country. Of course, when I expressed my views, the response I received was usually, "Shut up, sit down, and do what you're told."

author's collection

Hanoi, North Vietnam, circa 1967. Salvadoran FMLN (Frente Faribundo Martí de Liberación Nacional) revolutionaries were regularly trained in North Vietnam. While I was in South Vietnam, this particular group was being trained there. Here they're with their North Vietnamese instructors (photo courtesy of Eduardo Sancho, *Fermán Cienfuegos*, former FMLN military commander).

While in Vietnam I developed, almost by osmosis, a feel for what I now think of as the insurgency battle space, which reinforced the conclusion I'd reached while still in the Marines. We were losing the war in Vietnam despite the sacrifices of those in uniform, whether American, Vietnamese, Korean, or even, as was the case of an artillery training team in my district, Australians. I came to believe that, while our armed forces had the guns, it was the local White Mice, the Vietnamese National Police, and Ruff-Puffs, local militia, that were the most effective forces for combating these village networks. But rather than learning from them, we did just the opposite. The more we trained these militias and the Vietnamese Army in our own tactics and armed them with our modern weapons, the further they drifted away from their own people.

By the time I reached Vietnam, the Vietnamese Army had become road-bound and tied to logistical tails that were almost entirely dependent on us and unsustainable without us. It's an axiom that guerrillas alone don't win wars, armies do. Creating a force capable of invading the VC's sanctuary, North Vietnam, might have led to victory. But what we created was an essentially reactive force, perhaps capable of confronting insurgents, but entirely insufficient for defending the country against an invading regular army. So toward the end of our involvement, when we began to withdraw our military forces and reduce our support, the once inferior regular North Vietnamese Army became the superior force on the battlefield. This made it inevitable that sooner or later our erstwhile allies would be overwhelmed, as proved to be the case. Almost three decades later, I was to play a key role in the eerily similar defeat of yet another ally we'd led down the same primrose path, first supporting and then abandoning the Nicaraguan Contras to the mercies of their still armed enemies.

As I mentioned earlier, after leaving the diplomatic service for academe, I was able to document the existence, as well as the importance, of nearly identical clandestine support networks to the revolutionary forces in El Salvador, Honduras, Guatemala, Mexico, and Nicaragua. Interestingly, in the case of Nicaragua, many of the networks that were crucial to the Sandinistas during their anti-Somoza guerrilla revolutionary phase became equally crucial to the Contras that later opposed them.

Many years later, when I mentioned this one of my former-revolutionary friend, Farabundo Martí Liberation Front (FMLN) military commander *Fermán Cienfuegos*, he smiled and gave me a copy of the Spanish-language manual that the North Vietnamese had used to teach the FMLN's cadre how to prepare and stage an insurgency. Later former Mexican, Honduran, Nicaraguan, and Costa Rican Marxist revolutionaries told me that they too, had been taught how to organize an insurgency and launch a guerrilla war in Cuba, Libya, the Soviet Union, or Eastern Europe, out of essentially the same manual. *Ferman Cienfuegos* even gave me access to several hundred individual FMLN personnel files that confirmed that more than 30% of their members were trained in Cuba or elsewhere. Even a few Contra commanders had been trained there during their pre-Contra years, while they were part of the Sandinista forces fighting to overthrow the Somoza dictatorship.

Put simply, clandestine support networks are the guerrilla's equivalent of a regular army's rear echelon support system for a very simple reason, both regular soldiers and guerrillas have to eat, sleep, and drink, but neither grows its own food, makes its own clothes, nor manufactures its own weapons. Without these networks, no insurgency can prosper. It's that simple. As far as I can tell, it's also a lesson we've yet to learn.

But all assignments, good or bad, come to an end. And besides, the outgoing 280mm artillery fire was beginning to disturb my sleep, especially when the occasional premature airburst threatened to make my headquarters building collapse on my head. Further, it was time for me to get back to America's real first line of defense, the cocktail party. As usual, the State Department's personnel gurus came through like gangsters (excuse me—like gangbusters) and delivered on their promise that anyone that volunteered for Vietnam would get a choice onward assignment. In keeping with the fine print of that promise, I was given three from which to choose, opening a new Consulate in Songkhla on the Kra Peninsula in Thailand, becoming a political officer in Cairo in the wake of the 1967 Arab-Israeli War, or Mérida, Mexico in the aftermath of the Spanish Conquest.

Perhaps because I already had extensive experience in the county, the Department did its best to con me into taking on the assignment in Thailand, a posting that might have sounded like a dream assignment—to an idiot—opening a new Consulate in Songkhla in the middle of yet another war, this one accompanied by family. But I knew better. State may have thought that the Kra Peninsula, which connects southern Thailand to Malaysia, would be an ideal assignment for me since I spoke fluent Thai. But it was the late 1960s, the Cold War and the Vietnam War were both still in full swing, and Thailand was nothing like the tourist paradise it has since become. In those days the biggest industry in Songkhla was hunting sharks for their fins to sell to the Chinese to make soup. So the most exciting evening pastime was counting the number of fishermen that had lost an arm or leg to the sharks that day, as several always did, given the shark's tendency to bite back.

The biggest plus to taking the Songkhla assignment, at least from a family point of view, would be the multilingual school system that would give our children their choice of languages in which to study, Thai, Malay, or Chinese—take your pick. As an added bonus, I'd be free to choose my own house from among numerous walk-up wooden homes perched cheerfully on stilts one floor above open-air sewers. True, in those days none of them had air-conditioning. But they were cooled by the occasional ocean breeze, albeit minimally since both the average temperature and average humidity usually hovered steadily between 85% and 95%, although cracks in their split-bamboo floors did allow cooling breezes, along with the perfume of hog slop, free entry into the house. As an added bonus, we could raise pigs beneath the house like everyone else in town. And, as TV pitchmen incessantly say— wait, there's more.

As the first-ever American Consul in Songkhla, I would be free to choose my very own office building, provided, of course, it met Foreign Buildings Office (FBO) and State Department security standards while staying within budget. So if I accepted this outstanding assignment, I could look forward to spending two or three years supervising construction of a nice, new building for my successor to occupy, providing, of course, that FBO could speed up its normal process and approve the floor plans in less than ten years. Best of all was the job itself. I would have my very own guerrilla war not fifty miles from my family's home and the close company of every Malay CT, communist terrorist, the Brits could push over the border. My own war, my own Consulate, and my very own family disaster-in-waiting—how could anyone resist the temptation? Well, I could, for one.

So I turned my attention to Cairo, until I was told that I would not be taught Arabic, would be the only political officer in a nest of consuls, and would have to do all my political work in my free time, since I would spend most of my workdays chained to a visa line stamping *no* on passports. That left Mérida, where I would be the eleventh ranking officer in a two-man post, since numbers two through ten lived in Mexico City and only visited when they wanted to climb a Maya temple. But at least I already spoke the language and the house had air conditioned bedrooms. So, Mérida it was.

I left Vietnam with a heavier heart than when I arrived, satisfied that I had gone the extra mile, but more convinced than ever that, sooner or later, our hyper politically partisan approach to foreign policy that routinely puts short-term domestic political power before long-term national interests, would eventually trump the efforts of our troops and allies, no matter how well they did in battle. But at least the experience taught me a lesson or two that would be of some value later. In the interim I had other places to go.

TWENTY-SEVEN

MÉRIDA, MEXICO—*LA CIUDAD BLANCA*

The Post Report on Mérida was orgiastic in its praise of the city's myriad world-class attractions and the luxurious lifestyle that the chosen few assigned there were blessed to live. Of course, every Foreign Service post is required to produce a description of life at post. They just aren't required to tell the truth in it. In the case of Mérida, its Post Report went on forever about the idyllic tropical weather, the mansion we would inhabit, located just ten yards from the office and fully furnished out of Federal Government's General Services Office (GSO) catalog, the region's particularly melodious Spanish accent, and Mérida's excellent schools, great supermarkets, big hospitals and a welcoming American expatriate community. All in all, it described the Yucatan as a truly remarkable paradise on earth.

Rarely, if ever, have so many out-and-out lies been crammed into so little text, as we would soon find out. The schools sucked, even by Mexican provincial standards. There was no potable running water and no sewer system. As to sanitary conditions, the local Director of Public Health delicately explained to me soon after we arrived, "If feces were florescent, Mérida wouldn't need electric lights." Most roads consisted of worn patches of asphalt spread thinly between giant potholes. True, the hospitals were big, but only because they needed large patios in which to boil their soiled bed sheets in fifty-five-gallon drums over open fires. What the hospitals didn't have most of the time, especially at night, were doctors, which could be a real drawback in an emergency. As for public transportation, Mérida was a place where old American school buses went to die. The open markets were better stocked and cleaner than the supermarkets, but neither sold good quality fresh meat or vegetables. The fruit, on the other hand, was good, and the seafood was great.

Once we settled in; Leda recovered at the house from some infectious hepatitis she'd been given in Costa Rica as a going-away present (the Consulate doctor forbade her to go to a local hospital because it was too dangerous); the kids enrolled in a Spanish-language school run by sour-faced old nuns; our first shipment of edible food from Denmark arrived by boat and cleared customs; and we found a personal smuggler, it turned out to be a great place. The best part was being together again as a family.

There was one other professional Consulate in Mérida, that of Cuba. But, since relations between our governments were a bit strained and there were a couple of Cuban-armed insurgencies sputtering next door in Central America, we didn't mix socially. We did, of course, keep a wary eye on the Cuban Consul. But as far as we could tell, his main job wasn't to help foment those insurgencies. It was to assure that the Cuban Revolution's political elite received a regular supply of embargoed American luxury goods and spare parts for their aging American cars. American home satellite systems were in especially high demand by the Cuban revolutionary elites, since that was the only way Fidel Castro and his merry band could watch American professional baseball games.

That the Cuban Consul wasn't involved in promoting the Mexico branch of world revolution was apparently due to the existence of a rather obvious, if unpublished, agreement between Cuba and Mexico. Mexico would allow Cuba to use its territory to aid and abet revolutionary activities in third countries in return for its not doing unto Mexico what they were doing unto others. How this "pact" worked was explained to me decades later by a Mexican revolutionary friend. But the fact that it existed was obvious enough, since Marxist guerrillas regularly moved to and from Cuba via the Mexico. Besides, Mexico already had more than its fair share of radical revolutionaries quite able to do their own revolutionizing, thank you.

As for the Yucatecans, they were almost universally very warm and friendly, provided you never made the mistake of calling them Mexicans. They themselves called people from Mexico City *hwatch*, a Mayan word pronounced roughly like the sound made when you hack a really big goober and spit it on the floor. Being culturally sensitive, I took this as a clue that maybe, just maybe, there wasn't much love lost between them and their masters in Mexico City.

Soon after our arrival, we received numerous invitations to Yucatecan homes and soon felt we needed to reciprocate their hospitality. So we drew up an invitation list, sent out our invitations, and waited for the big night. Being from Nevada and therefore more laid-back than the average Ivy League FSO, our game plan was simple. Put some Latin music on the phonograph (merengues from the Dominican Republic worked especially well), set up an open bar, and then let the music and booze do the rest. When guests arrived, we'd greet them, show them where to find the food, make them stiff drinks, and let them have at it.

That evening we learned two lessons. One was that the preferred drink of Yucatecan men was anything alcoholic flavored with a small dash of Coke. But Yucatecan women preferred cognac, straight, and preferably a full bottle each (a truly remarkable feat!). The second was that, when it comes to rum, the Yucatán battle cry was "Bacardi or die." This I learned the hard way when I led a new friend, Santos Molina, to the bar and offered him Havana Club and Coke. (Yes, I knew there was a Cuban embargo. But sometimes one must make sacrifices for the greater good. And, besides, this Havana Club wasn't actually produced in Havana.) He took one look, made a face, and stalked out of the house. I was intrigued when his wife didn't go with him, though I assumed she would stay just long enough to finish her bottle of cognac. But then she sidled over, smiled, and said not to worry. Despite her reassurance, since his behavior seemed decidedly odd, I continued to worry that I'd somehow offended him, which turned out to be exactly what I'd done. Eventually Santos Molina returned carrying a full case of Bacardi Black Label, followed by his driver carrying a second case, and said, "Let's make a deal. You serve only Bacardi, and I'll see to it that you never run out of rum." Since he was the local Bacardi distributor, I had to resign myself to the ordeal.

As the posts only Vice Consul, my job was to deal with pretty much anything my boss wanted to throw my way, which turned out to be mostly consular scut work or just about anything else, save political analysis. The biggest part of my job involved nonimmigrant visas—trying to separate the 10 percent of the visa applicants that were bona fide tourists and businessmen from the 90 percent desperately trying to get into the United States to better their lives. Hour after hour, it was my job to stand at a counter listening to people's stories, knowing full well that nine out of ten of them were lying, and then making snap decisions, mostly to refuse their visa requests.

It was a bit like playing God, deciding the future of strangers based on the scantiest of information, crushing their dreams of better lives. I certainly had nothing personal against any of them. In fact, I liked and sympathized with the vast majority of them because they were almost all good, hardworking people looking for a way to improve their lives and those of their families, something the Mexican socio-political power structure still doesn't let them do with ease. If I'd been in their shoes, I would have done the same thing. But as an American Consul, my job was to approve visas only for people who didn't intend to stay in the United States. Since almost half of all illegal workers in the United States enter legally on valid visas but then overstay them, the visa line was as important as the border in efforts to control illegal immigration. I was also responsible for all sorts of other services, from delivering of Social Security and Veterans pensions, to helping Americans in trouble, and visiting the ones in Mexican jails. I also back-stopped my boss when he was out of the district. While few of our "clients" were as colorful as John of the Armpits or Hallelujah, Mérida did have its moments.

TWENTY-EIGHT

Show Time!

One of Mérida's saving graces was my boss, Bill Harbin, who'd been there long enough to have the place totally wired. He knew almost everyone and was liked by all. He was also exceedingly generous, even eager, to pass his knowledge and contacts on to me, although I chose not to take him up on a few of them. I passed, for instance, on the young ladies he and my predecessor as Vice Consul had regularly invited to skinny-dip in the swimming pool between our houses while the Maya gardener, barefoot in a tux, served drinks.

I suppose they thought that the trees between the pool and the main road in front of the Consulate fully screened their revelries from the view of passersby which, in a sense, was technically true. Almost everyone that later told me about the goings-on said they'd not passed by, but stood still on the sidewalk in order to watch the show. Most of them felt it was a much better spectacle than the movies in local theaters, although I never could confirm a rumor that one of them had bribed the gardener to prune the lower branches off the trees.

It should be explained to those less accustomed to the quaint customs of Latin males, that the only diplomatic problem caused by these incidents was the risk of their getting caught by their significant other. Up until the Vice Consul's wife's unexpected return from the United States after several months' absence, it may have been the best men-only show in town. From my own point of view, it all turned out rather well, since she became so screaming mad that she refused to let her husband go back to work at the Consulate, which is how the job in Mérida came open. As someone once said, all's well that ends well.

Harbin was, by education, a geologist. But intellectually he was a Renaissance man. Among his many hobbies, he kept a daily journal written in beautiful, Edwardian script. His comments were extraordinarily insightful, sharp-witted, and included hundreds of devastating descriptions of people he'd met. One evening over Bacardi and Cokes, after swearing me to secrecy and threatening to label me an incompetent cretin with a shriveled you-know-what if I dared so much as whisper any of it to anyone, he let me read much of it. It was a singular honor, really. Bill knew very well that he didn't dare let anyone he mentioned in it see it or even hear about it, unless he wanted to be ridden out of town on a rail or to be laid out on a sacrificial Chac Mool and have his still beating heart cut out of his body by a Maya priest with an obsidian knife.

Harbin guarded his journal with the sort of zeal and jealousy one normally reserves for protecting the family jewels and always kept it with him until - one day - he left it in a restaurant. Knowing what was in it, my reaction to this news was similar to hearing the sound of incoming fire in Vietnam. I frantically called everywhere Harbin had been that day that had a telephone (about two out of twenty spots) while dispatching local employees posthaste in cars, busses, on motor scooters, and on foot to check the rest. If we'd had a horse, I would have sent someone on horseback, if we'd had a saddle. The whole Keystone Cops routine reminded me of the time I accidentally stirred up a nest of baby scorpions and sent hundreds of them scurrying about, more than a few in my direction.

As ringmaster, or should I say search-master, I tried to keep out of the way, until a restaurant owner in Dzibilchaltún (try saying that ten times, fast!), a small town nine miles from Mérida, called to say he'd found a strange book of hieroglyphics with the American Consul's name on it. I don't remember the speed limit between Mérida and 'Zib in those days, but I doubt it was 110 miles an hour. I didn't even know the Consulate's official car could go that fast. Thankfully, I had diplomatic immunity in case I was stopped by the *chota*, Mexican slang for the cops. Murmuring fervent prayers to Kinich Ahau, the Maya Sun God, to let me recover Bill's journal before anyone who could read Edwardian script had a chance to examine it, I raced into the café, grabbed the journal from the startled innkeeper, dropped a few greenbacks on the counter, and drove sedately back to Mérida. Since no one tried to assassinate Harbin, I probably succeeded. My prompt action also helped earn me a great efficiency report.

TWENTY-NINE

Alarums and Excursions— and Shrimp

Of course, refusing people visas and reading seditious journals weren't my only jobs in Mérida, as I learned one day when an agent from an American insurance company dropped by to discuss a problem. They were having issues with claims made for the loss of shrimp boats that weren't making it back to Texas and Louisiana from fishing trips in the Gulf. To be precise, they were losing about twenty boats a year, each worth about half a million dollars, so they wanted the Consulate's help. Now, even though Consuls are responsible for shipping and seaman problems, I didn't see how we could stop boats from sinking, until he explained what was happening.

American Gulf Coast shrimpers were putting in at the port of Tampico in our consular district for a bit of recreation. They'd sail into the harbor, drop anchor, and promptly receive visits from scantily clad young ladies of the evening and petty merchants who were more than happy to sell them pot and booze at discount prices. A half-dozen or more shrimp boats were partying in the bay at any one time, spending the cash each Captain had for use in case of an emergency. While the owners of the boats didn't agree with them that procuring the services of prostitutes and buying booze qualified as an emergency, their captains weren't allowing such petty differences of opinion to slow them down. Rather, they were partying until the funds ran dry. At that point, a local merchant would appear to buy the shrimp the boats had caught, thereby helping them continue their parties. At first this seemed like a pretty good deal, but when they ran out of shrimp they were faced with another problem—reality. The captains really didn't want to go home reeking of whiskey to tell the owners of the boats that they hadn't been able to find a single shrimp in the entire Gulf of Mexico. So yet another local merchant would appear, offering to buy the boat's radios, fishing nets, refrigeration equipment, and so forth so they could keep on partying, which they did, until almost nothing remained they could sell.

Once a boat was stripped of everything salable and its Captain sobered up enough to realize he was in real trouble, another local merchant would drop by to suggest a solution. Caught between a rock and a hard place, all too many of the captains chose the rocks. They would sail their boat out into the Gulf and "accidentally" run it aground on a rocky reef known as the *Arecife Alacranes* (Scorpions Reef), gently, so the hull wouldn't be damaged. By prearranged "miracle," a Mexican boat sailing nearby would see them and "rescue" the crew. Once back in Tampico, the crew would contact the owners, tell them that they'd hit a reef, watched the boat sink and, thankfully, been rescued. All they needed now was to be repatriated. In the meantime, almost immediately after the crew had been rescued, yet another Mexican boat would "discover" the now-abandoned American boat, claim it as salvage, and tow it back to Tampico where it would be added to the rapidly growing Mexican shrimping fleet. It was quite a racket. And, since maritime law on such matters is "finders keepers, losers weepers," there wasn't anything the owners could do once a boat had been salvaged but file a claim with the boat's insurers.

But their insurance companies were getting tired of ponying up half a million dollars every time the owner's lost a boat. They wanted me to dash up to Tampico carrying legal documents, board every partying shrimp boats in Tampico harbor, and relieve its Captain of his command. It sounded more dangerous than Vietnam—board a shrimper full of drunken sailors and prostitutes, relieve the Captain, tell the crew that I, the American Consul, was now in command, and order the crew to sail the boat back to the United States without me aboard. Amazingly, when I finally did just that, no Captain or crew ever rejected my authority, although I did experience some tense moments on Tampico Bay.

Whenever I was in Tampico, I also visited an American being held in the local lockup. To ensure he was being well-treated, and not just being cleaned up for my visit, I'd appear at the jail unannounced and ask to see him immediately. Since he'd been a resident of the Tampico jail for about five years and had five or so to go, I wound up dropping in to check up on him every couple of months. Although it generally took a while for him to appear, my first few visits went well and he seemed to be in good condition and spirits.

After a few such visits, the warden called me aside and asked that, in the future, I give him some advanced notice of my visits. I patiently explained to him that, under the Vienna Convention, he was required to give me immediate access whenever I appeared. After listening to me patiently for several minutes, he started to laugh. "Señor Consul, I'm not asking you to do anything contrary to international law. It is just that he's not here most of the time."

When he saw that his comment had caught me off guard, he explained. "He's a model prisoner, married to a local girl, and has a small business downtown. So he's only here weekday nights. He leaves every morning for his shop and spends his weekends in town with his wife. So when you show up, he has to close up his shop and rush to the jail to meet with you." Only in Mexico.

One of our special Yucatecan friends was one of Mexico's most popular music composer and singer, Armando Manzanero, a short, charming, and very friendly Yucatecan who'd begun his professional life in Mérida as a bar singer and gone on to become one of Mexico's most famous singers and composers of popular ballads. Leda and I spent many an enjoyable afternoon at his beach home in Progreso watching his children and ours swim or play games while Armando whipped up a mean barbecue.

One day Armando unexpectedly came to the Consulate to ask me, "Why do you Americans hate me?"

I assured him that we didn't hate him at all. "Just the opposite, you're one of our best friends."

After repeating his question several time, he finally told me what had happened. The day before, he and his wife had decided on a whim to take their children to Disneyland, but needed visas. But when he went to the Embassy to get them, the Consul turned them down.

I just looked at him. "Armando, why didn't you come to me?"

He explained that he'd applied for their visas in Mexico City, not in Mérida, because that's where he'd been. Intrigued, I asked him to describe exactly what happened. He'd simply taken their passports to the American Embassy and joined the daily line of several hundred other Mexicans waiting their turns to speak with a Consul. (In those days you didn't need an appointment.) When his turn came, he put their passports on the desk in front of a very young man and asked him to please stamp visas in them. He hadn't bothered to dress up and was wearing a pair of old trousers, a loose hanging shirt, sandals, and a peasant hat. The Consul, who probably didn't speak much Spanish much less know much about Mexican popular music, took one look at him, decided he was an indigent Indian trying to get into the United States to find a job, and rejected his application.

I just shook my head. "Armando, would you have gone to a Mexican government office and asked for something if you weren't known to them? Of course not. You'd ask a friend to help you. Our system isn't really all that different." And with that, I issued him and his family visas.

Another friend, whose name I won't use for obvious reasons, was an official of Mexico's once and future ruling political party, the Partido Revolucionario Institucional, the PRI. His specialty was forecasting election results weeks in advance, and he was always right. Intrigued by his uncanny skills, I invited him to lunch, gave him a couple of stiff drinks, and began pumping him for information about the upcoming presidential and gubernatorial elections. When I asked how he thought they'd turn out, he said with a slight slur, "I can do better than that. I'll give you the results now. I have them right here."

Reaching into his pocket, he pulled out a notebook. While I had some experience with using polls to project the results of elections, I'd never seen such precise precinct by precinct results a month in advance, and I said as much. He responded,

"But that's my job. I fix elections so my party doesn't lose any." I asked how he could make that happen this time when the Partido de Acción Nacional (PAN) was projected to receive between 70 and 80 percent of the vote. He agreed that public opinion sometimes made his job difficult. Because the PAN was so popular, he had to make sure the PRI won by a very small margin. That way, they could defend themselves against what were bound to be screams of outrage. The numbers he showed me were just that—a PRI win by a very small margin.

On Election Day, I drove around the city and out into the countryside to visit polling places. At several of them, Army troops were busy burning ballot boxes in the streets, so I wasn't able to get close enough to observe the actual voting procedures. But it was fairly clear that, by hook or by crook, the PRI was determined to win, which is why I was surprised when they lost both the gubernatorial and mayoral elections, making Yucatán the only state and capital in Mexico governed by the PAN. That evening at the café, I ran into a very despondent Enrique doing his best to get totally smashed. I sat down next to him and asked that most diplomatic of all questions, "What the hell happened?"

As it turned out, every precinct had voted exactly as he told me they would, except one, the Mérida Army garrison. Since almost everyone stationed there came from somewhere else and owed their jobs to the government, he hadn't bothered to fix that precinct on the assumption that they would all favor the PRI. Instead, more than 90 percent of that precinct went to the PAN because virtually all of its enlisted men and most of its officers had voted against the PRI.

There was little he could do besides get drunk and wait for the ax to fall. But in the end, he wasn't the one punished. It was the Army. In retaliation, the garrison battalion was ordered to open a new border post deep in the Lacandon jungle on the Guatemala-Mexico border where no human foot, with the exception of an occasional intrepid hunter and maybe a few wandering Maya, had ever gone before. Located about three days march from the nearest road, it didn't even have a helicopter landing zone and was about as isolated as one could get while remaining inside Mexico.

Speaking of isolation, some of my readers may wonder how on earth anyone could feel isolated anywhere near Cancún, one of the world's premier beach resorts. The answer is simple. When we lived in Mérida, the islands of Isla Mujeres and Cozumel were the only places on the peninsula's Caribbean coast with relatively modern tourist facilities. Cancún hadn't yet been built. In fact, I didn't know it was even a gleam in anyone's eye until about halfway through my tour, when several executives from American hotel chains came to talk with me and show me their project plans for hotels in Cancún.

I had a few questions right away, like how are tourists going to get to it, since there isn't an airport? They responded that Mexico was going to build one not far from the beach opposite Isla Mujeres. They went on to explain that Cancún's being as far from any city as one can get and still be in Mexico was its major attraction for the Mexican authorities. All of Mexico's other large resorts were on the Pacific, and their proximity to some of the poorest places in Mexico had generated lots of problems, the Lucio Cabañas insurgency near Acapulco being a good example. They wanted to avoid experiencing similar problems by making Cancún a second Acapulco, but one located far enough from any population center that the upscale lifestyle reflected by the resort area wouldn't generate too much discontent among the poor. Even though Cancún was still very much in the planning phase, it was a gigantic project and already involved several American companies. I wrote a report on what the hoteliers told me and sent it into Washington. The Embassy Commercial Officer, instead of saying thank you for the information, sent a cable to Washington stating flatly that Cancún was a fantasy I'd invented, implying that someone should look into my mental stability. Six months later, construction began.

Overall, our years in the Yucatán were unexpectedly enjoyable, and having the family together again was a blessing. But stamping visas (or not) while eating imported canned goods and avoiding the local tap water just wasn't how we wanted to spend the rest of our diplomatic lives. So I began to cast about for a way to change my path from consular to something else, preferably political affairs. But, once again, fate sent me in a different direction.

When I was offered the Department's six-month post-graduate crash course in economics, I jumped at the chance, thus assuring that my growing family was in for yet another wrenching change of lifestyle. When we arrived in DC with four children in tow, there was no room at the inn—any inn. No one was willing to rent an apartment to someone with four small children for just six or seven months. So we had to adapt and improvise. The result was all to the good, for those who enjoy two-hour commutes.

We ended up buying a two-bedroom, single-wide trailer (now more elegantly known as a pre-manufactured micro-mansion) in the wilds of Virginia. Four kids, two bedrooms, no yard, and fifty miles from the Foreign Service Institute where I would be studying. It was hardly the diplomatic high life, and I still thank the good Lord for giving me a wife willing to turn what could have been a grisly grind into an adventure. When we left DC, we even sold the trailer-house for more than we paid for it. And so once I'd finished the Department's Economics Course, we moved for the eleventh time since we'd been married—as always seems to be the lot of the itinerant foreign affairs specialist and his, or her, family—this time to South America.

THIRTY

PARAGUAY—BIG RIVERS, BIGGER EGOS

Before starting the Foreign Service Institute's Economics Course, I'd dropped by to see my Career Development Officer, or CDO, who told me that, since my first three assignments had been overseas, the rules mandated I stay in Washington for the next five years. Besides, he added, there weren't any jobs coming available overseas. So when he called me halfway through the course to say a position in Asunción, Paraguay had unexpectedly opened up, I jumped at the opportunity. After all, Paraguay was a dictatorship. Who could resist such a golden opportunity to serve in yet another one? With my crypto Master's degree in hand, as soon as the course ended, off we went to the heart of South America for what turned out to be one of the very best assignment of my career for all sorts of unexpected reasons.

Paraguay offered decent schools, safe streets, great housing, and delightful people; its politics were a veritable snake pit of intrigues, jealousies, backroom machinations, plots, counterplots, and corruption; and its economic system was crawling with smugglers, money launderers, and drug traffickers. It was just my kind of place, since I was fast becoming a specialist in strong-arm regimes: First Somoza's Nicaragua, then Franco's Spain, and now Stroessner's Paraguay, a trifecta if there ever was one.

Along the way I'd learned a few things about such regimes. Most people assume that dictators rule by dictating. So to understand what's happening, all you need do is watch the dictator. But that's not true. Far from being simpler than open systems, dictatorships are merely complicated in a different way. In fact, there's never actually been an absolute dictatorship for the simple reason that no one person can be everywhere at once nor do everything. Even Genghis Khan depended on his staff to get things done. In Nicaragua, the Somozas managed to stay in power as long as they did because they received the support of three groups: A cabal of Army sycophants known as the ALAS (short for Anastasio, Luis, Anastasio Somoza) that dominated the military, a bureaucracy packed with civilian suck-ups and, most importantly, an unwritten but very real compact with the country's traditional oligarchy. In Spain, Francisco Franco had had all of these, plus God, or at least the Roman Catholic Church.

Besides doing my main job, I also wanted to test both the political side of the Stroessner dictatorship and my newly acquired quasi-understanding of economics against reality. I thought it would be easy. But it wasn't. As my Peruvian daughter-in-law loves to say, "Yeah, right!"

During my years in Paraguay, "Big Al" Stroessner was the man. He also had a classic authoritarian personality. Fairly tall, undeniably heavyset, and clearly happy with his job, Big Al had some strange habits, like holding cabinet meetings at five in the morning and leaving work around noon to go home, kiss his wife, take a shower and drive over to a female "friend's" house for the afternoon. According to a story whispered to me several times, one morning when the Minister of Defense's home phone rang at about three, he automatically answered, *"Si, Señor Presidente?"* When Stroessner asked how he knew who was calling, the Minister answered, "Because you're the only person in this country that would dare call me at this hour." An apocryphal tale? Perhaps. But one that rang true.

By the time I reached Asunción I'd become a reasonably competent simultaneous Spanish-English interpreter, so my first Ambassador, Ray Ylitalo, a non-Spanish-speaking Finn with a misleading last name, began taking me with him to his meetings with Stroessner or having me accompany visiting VIPS.

Once, when I arrived at the palace with a visiting group of congressional staffers, Stroessner's security asked us to wait a minute because the President was on his way out. When he emerged, Stroessner stopped briefly to say something to one of his aides, and then headed for his car. But before getting in, he lit a cigarette, took a few puffs, ushered his driver into the back seat, took the wheel himself, turned, waved to the nice people standing outside watching, and drove away. Grandstanding? Yes, but it made quite an impression on both the tourists and the congressional staffers.

One can convincingly argue that, on average, dictators are not very nice people. But one can't convincingly argue that they're dumb. They're anything but. To cling to power as long as he did, Stroessner may not have been very democracy-minded and may have been responsible for some pretty horrendous human rights violations. But he wasn't stupid. Nor did he lack public relations skills. It was a lesson worth learning. Latin American dictatorships can be far more durable than democracies, so never underestimate a dictator, especially one on his seventh term as President. And if they're the right, or should I say left, kind of dictator, they can even be loved by much of the outside world. Just look at how well Fidel Castro has done in the global popularity polls.

THIRTY-ONE

NIXON, STROESSNER, AND THE FRENCH CONNECTION

One of my visits to Stroessner's office was particularly memorable. The desk behind which Vuestra Excelencia El Señor Presidente de la República y Comandante en Jefe de las Fuerzas Armadas, Ingeniero Don Alfredo Stroessner sat, was almost as long as his title. But it was dwarfed by his sixty-by-one-hundred-foot corner office.

The issue was August Ricord, the narco-trafficker better known as the French Connection. He was in jail in Paraguay by accident and we wanted him. But Stroessner was refusing to allow him to be extradited. While I'd been to Stroessner's presidential office several times with Ambassador Ylitalo to discuss the Ricord problem, this time I was there as the interpreter for Nelson Gross, a tough street cop President Nixon had made responsible for Drugs and Thugs (narcotics and organized crime) in the State Department. Ylitalo had failed to deliver several earlier forceful démarches demanding Ricord's extradition forcefully enough, and then somehow failed to report his own failures. Instead, he'd succumbed to what's known in diplomatic circles as creative reporting syndrome (CRS, also known in the trade as Cover Your Ass

Syndrome). It was the same sort of ambassadorial fudging of reports to Washington that may have led to the 1991 Persian Gulf War years later, a war our second daughter, Rebecca, voluntarily attended as a Marine Intelligence Sergeant. So Washington had ordered Ylitalo not to be present when Gross met with Stroessner.

Ricord was in the can in Asunción after being accidentally arrested by the Policia de Aduana, the Customs Police, we wanted him, and Gross was in Paraguay to set Stroessner straight, even though Stroessner thought he had things fairly straight already, given his decades-long experience as President. The problem was that Gross didn't speak Spanish nor was he accustomed to talking to someone with his very own, private country, which is where I came in. After the obligatory introductions, I took my place standing quietly and unobtrusively between Stroessner and Gross, just behind the line of eye contact between them, close enough to interpret, but far enough away to avoid being a distraction. Since I was to be with a Presidential Envoy, I'd made sure to dress professionally in a pinstriped mall suit, red power tie properly adjusted, and well-buffed shoes, just as I'd done dozens of times before.

The meeting began cordially enough and, if I do so say so myself, I was doing a rather brilliant job interpreting, so much so that the only other person present, the Foreign Minister, who was seated several yards away across President Stroessner's desk, actually winked at me. His Excellency and Nixon's emissary exchanged pleasantries and my simultaneous translation party trick was going swimmingly, until Stroessner asked Gross a loaded question, "So why are you here?"

Gross actually told him, in plain language no less, a nearly unheard-of breach of diplomatic etiquette, and I quote, "We want Ricord, and we demand that you send him to us now!"

I was dumbfounded. Gross was actually demanding action from Alfredito, as he was known to his underage mistress, although those less intimate informally called him Don Alfredo or Big Al, which was a better fit in several ways. Shocked by this unprecedented affront to his dignity, Stroessner demanded that Gross stop demanding things of him in the capital of his very own country. The exchange that ensued revolved around Gross telling Stroessner that since he was a dictator and his country, Paraguay, was totally corrupt and didn't have an independent judiciary, Stroessner could send Ricord to the United States any time he wanted. Or, as Gross delicately put it, "You're a@#*ing dictator, damn it. So dictate!"

Shocked, Stroessner responded that Paraguay was a flowering democracy blessed with the rule of law and so honestly governed that he, as it's constitutionally elected President, dare not interfere with the judiciary. To do so just wouldn't be right.

Frankly, the arguments being made by both men were beyond bizarre. A top level representative of the United States, which routinely denounced Stroessner for being a dictator, was demanding that he act like one, while Stroessner was wrapping himself in the concepts of American democracy. The more Gross insisted the angrier Stroessner became. When Gross reacted by raising his voice (most Americans seem to believe that any non-English-speaking person can understand English if you shout loud enough), Stroessner responded by raising his voice even more. Finding it difficult to fathom why the President of a smallish country should be shouting at him, Gross actually rose from his chair, probably to better fill his expansive diaphragm. In turn, Stroessner also stood up, the better to match his interlocutor, the Foreign

Minister appeared to be trying to shrink-wrap himself in invisible plastic beneath the President's desk, and I stepped back to avoid the gathering storm.

Gross, sputtering and swearing as only a good cop can, suddenly switched languages from English to Brooklynese and began using words best found in my dog-eared copy of the *Dictionary of American Slang and Unconventional Usage* (New York, Crowell, 1960), which, despite my years as a Marine, I'd not fully mastered in Spanish. Quite frankly, while interpreting can be fun, trying to interpret simultaneously for two heavies (in every sense of the word) shouting at each other simultaneously in different languages while using increasingly unconventional words and phrases was beginning to strain my bilingual stock of the more colorful terms. And then Stroessner lost it.

Let me explain. Paraguay is the only country in Latin America in which a Native America tongue is the dominant language. While Paraguayans study and work in their delightful version of Castilian Spanish, they fight and make love to the melodious phrases of Guaraní, the country's mother language. Right there and then I became the first American to learn that Stroessner's mother tongue was neither Spanish nor German. It was Guaraní. At first, I saw his fascinating switch between languages as a challenge and began trying to learn on the fly various new vernacular phrases in an entirely new language. But, except for Pentecostals speaking in tongues with the help of the Holy Ghost, interpreting a new language into English at high speed can quickly become a drag. So while there were two true heavyweights in the ring, I became the first referee in history to be TKOed. In sheer desperation, I held my left hand up in Stroessner's face, my right in the face of Nixon's august spokesman, smiled, apologized abjectly to His Excellency for my failure to master his melodious mother tongue and, much to their surprise and mine, sat down on the floor. After all, what else was I to do?

Now, junior diplomats rarely send Presidents or White House emissaries, much less one of each, to their neutral corners, even in the most obtuse, oblique, and unctuous of terms. But that's what I did. In the White House corner first came shock, then dumbstruck silence, then a frown with small flashes of lightning foreshadowing the emergence of thunder. In the Paraguayan corner, surprise, a facial expression suggesting disbelief, a twitch of the mouth, a grin, a smile, and then Stroessner burst out laughing. The air cleared by the storm, Stroessner and Gross got back to business.

Of course, we didn't get Ricord immediately. Stroessner would have lost too much face. At the time of Gross's visit, it was much more important to Stroessner to keep the support of Ricord's Paraguayan godfather than to maintain good relations with Washington. Stroessner's power rested primarily on five pillars: the Army, the National Police, smugglers, money changers, and the Colorado political party. And Ricord was under the protection of one of the most powerful of them all, the Commanding General of an army division. Normally, that would have made Ricord immune from arrest. But because his arrest became public knowledge before Stroessner could order him released, he could neither let him go free nor give him to us immediately. Eventually we did get him, put him on trial, convicted him of a few crimes, and slapped him in one of our nicer penitentiaries. After his release, Ricord went back home to Paraguay where he died in 1985. As for me, refereeing the Stroessner vs Gross heavyweight bout convinced me that it might be useful to learn a little Guaraní in case there was a rematch and I found myself in the middle of yet another unseemly diplomatic brawl.

Another notorious criminal who flitted across the Paraguayan stage while I was there was Meyer Lansky, the notorious "Mob Accountant", once a prominent resident of Las Vegas in Nevada, my home state. In 1970, Lansky was a business associate of two other notorious Mafiosi, Bugsy Siegel and Lucky Luciano, when the Feds began threatening to indict him for tax fraud. Before they could arrest him, Lansky fled to Israel and asked for asylum, claiming he was being prosecuted because he was Jewish. As I knew from my Tel Aviv tour, and John of the Armpits experience, a Jew that reached Israel and claims to be fleeing persecution was usually guaranteed life-long asylum, since Israel always refused to extradite them—until Lansky. Given Lansky's decades-long crime record, from fraud to murder, the United States had been trying for some time to extradite him back to the United States, but Israel had been refusing until, eventually, we worked out a deal. Israel wouldn't extradite him. But given Lansky's criminal record they would expel him as an undesirable and let us know where he was headed. I wasn't aware of this until Lansky tried to enter Paraguay using a valid Paraguayan passport he'd bought somewhere, and I became peripherally involved in the scramble to convince the Paraguayans to deny him admission since he wasn't actually a Paraguayan. I was told later that he also had Argentine, Bolivian, Peruvian, and several other passports in his briefcase. Every Embassy from Tel Aviv to Panama had also had to scramble like mad to keep Lansky from gaining asylum.

Almost a decade later, while I was the Paraguay Desk Officer at State, the Lansky case would serve as a model for handling two other notorious cases. One involved two

Croat terrorists. The other involved Josef Mengele, the infamous Nazi "Angel of Death." My first brush with the saga of Mengele had come in Paraguay. When arriving at a new post, I always made it a point to seek out and develop contacts not just in the government and diplomatic corps, but also in the local political parties, commercial and civil communities. In Asunción, this included the Central American Consular Corps, the Embassies of El Salvador, France, and Israel, economist clubs, the Mormons, Protestant missionaries, members of the Jewish community, a couple of great Paraguayan musical groups, and some Mau Maus (explanation to follow). Once, to the surprise of the Paraguayan Foreign Minister, this led to our hosting the annual National Day celebrations of all five Central American countries at our home. I also received invitations to several Jewish events and several visits to my office by B'nai B'rith's Latin America circuit rider.

During my tour in Paraguay, we repeatedly tried to run down rumors that Mengele was living there. So during one of his visits, I asked the B'nai B'rith circuit rider, a Rabbi, what he'd heard about Mengele. He just smiled. But, on his next visit, he did more than just smile. He handed me a copy of Mengele's application for residence in Paraguay, complete with certification by the German government that Mengele had no criminal record in that country.

I was shocked. How could Germany possibly have given Mengele a clean slate in light of his notoriety as a Nazi war criminal? The Rabbi explained that when the certificate was issued Mengele hadn't yet been accused of any war crimes. He was from a prominent family that owned a factory that manufactured agricultural equipment, and allied authorities had detained him for a short time just after the war. But at the time, they were unaware of his gruesome role in the

Holocaust, so they released him, and Mengele went back to work at his family's factory until war crimes investigators began to zero in on him. But before he could be detained, he fled to Argentina. From there he'd gone to Paraguay and, German Certificate of Good Conduct in hand, applied for permanent residence. Rosenthal's description of the events was very different than what I've heard since. This was to come back to me a few years later when the saga of Mengele reared its bloody head once more.

THIRTY-TWO

FAT COLONELS, MAU MAUS, AND CHILEAN BLONDS

As for Paraguay's politics, they were as fascinating as any snake pit I'd ever seen, and I'd seen a few real ones in Thailand. But, at first, I found its economic system baffling. Ninety percent of economic theory presupposes the availability of at least a few trustworthy statistics, the operative word being trustworthy, and there weren't any available in Paraguay, at least none that were public.

The Paraguayans could produce any set of statistics you wanted and were especially adept at delivering the masses of data foreign aid donors or international organizations need to justify growing their empires. At first, when I went looking for economic data out of sheer curiosity, I thought I'd hit the mother lode in the US Agency for International Development (USAID) mission's files. But when I looked closely, I noted that the data didn't correlate with what I could see with my own eyes as I moved around the country. In fact, their data sets looked like fool's gold. So I looked at statistics that the government had published without input from foreign aid experts, and they weren't any better. According to both sets of data, Paraguay was a deeply impoverished country in dire need of oodles of foreign money to clothe, house, and feed its near-naked, starving, and disease-ridden masses. The problem was, I couldn't find any huddling masses. All the Paraguayans on the street, in the markets, and even in isolated villages reachable only by dirt roads, looked decently clothed and well fed. Their homes, even in the poorest neighborhoods, showed a pride of ownership that belied the idea that they were downtrodden sufferers. And I have a rule. If the statistics don't match what you can see with your own eyes, it's probably the statistics that are lying, not your eyes.

When I tried to discuss this with the economists from the massive AID mission, it quickly became apparent to me that they had no interest whatsoever in looking behind Paraguay's statistical façade, perhaps because what they might find could break their rice bowl. My boss in the Embassy wasn't interested either. If everyone was happy with the status quo, why rock the boat? Well me, for one. I'm perfectly happy to rock a boat when it's so full of holes it's leaking American taxpayer dollars by the millions, and the hull of the foreign assistance boat in Paraguay had more holes in it than a sieve.

Since no one knew, or was even interested in, Paraguay's real economy, I decided to build a personal network of local economists, legislators responsible for economic policy, and policy planners. Being a strong believer in the Eleanor Parker theory of seduction, "Candy is dandy, but liquor is quicker," I began by inviting some of them to our home and getting them drunk.

Finally, one well-lubricated evening, after several hours of increasingly slurred chitchat, one of my guests blurted out, "Actually, we have two sets of books - one for people that will give us money and the other to run the country. Wanna see 'em? Come with me to my office and I'll show them to you."

So off we went with me driving, since I was relatively sober. He took me to his office, opened a file cabinet, and pulled out a well-thumbed file containing data that made a lot more sense than what AID was using. One of the biggest differences was that it showed both legal and illegal foreign trade, not just the smaller legal stuff. In other words, it included smuggling and money laundering.

In the AID data set, Paraguay was legally importing, but not exporting, immense quantities of cigarettes, Scotch, Cessnas and other luxury goods, which was obviously not true. The real Paraguay economy included massive smuggling operations, something that was immediately obvious to anyone who shopped outside the Embassy commissary. The second set of statistics clearly showed that the government knew all about it and not only didn't care, but quite possibly was involved. It also showed that Paraguay was not nearly as poverty stricken as AID claimed it was. When I reported what I'd seen to the Deputy Chief of Mission (DCM), the number two in the Embassy, he got mad and said, using a word I'd heard a few times before, that what I'd seen was bullshit. There was no way the Paraguayans were keeping two sets of books. If they so much as tried to do that, the brilliant economists in our AID mission would catch them out in a heartbeat.

So I went back to my office and ran the numbers the way the DCM said they should be run. Paraguay did publish statistics on legal imports and exports by product. So, if you assumed that Paraguay's published foreign trade statistics and census numbers were correct, then the tens of millions of dollars' worth of cigarettes, whiskey, luxury goods and Cessnas that Paraguay was legally importing weren't being re-exported. And if they weren't re-exported, then the Paraguayans were either consuming everything they imported or dumping all of it in the river, which was unlikely. If, instead, they were consuming all of their imports themselves, which is what the statistics being used by AID said and the DCM believed, then every man, woman, and child in Paraguay was smoking, on average, four and a half cartons of cigarettes a day and eating two and a half pounds of beef washed down with three quarts of Johnny Walker Black. They would then stagger to the airport, jump into their private Cessna, and fly away to Lord knows where to die of lung cancer or liver failure.

My alternative hypothesis never did go over well with the Embassy's head-in-the-sand set, not even after some unexpected, outside players—President Allende of Chile, El Salvador's Ambassador to Paraguay, Jose "Chepe" Mixco Fischnaler, and a tribe of Mau Maus—rode to my statistical rescue. The Mau Maus were professional smugglers; "Chepe" Mixco, El Salvador's Ambassador to Paraguay, was a short, black-haired Austrian-Indian with a penchant for tall, blue-eyed Chilean blondes; and Allende was either the Savior Himself returned to earth or a Communist revolutionary in socialist clothing, depending on who you chose to believe. Regardless, "Chepe" and the Mau Maus both made it clear when I talked with them that Chile's economy was going to hell in a hand-basket, but Chileans with the right connections, including with Paraguayan smugglers, were getting filthy rich. To prove his case, one Mau Mau took me with him to a meeting with a Chilean official from Allende's palace. During the meeting, the Chilean placed an order for a plane-load of— guess what —cigarettes, whiskey, and other luxury goods, to be flown by him to Santiago for sale on the black market. He had just been to another quintessentially typical institution of Stroessner's Paraguay—a sanctified, illegal Mennonite money exchange—and bought a few briefcases full of Yankee dollars so he could pay for his order in cash. I assume that those who believe Allende was a secular saint will also refuse to believe what Chepe said when I told him about the meeting, "That's nothing. I just bought two mansions worth several million dollars for ten thousand dollars each. I'm going to use one as my Embassy and the other as my residence, since I just got orders to go to Chile as El Salvador's new Ambassador."

author's collection

Sapucai, Paraguay, 1972. I always tried to balance the inevitably capital-city centric view out my office window by visiting, whenever possible, the rest of the country. Here I'm in the small village of Sapucai herding cattle, Paraguay's biggest "non-export."

Intrigued by the stories, and with a long family vacation planned in the months after Chepe left for Chile, I loaded our Volkswagen microbus with junk food, games, Leda, and our four kids, and we went to see for ourselves. Following Mixco's recommendation, I bought enough Chilean *escudos* in Córdoba, Argentina, to pay our expenses and then drove through a seemingly endless one-way railroad and car tunnel under the Andes to Chile. Our first stop was a gas station to fill up the tank. When I looked at the price I did a double, and then a triple take, before asking the attendant if the meter on the gas pump was accurate. He confirmed that it was. In brown market *escudos*, the tank of gas cost less than fifty US cents. We then drove to Santiago where an Embassy friend had made us hotel reservations. Again, I couldn't believe the prices. Two connecting suites at a four-star hotel, with a diplomatic discount, cost $3 a night. A superb, gourmet meal at the best restaurant in town for all six of us, complete with strolling violinists and a live orchestra, set us back about $6. And buying several changes of clothes for each of our four children, my wife, and me at a good clothing store (from admittedly depleted racks) set us back $25. The economy was clearly imploding, which was great for tourists carrying *escudos* they'd bought outside Chile, but disastrous for the country. In Allende's Chile, even more than in Stroessner's Paraguay, classic economic theory had clearly given way to Alice in Wonderland reality.

Back in Paraguay trying to make better sense of that country's economy, I began casting about for a more objective way to gauge conditions, something better than asking Mau Maus, black marketers, or hung-over officials. And I found one. My new method involved sitting on a park bench drinking a cool soda. Not just any park, the nice one in downtown Asunción between the Ministry of Finance and the Central Bank. In those days, Paraguayan Army officers weren't paid in cash by the Ministry of Defense. They were given vouchers they had to take to the Central Bank to cash. When the Bank was flush with cash, officers of all ranks would pick up their vouchers at the Ministry and then stroll leisurely across the park to the Bank. But when the Central Bank ran short of cash, it stopped honoring the vouchers, generating a fascinating economic phenomenon. Paraguay's foreign exchange situation could be roughly estimated by observing the rank and body weight of the Army officers heading across the park. If Lieutenants and Captains were strolling, and Colonels were shuffling to the Bank, things were good. The higher the rank and faster they were running, the worse the situation. I called it my Fat Colonels Theory.

THIRTY-THREE

RUTHERFORD B. HAYES, NATIONAL HERO

While in Paraguay I even learned some American history. The lower half of the country sits in the crotch of two major rivers, the Paraná, that forms its southeastern border with Brazil and Argentina, and the Paraguay, that flows from Bolivia through western Paraguay to the Atlantic via the Mar del Plata, the broad estuary between Uruguay and Argentina. Asunción, the country's capital city, sits on the eastern bank of the Paraguay River, across from a Paraguayan province named after American President Rutherford B. Hayes, one of the country's national heroes. And therein lies a tale.

One Sunday, while out boating as a guest of the local Ford dealer, we motored up the river to Villa Hayes, the capital of that province, where the Mayor met us and took us to city hall for a cool one. While we were sipping our libations, the Mayor called my attention to a document hanging on the wall. It was the city's pride and joy, a copy of President Rutherford B. Hayes's arbitration decision on a territorial dispute between Argentina and Paraguay awarding the province to Paraguay, signed both by then President Hayes and his Secretary of State. Because of Hayes decision, the province had been named after him. When I looked closely at the document, I could see that it was being slowly eaten by mold. So, as a gesture of friendship, I said to the Mayor that, if he were interested, we might be able to have it restored. He was pleased with the possibility.

When I took my idea to Ambassador Landau, he was all for it. The very next Sunday we all sailed up to Villa Hayes where the Mayor hosted an elegant dinner of river fish for us, washed down with smuggled wine. When Landau mentioned that if the Mayor was interested, we could send his priceless document to the United States to be restored, he immediately accepted the offer. Signed copy of Hayes's arbitration decision in hand, off we went back to the Embassy, where I carefully pack it in a wood box for shipment to Washington in the diplomatic pouch, included a Limited Official Use Only memo (LOU) explaining what it was and what needed to be done, and took it to the mail room. That done, we left for Chile for the vacation I described earlier.

The morning after we returned, Ambassador Landau asked me to come to his office and handed me a cable he'd received from the State Department's Undersecretary for Management. In it the Undersecretary reprimanded the Embassy for sending a souvenir in the classified pouch in violation of who knows how many State Department regulations, a dozen federal, state, and local laws, and, for all I knew, the Geneva Convention. It ordered Landau to punish the officer that had signed the memo, meaning me. After an unusually pregnant pause, Landau then handed me his response. I can still quote it verbatim, "I want to let you know someone is sending stupid messages and signing your name to them. I'm the one that ordered this particular shipment be classified, because it is not a personal souvenir. It's a national treasure of Paraguay. Not only did I order it to be classified when we sent it out, I expect it to be classified when it's sent back, even if that means sending a special courier with it." Needless to say, I was relieved.

author's collection

Villa Hayes, Paraguay, 1972. The Mayor of Villa Hayes (center, behind the US flag) the day he loaned us his town's prized possession—a signed copy of President Rutherford B. Hayes's arbitration decision awarding his province to Paraguay. The tall gentleman on the right wearing glasses is Ambassador Landau. Our son Timothy, then in elementary school, is holding the American flag. I'm the man with the mustache and silly grin.

THIRTY-FOUR

THE RETURN OF PHOENIX

All in all, my career seemed to be going rather well until one day when, out of the blue, a letter from the DG, Director General of the Foreign Service, appeared in my in-box informing me I'd been ranked in the bottom 10 percent of all officers eligible for promotion. The low ranking was based on a comment made in my performance evaluation report by the Deputy Provincial Advisor in Vietnam, an Army Colonel, saying I had "refused to obey a direct order." And, if I was "low ten-ed" again I'd be dismissed from the service. It was quite a blow. In his comments the Colonel hadn't identified the order I'd refuse to obey. But I knew exactly what he was alluding to—my refusal to sign off on the Phoenix assassination mission I mentioned earlier.

So what should I do? Pray my next report would put me back on track? Challenge his comment? I decided to do neither. Instead I sent the Director General a letter saying that the Colonel's comment was true. I had, indeed, refused to obey a direct order from him. All I asked was that a letter from me be placed in my file beside the Colonel's comment explaining what that order had been, and why I'd refused to obey it. In my letter I explained that, as District Senior Advisor, all operations in my district had to be authorized by me in writing.

And when it came to Phoenix squads, I was extremely reluctant to sign off on operations that might result in someone being killed, unless we had convincing intelligence that it was absolutely necessary. In the instance the Colonel alluded to, he had given me a direct order to sign off on the assassination of a village headman because someone had denounced him as a Viet Cong collaborator. But I'd refused to do so for three reasons. One, because his order was unlawful. He had the authority to authorize the Phoenix mission. But he couldn't order me to authorize and take full responsibility for one with which I disagreed because it was against my better judgment. Two, because the Phoenix team assigned to that particular mission had recently assassinated the wrong person and then blown its own cover, forcing me to risk lives to extract them, so I didn't have confidence in them. And three, because my intelligence information did not support the charge that the target was a collaborator. If the Department wanted to punish me for refusing an unlawful order to have someone that might be innocent assassinated, I wanted both the Colonel's evaluation and my letter on the record so I could share them with my Senator. Within weeks another letter came from the DG saying they'd removed the Colonel's report from my file and taken my name off the low 10 percent list.

But, despite the DG's positive response, I was still uneasy. So when I was unexpectedly given an opportunity to do so, I invoked a rule I'd learned from my father and relearned while I was in the Marines. If you're setting a booby trap that only needs about a half kilo of C-4 explosives to be effective, but you have ten kilos to spare, use all ten. So when my boss handed me a golden opportunity to do just that, I jumped on it. The State Department's annual performance evaluation season was well underway, and by the time I got the DG's second letter, my boss should have given me a copy of his report on me so I could comment on it. But he hadn't even started writing it. So, in a clear violation of the regulations, he asked me to write my own evaluation and just give it to him to sign. My father had taught me what to do when you're given such a golden opportunity. A Pentecostal minister, whenever someone claimed to know the Bible better than he did, his favorite response was to ask them what they thought of his favorite Bible quote from Hezekhia 2:3: "He that too-teth not his own horn, the same shall not be tooted." When they said it was one of their favorites, too, Dad would just smile. The meaning of the quote was clear as a bell. When asked to grade yourself, that's the wrong time for modesty. Give yourself an A+++, which is exactly what I did. I called myself the best officer my supervisor had ever known, able to fly without wings, walk on water, and leap tall embassies in a single bound. When I gave it to him he blanched and asked, "Do you really think you're this good?" I answered, "Yes sir, I do." I was promoted within months. Of course, there's no such quote in the Bible. There isn't even a Book of Hezekhia. But if your boss thinks there is, why argue?

THIRTY FIVE

Itaipu — The $ 19 Billion-
Dollar Dam

While many of my experiences in Paraguay were fun, for me the most important thing I did while I was there was develop commercial opportunities for American companies, because they could create jobs for my fellow Americans back home, and they were the people I really worked for. While I was in Paraguay, the biggest and potentially most lucrative commercial opportunities involved projects to build two of the world's largest dams, the nineteen billion dollar Itaipú high dam between Brazil and Paraguay and the eleven-billion-dollar Yacyretá-Apipé low dam between Argentina and Paraguay, both on the Paraná River. Since sales of booze, cigarettes, and Cessnas were doing just fine without me, I spent most of my time on the dam things.

Itaipu, since completed and now the world's largest single producer of electricity, was the bigger nut to crack. Since a dam anchored on only one side of the river doesn't work very well, it couldn't be built without first solving two geopolitical problems. The first was that, once up and running, Brazil would be the only market big enough to need that much electricity. The second was that Paraguay didn't have the means to finance its half. With the Ambassador's blessings, I'd joined the Economists Clubs of all three major political parties, the Christian Democrats, the Febreristas, and Stroessner's Colorados. And despite their political differences, all three were in agreement that, since Brazil needed the dam but Paraguay didn't, Paraguay not Brazil was in the driver's seat.

But, for whatever reason, and lots were later bandied about, Paraguay's treaty negotiators let the Brazilians eat their lunch. When the Paraguayan negotiators returned to Asunción, I threw a party at my house for them and some of my contacts, including several members of the political opposition to Stroessner. The negotiators were upbeat about the deal they'd signed, but no one else was, and it took less than twenty-four hours for the attacks to begin. In describing the draft treaty, one especially colorful TV commentator said, using sweeping hand and arm gestures to emphasize his point, "The Brazilians shoved it right up our ass all the way to the elbow. And they didn't even use Vaseline!" And he was just the leader of the pack.

Stroessner had rarely if ever faced such a massive political uproar, and became a bit irritated. And, since I was both a foreign diplomat and a member of all three economics groups that were publicly attacking the treaty, word came from the Presidential Palace that he was considering declaring me *persona non grata*. Thankfully he didn't, so I stayed on for a while longer.

Now, it's a truism that an agreement between countries works best when it serves the interests of both, not just one. So while the uproar may have been mostly in Paraguay, it was the Brazilian Congress that settled matters by refusing to ratify the treaty as written. They forced their own negotiators to rewrite it on the grounds that it was too favorable to

Brazil and could create "a Panama Canal problem" for them. In diplo-jargon, the Brazilians had over-negotiated.

Asunción, Paraguay, 1973. I spent much of my time in ParItaipu promoting American participation in building the Itaipu high dam. Here, during a reception I hosted in honor of the Paraguayan negotiating team at our home, we're celebrating the signing of the Paraguay-Brazil Itaipú treaty (prematurely, it turned out). From left to right are Ambassador Landau, Enzo Debernardi, the Director of Paraguay's electric power administration, and Myron Kratzer, the Embassy's scientific attaché. Half of me is standing at the far right.

Toward the end of my tour, as the Itaipu project was nearing the bidding stage, a colleague at Commerce obtained an almost unheard of approval by the Attorney General to let a consortium of major American companies negotiate a turnkey offer to build it, from design and finance to construction and management. Normally a big antitrust no-no, he'd managed to work out with the Attorney General's office a process that avoided this legal barrier. I'd already received orders transferring me to El Salvador, and I'd sent my family to Nevada. But the Ambassador asked me to stay long enough to help organize the visit of the trade mission this produced, made up of senior executives from American banks, engineering and construction firms, and equipment suppliers. As I recall, it included top officials from Chase Manhattan, Bank of America, Bechtel, Morrison-Knudsen, Allis-Chalmers, Caterpillar, and Harza Engineering, among others. Their Asunción dog and pony show—excuse me, technical presentation—took most of a day at one of the major local hotels and attracted almost everyone in the Paraguayan government and private industry, including the treaty negotiators, the administrators of the national electric power agency, and a number of ministers, and ended with a gala dinner. The only one that didn't come was Stroessner.

After the dinner, just as I'd suspected, several participants in the mission decided to unwind from their arduous task at some local entertainment establishments. I'd suggested they not get too happy, just in case Stroessner decided he wanted to see them before they left. But a number of them had, needless to say, ignored my suggestion. Sure enough, at about 1:00 a.m. a call came from the Presidential Palace saying that Stroessner wanted to receive the delegation in his office at 6:00 a.m. So I put in motion a plan we'd prepared in advance just in case. One officer went to the delegation's hotel to alert those who were there, while the rest of the Embassy's officers quickly drove to the most likely Asunción watering holes to round up stragglers. With a combination of hard work, night driving, and gallons of coffee, we managed to round them all up, get them to their hotel to put on clean shirts, and drive them to the Palace for their command appointment. I can still see their bloodshot eyes.

We were met at the Palace door by the Minister of Economy, who led us to a large hall. When he saw me, Stroessner asked me to accompany him as his interpreter as he walked up to each member of the mission, shook their hand, thanked them for their visit, and gave them a small souvenir. When they began to leave, and before I could join them, Stroessner then reached over and took hold of my left arm, signaled for Ambassador Landau to join us, took him by the right, and began walking us toward the main entrance, and made the evening even more memorable for me. Turning to the Ambassador he said (and I'll never forget his words), "I understand Mr. Brown will be leaving us on this morning's Braniff flight for his next assignment in El Salvador. I just wanted to say how much I appreciate your having made him available to me during his stay here. His help has been invaluable, and we'll miss him. I wish him the very best."

I must admit that having the President compliment me so warmly to my Ambassador caused my ego to swell and made me feel warm and fuzzy all over, until he went on to ask, "By the way, Mr. Brown, your friend Mr. Gross that came down to lecture me about Paraguay's lawlessness and demand that we send Auguste Ricord to the United States regardless of our laws. Is that the same Mr. Gross that was indicted yesterday in New Jersey for campaign fraud?" Needless to say, his mock farewell deflated my ego, especially because I later confirm what he said about Gross was true. But apparently it wasn't all show on his part since some months after I arrived in El Salvador the Paraguayan Ambassador handed me a photograph dedicated to me by Stroessner. As for Itaipú, some years later an unscripted confrontation between the US and Paraguay over human rights at a conference in Geneva resulted in our being cut out of the nineteen-billion-dollar contract.

Asunción, Paraguay, 1972. This photograph with Ambassador Landau (center) and President Stroessner in the Presidential Palace reached me in El Salvador after I left Paraguay.

THIRTY-SIX

EL SALVADOR—BACK TO MY FUTURE

Toward the end of my tour in Asunción, I'd received orders transferring me from Paraguay to Costa Rica, which would have been great. But they were broken at the last minute and I was sent to El Salvador instead. I learned later that Pete Vaky, then the American Ambassador in Costa Rica, had objected to my assignment because my wife was originally Costa Rican. We were disappointed, but there was nothing for it. Six months after we arrived in El Salvador, when Vaky was replaced as Ambassador to Costa Rica by Anthony Lake, whose wife was also Costa Rica-born, I could only shake my head. But that's life in the diplo-tropics. And at least El Salvador was in Central America.

When we arrived in San Salvador we checked into a B&B and went house hunting. The first one that caught our attention was a mansion just off one of the main highways. A plantation home at the far end of a long colonnade of magnificent Italian cypress trees, it had gorgeous grounds, came with gardeners, was fully walled for privacy, and looked like a set from *Gone with the Wind*. It even had a portico over the main entrance just like Tara Hall. The main entrance hall opened onto a series of formal rooms, including a library and separate study, and was dominated by a magnificent curved staircase leading up to the second floor where there were a half-dozen bedrooms.

Our enthusiasm for it was immense, until we looked more closely. Cheek-by-jowl with its main gate, there were dozens of squatters living in cardboard and tin hovels seething with children, dogs, chickens, and the occasional pig. The poorest of the poor, they didn't have electricity or running water and used an open ditch that ran in front of their hovels to dispose of their sewage and garbage. In the end, despite its being one of the most beautiful homes in San Salvador, we realized that we simply couldn't live beside such abject squalor. It was our first lesson in the stark divide between El Salvador's rich and its poor. In the end, we settled for a colonial-style house in a middle-class neighborhood.

As an American diplomat, I lived quite well with my family in El Salvador and, since we were in Central America, we were able to travel regularly back and forth to visit Leda's family in Costa Rica. But, even though the country's 1970s Civil War was still in the incubation stage, we were very uncomfortable with El Salvador's deep social divides and shocked by the level of everyday violence. While open class warfare hadn't yet broken out, the divide between its social classes was as sharp as any I'd ever seen. Several times while driving on the main highway, we had to swerve around drunks fighting with machetes. That was bad enough. But we also saw several machete fights just outside the supermarket where we shopped, and twice we had confrontations with men stealing plants from our front yard who, rather than fleeing, simply looked at us and the children, brandished their machetes, and defied us to try and stop them.

Only years later, after I retired and was researching Central America's recent civil wars, did I find a somewhat plausible explanation for El Salvador's violent nature. Before the Spanish Conquest, El Salvador was populated mostly by Nahua Indians, originally from the Puebla region of modern Mexico. The vast majority were essentially slaves and worked for a small but all-powerful oligarchy of Nahua princes and overseers. The Spanish Conquest hadn't changed their way of life, just their masters. Nor did their lot improve after El Salvador gained its independence from Spain. To them, independence merely brought yet another change of masters, this time from Iberian Spaniards to homegrown oligarchs. Real change had begun to arrive only recently, in great part thanks to modern mass communications that made them conscious of how poorly they lived compared to the rich among them. And this had begun to generate an increasing sense of anger and resentment. It was this anger and resentment that later gave its revolutionaries the tinder for their movement. But, back to my years in El Salvador.

Since my job was to analyze El Salvador's economy and find commercial opportunities for American companies, most of my contacts were members of the country's business leadership, not potential revolutionaries. And they reminded me yet again of an underlying Central American reality few outsiders understand, the importance of the family networks that knit together across borders not just Central America's political and economic elites, but also its revolutionaries.

A few months after we arrived, whom should I meet at a cocktail party but Carlos Tunnerman, the kid brother that had been his sister Iliena's chaperone during my Marine days in Managua. Now he was manager of TACA Airline's operations in El Salvador. Later, after the Sandinistas took power in 1979, Carlos was to be the Nicaraguan Sandinista's first Ambassador to the United States. More decades later while researching the revolutionary side of the region's civil wars, when I mentioned this to "Pepe" Puente, one of my key post-Foreign Service Communist revolutionary contacts he laughed, and asked if I'd known that, while I was in El Salvador, Carlos had been running guns to the Sandinistas. Another post-Foreign Service revolutionary contact I've mentioned earlier, Eduardo Sancho, *Fermán Cienfuegos*, added that Carlos had also been actively supporting El Salvador's Faribundo Martí Liberation Front activities, and showed me documents to confirm it.

Another example of the region's complex cross-border connections emerged when I met Nicaragua's Ambassador to the Organization of Central American States (ODECA), Román y Vega. Román y Vega turned out to be a cousin of two later leaders of the Sandinista Front, Jaime and Ricardo Wheelock Román. He was also first-cousin of the husband of one of my wife's relatives, Victor Román Jara, Deputy Foreign Minister of Costa Rica while I was in El Salvador, and the husband of yet another of my wife's relatives was Guatemalan Army Colonel Román.

Years later over breakfast at a McDonald's in Managua, when I mentioned this to Nicaraguan Army Colonel Ricardo Wheelock Román, the brother of one of the members of Nicaragua's ruling Nine Comandante Junta, Ricardo confirmed that they were related to both Román Jara and Román y Vega. One of Somoza's Ambassadors, two top Sandinista Comandantes, a Costa Rican Deputy Foreign Minister, and a Colonel in the Guatemalan Army, were all cousins. And so, a rule: Never speak ill of one Latin to another, especially not in Central America, no matter how much at odds they may appear to be, because they may be cousins. And, in Central America at least, while cousins may hate one another, they will still close ranks against outsiders. And Gringos are almost always outsiders.

On occasion Central American friends would also tell me things I'd just as soon not have known, but felt obligated to report once I did. For example once, while driving from El Salvador to San José, I stopped in Managua for lunch with Remy Rener, who, as you may remember, was a best man at my wedding. At the time, El Salvador and Honduras were officially at war. So, diplomat or not, to drive from El Salvador to Costa Rica you either had to take a former Staten Island ferry boat from La Libertad in El Salvador to Corinto in Nicaragua or drive to the El Salvador-Honduras border, remove your Salvadoran license plates and put different ones on, so the Hondurans would let you through their customs,. The plates didn't have to be valid, just not Salvadoran. So I used an old set of Nevada plates that had expired in the 1950s.

When I commented on this to Remy over lunch and wondered if the two countries were ever going to settle their war, he laughed and told me he was the executor of late President Luis Somoza's estate and that it included a half interest in the La Libertad-Corinto ferry. So, from his perspective, he didn't care if they never made peace because, once they did, the ferry would no longer be the only way for truckers to move cargos to and from El Salvador. And that was a major source of income for Luis Somoza's estate, because the ferry was jointly owned by Somoza and a Salvadoran by the name of Borgonovo. When I looked startled, Remy said, yep, the family of Salvadoran Foreign Minister responsible for negotiating a peace agreement with Honduras.

Back in Salvador I called the owner of a trucking company I'd come to know fairly well, who not only corroborated Remy's story but claimed to be the Salvadoran go-between for the partners. I was never able independently to confirm this story. But it may have explained why, when several times the two countries seemed to have reached a peace agreement, it was shot down at the last minute by the Salvadoran Foreign Ministry. It was just the sort of behind the scenes "arrangement" that all too often exists throughout Central America.

While in El Salvador, another ghost from my Marine past appeared at a reception at the Spanish Ambassador's residence. An elderly gentleman walked up to me, gave me an *abrazo*, and said, "Sergeant Brown, how nice to see you again. It's been a long time."

I had no idea who he was but tried hard not to show it.

"The last time I saw you was in Guatemala while I was President. You were with the American Ambassador."

It was General Ydigoras Fuentes, and I'd met him just once when, as I mentioned earlier, I was in Guatemala as part of Ambassador Sparks' security detachment and went as his bodyguard to a reception at the Spanish Ambassador's residence. Ydigoras, the guest of honor at the reception, had reached behind the Ambassador to shake my hand and asked my name. It was an astonishing feat of memory.

Ydigoras explained to me that he was in San Salvador in political exile with his daughter. He called her over and introduced us. Intrigued, and more than a little curious, after chatting a bit, I invited the two of them to dinner. They soon became regular guests at our home and I was to spend many evenings listening to stories of his experiences in Guatemala. One of his stories involved Belize's former Prime Minister, George Price, whom I'd come to know while I was serving in Mérida, Mexico. During Ydigoras' presidency Belize was coveted by both Mexico and Guatemala, and Price regularly came to visit him to discuss Guatemala's territorial claims and argue against them. By the time we met again, and Ydigoras told me about his visits with Price, Belize had gained its independence, so it was just history. But it was something that happened in Costa Rica that put me in a real bind.

THIRTY-SEVEN

QUE PUTAS ANDA HACIENDO TU GOBIERNO? (WHAT THE @#* IS YOUR GOVERNMENT DOING?)

During one of our visits to Costa Rica, Victor "Vico" Román who, as I mentioned earlier, was then Costa Rica's Deputy Foreign Minister, and his wife, Virginia, one of Leda's first cousins, invited us over for what I thought would be just a family dinner. It was 1978, the Sandinistas were closing in on Somoza from their sanctuaries in Costa Rica but had not yet taken power, and the Carter administration was secretly looking for a solution that would keep them from doing so. When we finished dinner Vico handed me a cognac, led me to the balcony, closed the door, looked me in the eye and asked, using a phrase redolent of Costa Rican vernacular, *"Que putas anda haciendo tu ---- gobierno?"* (what the @#* is your government doing?) Just a few days ago, your Ambassador to the OAS asked for the creation of a multinational force to be sent to Nicaragua to separate the Guardia from the Sandinistas so that a plebiscite can be held. But I just got back from a meeting in Liberia where one of your officials told us to ignore

what you said in Washington, because your real policy is to
help the Sandinistas take over. So should we keep on helping
them or not? We'll support whatever you want. But we need
to know what the @#* it is!" I told him I wasn't in the loop
and only knew what I read in the papers. But if he wanted
me to, I'd ask around. But was he sure it was someone from
Washington? He said yes, he was.

The next morning I went to the San José Embassy to see
Lyle Lane, at the time the Embassy's Deputy Chief of Mission,
to tell him what Vico had told me. He was stunned. As far as
the Embassy knew, no senior official from Washington had
been in Costa Rica recently. With the plot thickening by the
hour, as soon as I got back to San Salvador I called a Seventh
Floor friend and asked who had just visited Costa Rica (the
offices of the Secretary and Deputy of State and their staffs are
on the seventh floor of Main State). No one, as far as he knew.
So I called the chief of Costa Rican Presidential Security, yet
another of Leda's cousins, who confirmed that a senior official from Washington had just been in Costa Rica and met
with representatives of several governments, including his
own, although he didn't know the gist of their conversations.

Decades later, former Costa Rican Minister of Public
Security, Johnny Echeverria who, at the time, had been Costa
Rica's key liaison to the Sandinistas, also confirmed during a
videotaped interview in his office in San José that the meeting
had taken place, and he'd been there. He told me that, until
that meeting, the Venezuelans, Panamanians, Americans, representatives of the Somoza government, and the Sandinistas
had been secretly negotiating in Panama and reached an
agreement that involved Somoza being replaced by a tran-
sitional government. The Sandinistas had even agreed on
some cabinet members, including Nicaragua's then Military

Attaché in Washington, Colonel Enrique Bermúdez, later commander of the Contra army, as Minister of Defense. If a senior official had, indeed, held such a meeting, it would have been an astoundingly brazen example of playing a double game. And if not, it was an astoundingly wild story for Román, Echeverria, and a presidential security officer to have cooked up.

Another "situation" in Costa Rica came a few months later, when Lyle Lane called me in San Salvador to ask for help. Embassy San José had received urgent instructions from Washington to contact the President of Costa Rica to deliver a message to him personally. But they couldn't find him because neither the Foreign Ministry nor the President's staff would tell them where he was. The State Department apparently refused to believe Embassy San José couldn't even find their country's President and was driving them crazy. Lyle was calling me out of desperation in hopes I could find him for them. It took two phone calls. The first was to one of the President's former paramours I'd once met, who told me with considerable malicious relish not just where he was, but what he was up to and how good (or bad) he was at it. The second was to Leda's cousin that was Chief of Costa Rica's Presidential Security to confirm the former's rather florid response. Information confirmed, I sent a quick message to Embassy San José saying their President was in Mexico for the weekend with two fellow heads of state doing some thinking from the waist down. When I think back, it may have been just as well that my assignment to Costa Rica hadn't worked out, since my contacts there kept landing me in the middle of touchy problems in Costa Rica, like the ones I describe above.

THIRTY-EIGHT

ACCIDENTAL COUP D'ETAT

One day one of my Salvadoran contacts, Colonel Jaime Abdul Gutierrez, then Deputy Director of ANTEL, El Salvador's telecommunications administration, called me to say they wanted to buy a few million dollars-worth of new radios for the armed forces. But they wanted to do so on the open market not, as they usually did, through our military sales system. So, hot tip in hand, I arranged for some American manufacturers to make offers. In the process, I began inviting Gutierrez to the house every couple of weeks for drinks, largely because, contrary to the stereotype of a Latin American Colonel, he was politically quite progressive and eager to say things to me he would not have dared say at the Officer's Club.

The better I got to know him the more I began to think he had considerable leadership potential. So I recommended him for a Future Leader Grant, one of the juiciest plums an Embassy can pass out. But, when I proposed his name, those who were, or should have been, much better informed than me, including the Military Attaché, the Chief of the Military Advisory Mission, and the Chief of the Political Section, looked at me in disbelief and unanimously insisted that he was just a second level officer in an unimportant position with no leadership potential. I responded, perhaps. But, if nothing else, he was the key to several million dollars-worth of sales of American products.

So, despite their reluctance, they finally agreed to do me a favor and support giving Jaime Abdul Gutierrez one of our precious grants. He was delighted and accepted immediately. To make his trip even more memorable, I arranged for one of his stops to be in Sparks, Nevada where John Ascuaga, the owner of the Nugget Hotel-Casino where I'd waited tables while finishing my undergraduate degree, made his visit memorable. Ascuaga sent a limousine to the airport to meet him, put him and his escort-interpreter up in the Nugget's best suites, and gave them complimentary dinners in its main showroom. He also dropped by their table to say hello.

Not long after Gutierrez returned, ANTEL signed the purchase orders for several million dollars in American radio equipment. And shortly after we left for my next assignment in Amsterdam, he and the Director of ANTEL staged a coup and took over the country. So much for his not having any leadership potential, although that wasn't quite what I'd had in mind.

Decades later, during my most recent visit to El Salvador as a member of a DOCA (Defense Orientation Conference Association) trip to Central America, when Gutierrez came to my hotel to say hello, I asked him about a claim made by *Fermán Cienfuegos*, the former military commander of the Faribundo Martí Liberation Front that I've mentioned several times earlier. During a post-Foreign Service interview, *Cienfuegos* had asserted that Gutierrez had been one of their supporters. Was that true? He said no, it wasn't true that he'd supported them. But he did share one goal with them. He, too, wanted to break the stranglehold the traditional elite had on the country's political, economic, and social systems. I must admit that we drew more than a few stares as we spent most of the evening together while he told me his version of what had happened during those fateful months, both known and unknown. But that was in the future.

El Salvador's bloody civil war had not yet started when Leda and I, our four now teen-age kids in tow, left El Salvador for my next assignment as Deputy Consul General in Amsterdam. But the warning signs were there for all to read, especially the deputy in the Political Section, Charlie Blum, who later became an Ambassador. I remember him carefully laying out for me the evidence that had convinced him a revolution was brewing and was on the brink of exploding. But only his boss, Bill Walker, who also went on to become a distinguished Ambassador, seemed to believe him. If others had done so as well, just maybe it would have been possible to avert the war that later broke out. But we'll never know.

THIRTY-NINE

WOODEN SHOES, WOODEN POLICIES

Amsterdam was a new world. The Consulate General was on one of the city's most beautiful parks, the Museumplein. Three of the city's premiere cultural attractions—the Van Gogh Art Museum, the Concertgebouw (Amsterdam's premiere concert hall), and the Rembrandt Museum—were just a short walk away. The building itself had been a private home until World War II, when the Gestapo commandeered it and used it as its headquarters. After its use by the Gestapo, its owners didn't want to move back into it. But they did want it put to good use. So they sold it to the United States government for a dollar in appreciation for our spearheading the liberation of the Netherlands. I soon learned to take full advantage of what the surroundings offered, first going to the Concertgebouw for a free noon concert and then strolling to the Van Gogh or Rembrandt for a light lunch among the masterpieces, complete with a glass of wine. For a change, occasionally I'd walk to a nearby fast food stall run by a couple of Texan expats to have a raw herring taco—with lots of onions. From time to time I also did a little work.

I was dual hatted as the Consulate's commercial officer and as deputy to Consul General Alex Davit, who'd been the director of my orientation course when I entered the Foreign Service. This gave me two masters, Davit and the Commercial Attaché at the Embassy in The Hague, Joe Harary. My staff consisted of a secretary and a senior local commercial specialist, Conrad Van der Knapp, who had managed one of the largest factoring (trading) companies in Curacao for several decades before retiring and knew more about commercial promotion work that all of us combined. On my first visit to The Hague, Harary told me my job was to sell Boeing 707s and IBM computers, although, if I had any spare time, I could waste it on lesser American exports. It could all have been rather cut and dried — and boring — except that, just as in Paraguay a few years earlier, I took a great deal of personal satisfaction from "selling American" because more sales abroad meant more jobs back home.

The biggest barrier turned out to be *les idees fixes*, the preconceptions, of both American businessmen and my supervisors, who all strongly believed that most American products, especially consumer goods, would never sell in the Netherlands, because, well, they were too foreign. So why try? Well, because of the challenge, for one thing. Besides, I didn't agree. To the contrary, I was reasonably sure that with a bit of effort and a little tweaking of our marketing strategies, lots of American products, even those less sexy than 747s and IBM mainframes, would sell on the Dutch market. Besides, Boeing and IBM didn't need my help - they were doing just fine, thank you, but lots of smaller American companies did. So whenever IBM and Boeing didn't need my help, which was always, I concentrated on promoting other American products.

Initially, when Harary and the Commerce Department realized what I was doing, they were horrified. They demanded that I stop wasting my valuable time trying to help little guys and get back to promoting big-ticket sales. When I pushed back, arguing that major corporations didn't need my help, but small American companies did, they retorted that it would be a monumental waste of my time but reluctantly agreed— as long as Boeing and IBM didn't complain. I don't remember telling them I'd already met with the local representatives of both companies and told them they had first dibs on my services if and when they needed them. Nor did I mention that their responses had been a polite, "Don't call us, we'll call you." With my bosses unenthusiastic commitments not to lynch me if I were to stray from the straight and narrow onto other trading grounds, I was off and running.

One idea came to me when I visited one of Europe's biggest trade fairs, the Boating Show at Amsterdam's RAI exhibition center, an annual event promoting everything nautical from yachts to signal flags. The Netherlands was awash with waterways, the Dutch were boating enthusiasts, and every other American household seemed to have a boat or two or three, so the Netherlands should have been a natural market for American boating goods. But there wasn't a single American product on display at the show. Not one. So I began looking for American boating-related products that might reasonably sell in the Netherlands, found literally hundreds of possibilities, and began contacting the American companies that manufactured them, recommending they consider mounting displays at the next year's show.

Two years later American boating goods, from Hatteras yachts to canoe paddles, dominated the show, which was nice. The question was whether or not they were selling anything. So I made the rounds of the American exhibitors to ask them how they were doing. When I came to an enormous Hatteras yacht, the sales rep told me they didn't expect to sell any. They were just there to introduce their name to the market, which seemed strange given the long line of visitors waiting to look inside it, and I said so. Caught out, he admitted he'd sold five of them for cash with delivery in other countries—not bad, at about four hundred thousand dollars a pop—and mentioned dryly that, while he didn't know for certain, maybe delivery in another country had something to do with it, since the Netherlands' 18 percent value-added tax on sales made them a bit pricey on the local market.

I found what looked like another ripe opportunity at a trade show featuring travel trailers. But in that case, I was much less successful. The problem was not quality, price, or demand, since American trailers were of better quality and cheaper than European ones, and the market for them was enormous. The problem was that they couldn't be licensed in Europe because their axle strengths, brakes, and lighting systems didn't meet European safety standards—they exceeded them. It was a classic example of the biggest loophole in almost every trade agreement—nontariff trade barriers (NTBs) that can be, and routinely are, exploited to keep competitors out of a market. It was just one of many instances in which the Europeans were shamelessly using them to get around their trade agreements with us.

Automobiles were another, even bigger, example of this. Supposedly, American-made cars wouldn't sell in Europe, since everyone "just knew" that Europeans don't like them, because they're too big. But that wasn't true. Or at least it wasn't true while I was in the Netherlands. The Dutch loved big American cars. They just couldn't afford them. Not because of their base price or quality, those were competitive, but because the Europeans had found a way to make them prohibitively expensive at the point of sale. We could have sold American cars by the tens of thousands a year in the Dutch market alone had it not been for something that had nothing to do with their size, quality, purchase price, or import duties, since, by treaty, we both levied the same import duties on automobiles. Our cars were too expensive because Europe's annual registration fees were based not on the value of the vehicle but on the cubic centimeter displacement of its engine's cylinders, and went up exponentially as they got larger. If I hadn't been a diplomat, the annual registration fee for my Ford Grand Torino would have been more than 100 percent of its original sale price.

I did have other successes though, especially in Western clothing and boots and in furniture. When I first proposed campaigns to promote these two items, both Harary and the Commerce Department were incredulous. They simply knew beyond a shadow of a doubt that it was impossible to sell American clothing, shoes, or furniture on the European market. But when I persisted, they finally agreed to let me try. In the end, Western clothes and boots proved easy to sell for one simple reason. It was in vogue in the Netherlands to dress in cowboy clothes. And while foreign suppliers had largely taken over the traditional shoe and clothing markets, they hadn't taken over the niche market for cowboy boots and hats, blue jeans, and square-dancing shirts. But the biggest success story proved to be furniture.

At first my efforts to promote the sale of American furniture in the Dutch market were met with a great deal of resistance from both my colleagues and Dutch retailers. When I made a presentation to the Dutch furniture retailer's organization, it was met with skepticism bordering on the discourteous, especially from Dreschler, the President of the

Association and owner of a large chain of upscale furniture stores. So it caught me by surprise when Dreschler called me the next week to ask if I could suggest some American furniture shows he might go to. Always on the hunt, I invited him to lunch to talk it over.

It was clear that, while he had pretended to be skeptical, in fact he'd been intrigued. But he hadn't wanted to show his interest in front of his competitors. So I sent messages to several major American furniture manufacturers and arranged for them to give him private tours of their showrooms. Surprised by my direct approach, a number of them went out of their ways to wine and dine him. When he got back he called to say that he'd been so impressed that he'd placed a large number of purchase orders, especially with Drexel Heritage in North Carolina. In fact, he'd ordered enough American furniture to change more than 70 percent of his offerings from European to American, an immense gamble even though we had only three advantages, better quality, lower prices, and quicker delivery.

You can imagine my concern when, about six weeks later, Dreschler called to say he had changed his mind. He'd discovered that, while the goods themselves were competitively priced, the cost of shipping assembled furniture from the United States to Europe was simply prohibitive. When I told my commercial wizard, Conrad Van Der Knapp, about the call, he grinned and said, "There's a fix for that. Change the ocean shipping content of the containers from assembled furniture to home decorations by making them more valuable than the furniture." What Dreschler needed to do was buy more American products like lamps and decorator items and have Drexel pack them for shipment in the otherwise empty spaces inside the assembled furniture.

At first I found his recommendation beyond bizarre and said so. So, as usual, Conrad had to patiently explain to me the realities of commercial life. In this case the problem was yet another major NTB that put American products at a disadvantage, North Atlantic Conference (NAC) shipping tariffs. The cost of shipping a container load of unassembled furniture, known as KD, for knock down, was much lower than for assembled furniture. But, if more than half of the cost of what you were shipping was for non-furniture household items, it was surprisingly low. So the solution was to change the nature of the most expensive product in a shipment from furniture to household items by filling the empty spaces in the furniture with expensive lamps, table clothes, curtains and decorator items of greater value. That would change their NAC tariff category and lower the cost of shipping enough to make the assembled furniture competitive. That this would also sharply increase the sale of other American products would be a bonus.

It was all Greek to me, or maybe Swahili. But before coming to work at the Consulate that sort of thing had been Conrad's daily bread and butter, so I sent him to Dreschler to explain this to him, at which point Dreschler called me to say it was Greek to him too, or maybe Surinamese Papiamento. But he decided to try it, and he bought lots of curtains, towel sets, lamps, and decorator items that Drexel Heritage agreed to pack into the furniture's empty spaces. He even agreed to pay for bringing several American cultural exhibits to the Netherlands to help him promote his new line, including an art collection from the San Francisco Museum of Modern Art, complete with a curator, an artisan from Colonial Williamsburg to sit in the window of his main store in The Hague making furniture by hand, and a reception to be hosted by the Ambassador.

That problem solved, or so I thought, I went on to other things. Then one day Dreschler called me to say the goods had arrived, but when he ran the numbers, he found he had a serious problem. He'd applied his standard multiplier, a common practice in the retail trade, and come up with prices at which he wouldn't be able to sell the American furniture. It wasn't because they would be too high. It was because they would be so low his customers wouldn't buy them for fear they were inferior goods. So he said, with mock sorrow, he'd just have to price them higher and make more money than he'd expected to make. He hoped I didn't mind. We should all have such problems! Not that everything came up tulips while we were in the Netherlands.

FORTY

TERROR IN THE TULIPS

Realizing the value of a second language, and knowing our children would learn English at school, even before Barbara was born, Leda and I had agreed to use Spanish at home as our primary language. So our children had grown up both bilingual and bicultural in that language. When we arrived in the Netherlands, we found an opportunity to expose them to even more languages. So we rented a house in a small North Holland town called Bergen-Binnen, an hour or so from Amsterdam, and registered them in a multilingual K–13 European Union school that catered mostly to the European Atomic Energy Agency (Euratom) set. The school's three hundred or so students studied in five languages, French, German, Dutch, Italian, and, at the lower levels, in English. So we put our three daughters in the French section, only to find they had to take classes in German as well. Rarely have my children been so angry with me, since they didn't speak either language. But they buckled down and, despite constantly gnashing their teeth, all managed to pass.

We also made friends with several Euratom families with children in the same school, including that of Jaques Geist, a French nuclear physicist and proponent of molten salt fast breeder reactors who insisted on trying to teach me how they worked. Even though I could barely understand what he was talking about, I spent many an evening listening to Jaques "talk nuclear" while he whipped up some of the best dinners I'd ever had. Spending hours trying to look smart while feeling stupid was a price I willingly paid. As so often happens, even though I barely understood what he was talking about, enough stuck to give me a leg up several years later when I was the State Department's Deputy Director of European Political and Economic Affairs, with a portfolio that included the International Atomic Energy Agency (IAEA).

Our biggest problem in the Netherlands turned out to be terrorism, not molten-salt fast breeder reactors. The Netherlands' rather liberal immigration policies, especially for people from its former possessions, had resulted in large colonies of Surinamers, Indonesians, and South Moluccans. Most seemed to be reasonably content, and there were lots of Indonesian restaurants that served up *nasi goreng* and other delicacies we'd learned to love in Paraguay (that's another story). But a handful of them had turned to petty crime. Once, on a tram, a Surinamer managed to get his hands on our daughter Barbara's coin purse until Leda saw what he was doing and broke a loaf of bread over his head.

As for the Moluccans, I'd never even heard of them before Amsterdam, although that quickly changed when a seven-man cell of South Moluccan terrorists hijacked a commuter train carrying several hundred people and held it for a week, demanding, as ransom, independence for their remote archipelago. But it was while we were in the Netherlands that we had our scariest brush with terrorism in all our years abroad. And it didn't involve Moluccans, Surinamers, or any other minority. It came in the form of a bona fide, home grown Dutch terrorist.

author's collection

The Netherlands. Here we're all "going Dutch." Left to right, Tamara, Rebecca, Leda seated at a spinning wheel, me with a pipe, Barbara, and Timothy Patrick with the accordion.

One morning a couple of months after we'd settled down in Bergen-Binnen to be near the children's school, no more than a minute or two after I left for work, the phone rang. When Leda picked it up, a male said to her in Dutch-accented English, "I see your husband just left for work. So the children will be leaving on their bicycles for school in a few minutes, and you will be alone, won't you?"

The caller was a convicted terrorist who had just been released from jail after completing a sentence for setting off bombs at a couple of military and police facilities. You can imagine how Leda reacted, especially since he clearly had us under constant surveillance and knew our movement patterns. As soon he hung up, she called me, I called the Embassy security officer, he called the police and I raced home. By the time I got there, the police had already arrived. And, although they immediately started an investigation, they let me know that they were more than a little surprised—and peeved—that an American diplomatic family was living on their turf without their knowledge, since it was *de rigueur* that everyone inform them immediately when they moved in or out of their bailiwick.

It was to be just the first of dozens of calls our terrorist "friend" was to make at all hours of the day and night, almost all threatening, and all recorded with my permission by the police in hopes that he'd say something that would open him up to criminal charges. But, being an experienced terrorist, he knew exactly where to draw the fine line between making threats by innuendo, which was deeply worrisome but not illegal, and making direct threats that would have constituted criminal acts.

He lived on a houseboat in Amsterdam and spoke English well. But he did have one weakness, math, as our oldest, Barbara, discovered one evening when one of his calls interrupted her while she was doing math homework. Since he'd interrupted her in the middle of trying to solve a problem, she asked him to help her solve it, and he did, and got it wrong. Competent math tutor or not, he aroused our constant fear that he might go beyond making phone calls and take some sort of action, and the uncertainty soon began to grind us down. The children continued to ride their bicycles to school, but now they were followed by a police car. Once they were in class, police officers would stand guard just outside their classrooms, a novelty that soon wore off for both them and the school administrator. Finally, one day I received a visit from an officer of a special police unit who told me that our terrorist friend wouldn't be bothering us anymore. Acting on a tip, they'd raided his houseboat and found some illegal drugs he claimed he didn't know existed. But in return for not being arrested, he'd agreed to stop harassing us. It was the worst terrorist threat of my career, because it wasn't aimed just at me. It was also aimed at Leda and our children. And it took place in a country that should have been one of the safest places in the world for my family.

author's collection

West Point, NY. Our oldest daughter, Barbara, in her West Point Cadet uniform.

Just as we were becoming truly acclimated, our oldest daughter, Barbara graduated from high school, Senator Laxalt appointed her to West Point, and we realized that it was time for us to take our brood back home to the United States to finish their educations. So I asked for and was granted and early transfer back to Washington to coincide with the school schedules there.

FORTY-ONE

TURF WARS — THE OFFICE OF PARIAH STATES

A bit more affluent than we'd been during our earlier sojourns, we settled into a nice suburban home in Chevy Chase, Maryland, put the two younger girls, Rebecca and Tamara, in the Georgetown Visitation Convent girl's school, our son in St. John's College High School, then a boy's school, and began digging ourselves into debt, although there were many bright spots as well. One came a year or so later, after Barbara had left West Point, when the Nevada delegation to Congress in Washington, DC, chose her as Nevada's 1983 Cherry Blossom Princess and my Congresswoman, Barbara Vucanovich (she preferred Congressman) escorted her to the presentation ceremony.

Over the next five years I was to have three different jobs in the State Department, the first as Desk Officer for Paraguay and Uruguay, the second as Deputy Director for European Political/Economic Affairs, and the third as Deputy Coordinator of Cuban Affairs. The Paraguay/Uruguay Desk was in what was officially called the Office of Southern Cone Affairs that included the Brazil, Argentina and Chile Desks. It was the era of Jimmy Carter's human rights *uber alles* approach to foreign policy, and we spent so much of our time working on issues related to political prisoners, torture, disappearances, and so forth that we privately called it the Office of Pariah States.

author's collection

Washington, DC, 1983. Left to right, Congresswoman Barbara Vucanovich (R-NV), the author, and our third daughter, Tamara. At the time, both daughters were students at Trinity College in Washington DC, then an all-girls college.

In the cases of both countries for which I was responsible, Paraguay and Uruguay, we had two different foreign policies, rather than the usual one. The first, championed by my Bureau, American Republics Affair, (ARA - since renamed Western Hemisphere Affairs—WHA) was to advance the broad range of our interests—trade, aid, and the like—even though Paraguay was ruled by a dictator and Uruguay by a military junta. Especially in the case of Paraguay the second policy, championed primarily by the Human Rights Bureau (HR), almost always at odds with that of ARA, was to beat up on Stroessner at every possible opportunity, regardless of our other interests, because he was a human rights violator. This led to lots of disagreements between the two bureaus that had to be elevated to the level of the Deputy Secretary of State, Warren Christopher, for decision. As a consequence, while the average Desk Officer might, during a two year tour, deal with three or four issues that had to be elevated to that level for decision. I had five or six a week.

One of the oddest decisions we had to elevate all the way to the Deputy Secretary, involving the Paraguayan Army's pants, became my all-time favorite. For decades we'd been selling surplus army uniforms to Paraguay as part of our military assistance program because we felt this gained us a certain amount of leverage with that establishment. But all Foreign Military Sales needed the State Department's approval. So, when a Paraguayan request came across my desk for permission to buy more surplus army pants for their soldiers, I assumed it was simply a routine sale, until HR chimed in. They wanted to deny the request because, they argued, selling used military clothing to Paraguay implied approval of the dictatorship and therefor abetted its violations of human rights, which is how we wound up arguing all the way up to the Deputy Secretary of State whether or not the Paraguayan Army should wear pants. Human Rights insisted that either they should buy them somewhere else or wage war in their underwear: We argued that having Paraguay's soldiers running around the country in their underwear was not in our national interest.

By now you've probably guessed that having to deal with Paraguay and Uruguay in the super-heated Carter-era atmosphere was endlessly fascinating, challenging, and a royal pain in the ass. Personally, I tended to spend more time on Paraguay than Uruguay, much to the irritation of the Uruguayan activist community. This was in part because I knew many Paraguayans personally, including Paraguay's Ambassador to the United States Mario Lopez Escobar, who had been a personal friend and unusually valuable contact of mine during my earlier tour of duty in Asunción. Because we were friends, I had immediate access to him, and this made it possible to nip some problems in the bud before they had time to fester.

By way of contrast, the Uruguayan Ambassador and Embassy staff let me know early on they felt it was beneath their dignity to deal with a mere Desk Officer, leaving as my primary Uruguayan interlocutors a collection of human rights activists and ambitious politicians bent on using Carter's human-rights policies as a springboard back to power. Dealing with them could be as difficult as dealing with the Bureau of Human Rights, as I was to learn when, after I didn't enthusiastically adopt all the positions espoused by everyone in the Uruguayan activist community, several of them took to bad-mouthing me around town.

Eventually I was able to make a trip down to visit my two countries and found Uruguay fascinating, similar in many ways to its much larger neighbor, Argentina, but with its own very distinctive personality, charms, and quirks. The Embassy in Montevideo went out of its way to welcome me and introduce me to as many key players as possible, which helped. The DCM, John Youle, even invited me to stay with him, a gesture that made my visit much more comfortable.

One formal call I made during my trip to Uruguay, in the office of the head of the then ruling Military Junta, General

Quierolo, proved especially enlightening. After we'd chatted for a while with him and the other members of the Military Junta then ruling Uruguay, Quierolo suddenly stood up, invited us to go with him for a cup of coffee, and headed down the hallway outside his office toward the building's exit. Along the way he paused several times to show me photos of some of the "atrocities" committed by Uruguay's Marxist Tupumaro "terrorists" that had forced the military—against its will—to temporarily take over the country to save it. He took special pains to tell me how many innocent civilians, police, and soldiers the Tups had killed. Before the Generals took over, Uruguay was one of the few truly democratic countries in Latin America. So when he repeated this casualty count for the third time, I was sorely tempted to retort that I'd lost twice as many men in my district in one year in Vietnam as he'd lost during his whole war. And for this he'd overthrown a functioning democracy? But I bit my tongue.

Finally past the photo gallery, we all marched out the door and about a block down the avenue to a small café where he ordered coffee and snacks all around. Apparently this was intended to demonstrate that Uruguay could hardly be a nation under siege if the entire General Staff could stroll freely out of its headquarters and down the street to a café without a single guard. It was an interesting piece of political theater. But it would have been more convincing if my former Marine Embassy Guard-eyes hadn't spotted the plainclothes security personnel trying to blend in with the "spontaneous" crowd of spectators watching us. Still, and despite the theatrics, the experience told me a few things, including how sensitive the Generals were about their image, something that came in handy several months later when Quierolo came to Washington.

One day a message from Embassy Montevideo came across my desk saying that General Quierolo wanted to make an official visit to Washington, a request that posed a problem for us. He might be the real power in Uruguay, but he wasn't an elected head of state. So receiving him at an overly senior level could be perceived as an endorsement of the Junta and that was something neither Bureau wanted to do. The request caused quite a stir, especially in the Human Rights Bureau. But after a couple of hand-wringing sessions, HR reluctantly agreed that he could be received at the State Department but not the White House.

The next question was who at State should do the honors. This led to yet more hand-wringing, including by my boss in Pariah States, Klaus Ruser, my Office Director, who became especially agitated when I gave him a draft Memorandum to sign suggesting that Quierolo meet with Deputy Secretary Warren Christopher at a specific date, time, and place. He was outraged. Mere Office Directors did not advise Deputy Secretaries what they should do, much less when and where they should do it. Besides, the Deputy Secretary was extremely busy, so we'd be lucky to get Quierolo an appointment in anything less than a couple of weeks. "Not to worry," I gently responded, "I've already made the appointment. I just strolled up to Christopher's office and asked his secretary when he might be free." When she showed me his almost completely clean schedule for the next couple of weeks, I'd simply selected the day and time that was most convenient, and she'd put it on his schedule. The Memo was just a formality. Shaking his head, Ruser just signed it and walked away.

Proud of myself for having successfully made an end run around the system, when the day arrived I put on my very best suit and tie and was just about to go down to the main entrance of State to greet Quierolo and escort him to the Deputy Secretary's office, when the phone rang. It was Christopher's staff aide who had just noticed I'd failed to arrange for Language Services to provide an interpreter, so it might be necessary to postpone the meeting until they could send one. Thinking quickly, and with my ass suddenly on the line, I took a deep breath and winged it. I told him not to worry. I planned to do the interpreting myself. He didn't sound terribly convinced, and let me know in no uncertain terms that if I blew it I'd be in trouble. When I escorted Queirolo into Christopher's office his aide was there with him and, when Christopher asked where the interpreter was, pointed at me. Christopher raised his eyebrows ever so slightly, the diplomatic equivalent of shouting out loud and saying, in effect, "I hope so, or you're in deep trouble." When I was, as usual, brilliant and didn't miss a beat during their twenty minute meeting, his aide sighed in relief. *Sic transit gloria* Desk Officer.

FORTY-TWO

CROAT TERRORISTS AND THE NAZI DEATH DOCTOR

One of the more bizarre incidents while I was on the Paraguay/Uruguay Desk took place when the body-guard-chauffeur of my Paraguayan friend, Ambassador Mario López Escobar, beat the crap out of the son of Washington, DC's Congressional Delegate, the Reverend Walter Fauntroy. Now, in the diplomatic world at its best, or even at its worst, Ambassador's chauffeurs don't beat up anyone. In this case it was even worse. The Paraguayan Ambassador's chauffeur-bodyguard turned out to be a Croatian terrorist with a black belt in karate who was in the United States under a false name on a Paraguayan diplomatic passport.

The name on his passport was Toni Saric, but his real name was Miro Barešić. In a prior incarnation he'd headed an assassination team that killed the Yugoslavian Ambassador to Sweden. The Swedes had promptly arrested, tried and convicted him and his team and had them in a high security prison when another team of Croat terrorists hijacked a Swedish airliner full of passengers and threatened to blow it up if their comrades were not released. Sweden caved in to their demand and arranged for the team's expulsion to Spain.

From there Barešić and a comrade named Vuyasevic traveled to Paraguay where they received the protection of the Stroessner government.

In Paraguay, Barešić became a karate instructor at the Military Academy, which is where Ambassador López Escobar, who was at the time a Navy Captain, came to know him. It wasn't clear whether López Escobar had personally asked that Barešić be sent to Washington or if that decision had been made by someone else. Regardless, shortly after López Escobar arrived in Washington, so did Barešić, who proved to be quite protective. When a motorcyclist cut off the Ambassador's car at a stop sign, Barešić initially just honked the horn at him. But when he then turned around and flipped off both him and the Ambassador, Barešić got out of the car and beat the crap out of him. The cyclist ended up in the hospital and I wound up with a real diplomatic mess on my hands. Of course, by the time we learned what had happened, Barešić had fled the country and returned to Paraguay, which is when things really got interesting.

With the Yugoslav Embassy chanting, "I told you so, I told you so," the FBI began looking into the matter and discovered that, during the time Barešić was in the United States, he'd accompanied the Ambassador on several trips. Apparently, Barešić's buddy, Vujasevich, who had stayed behind in Paraguay, was sending letters to members of the Croatian community in the United States asking for money to support their cause. And, in his spare time during the Ambassador's trips outside of Washington, when he wasn't driving the Ambassador around, Barešić would pay visits to those that hadn't coughed up, Whether or not he wore his karate black belt while he did so, I'm not sure. But, apparently, a few times when one of the businessmen refused to pony up a donation to the cause, their stores later burst into flames.

Paraguayan Ambassador López Escobar and his government insisted that they'd not been aware of this activity, nor were they aware that the Ministry of Foreign Affairs had issued a passport to Barešić using a false name. The disclaimers were received with skepticism in some circles around Washington. Still, there was no proof, so we decided that the best solution would be to bring Barešić and his buddy Vujasevich back to the United States to discuss their problems with our courts.

After a great deal of negotiating the Paraguayan government responded, echoing their previous comments regarding Auguste Ricord, not just no, but hell no, because agreeing to extradition would be an admission of wrongdoing. However, thanks to a great deal of work and pressure brought by our Ambassador in Asunción, the Paraguayans concluded that, in the name of good relations with the United States, the presence of Vujasevich and Barešić in their country was not in their best interests.

So, one fine day, a reservations clerk at the office of the Paraguayan airline made a telephone call tipping us off that both men had booked reservations from Asunción to Washington, DC and we, in turn, prepared to receive them with proper honors. But, like Ricord earlier, Barešić and Vujasevic had good friends in high places in Paraguay that might not want them in the hands of the American judicial system. Since the Stroessner dictatorship was really a modern version of a medieval kingdom in which princes and dukes had their own fiefdoms and gave loyalty to the king in return for his protection, this didn't come as a surprise. I knew from my years in Asunción that there were Generals with smuggling franchises in whiskey, cigarettes, cars, airplanes, flour, and more. There was even an Admiral that reportedly specialized in fencing goods pilfered out of shipments intended for the commissary of the American Embassy. (In my day, the Paraguayan Navy had six river patrol boats and seven Admirals.)

The appearance of the names of Barešić and Vujasevic on a list of airline passengers with reservations on a future flight became the key to our getting both to the United States to face justice. As soon as we confirmed their flight time, date, and seating arrangements—in First Class no less—we set our plan in motion. When their flight arrived in Asunción, the Paraguayan authorities ordered all passengers to debark and go to the transit lounge, where armed police made an unusual effort to keep the drapes closed. A squad of Paraguayan police then appeared, escorting two men who were carrying their own suitcases, indicating they were leaving of their own free will, not being kidnapped. When the police accompanied them to the foot of the ramp and invited them, voluntarily and without coercion, to climb aboard they did so, removing all doubt. There just happened to be a Croatian-speaking United States Marshal standing at the top of the stairs who looked in surprise at the flag painted on the tail of the airplane, then at them, and said, "I recognize you! You're Croat terrorists wanted in the United States! And this is an American airplane! And I'm a United States Marshal! Welcome aboard."

Barešić reportedly blanched and asked, "Yugoslavian?" When the Marshall answered, "No, American," he was so relieved he simply held his hands out to be handcuffed. Both were then escorted to the rear of the airplane, where the Marshal proceeded to make them strip naked, did full body-cavity searches, and put Barešić in a straitjacket, just in case he decided to demonstrate his karate while in flight. Thus began the second part of the show.

Now, by and large terrorists are not nice people. Nor do they work alone. So, just as we had suspected they would, other Croat terrorists in the region learned almost immediately of their comrades' detention. This led us to fear that an attempt might be made to free them at one of their intermediate points: Lima, Buenos Aires, La Paz, Panama City, or wherever. To prepare for this possibility, we had sent FLASH/STADIS messages to all of the embassies on or near their route, alerting each to the possible immediate need for action at their respective airport. (STADIS stands for State Department distribution only, not to be shared, even with military attachés or spooks.) But, to maximize security, we didn't tell them why.

The moment Barešić and Vuyasevic were detained by the Marshal, an Embassy officer who was standing on the tarmac called the Embassy, which in turn sent FLASH/STADIS/ACTION messages to each of the Embassies located along their scheduled flight path, informing them of what was happening and instructing those involved to do their best to make sure the two weren't freed by some stray Croat terrorists, or even allowed to get off the plane. As it turned out, no one tried to get them released while they were traveling. And, when they arrived in New York, they were arrested.

It would be nice to be able to report that they were then tried, convicted, and jailed in the US. But that's not what happened. The only charges filed against Barešić turned out to be for visa fraud, and those were dismissed because he' had entered the US on a diplomatic passport, false or not. And that gave him immunity. As for Vuyasevic, he was convicted of passport fraud because his name was misspelled on his passport. But at least we held them long enough for the Swedes to come up with extradition orders, at which point they were picked up and taken to Stockholm. Of course, modern justice being what it is, since then they've finished their jail sentences and been released. I heard later that Barešić went back to Paraguay to teach karate.

A few months after the Barešić affair, we received a tip from the same source that yet another wanted criminal had booked a flight from Asunción to New York. This time, the name on the reservation was no less than Dr. Josef Mengele, the infamous Nazi Angel of Death. Devotees of late-night movies have no doubt seen Gregory Peck's masterful depiction of Mengele in *The Boys from Brazil.* And those that went to school before they stopped teaching history may remember reading somewhere that Mengele fled to South America before he could be tried for war crimes and, after a short stay in Argentina, moved on to Paraguay. Since, as I mentioned earlier, while I was in Paraguay the B'nai B'rith's circuit riding Rabbi had given me copies of Mengele's application for permanent residence there, I knew the information might even be true. So I gave the tipoff some credence and we began to prepare a choreography patterned after the one we had used in the case of the Croats, just in case he should actually appear. We also informed the Israeli and German Embassies. In the end, someone tipped off the press, and when the great day arrived, the Asunción airport was swarming with journalists, and Mengele did not appear. Was it a hoax? Maybe. But like so many things, I'll never know.

Those weren't, I must admit, the only exciting happenings during my sojourn on the Paraguay/Uruguay Desk. Another involved a personal friend from my Asuncion days. One day rumors began to fly that an opposition politician, Domingo Laino, had been detained in São Paulo by the Brazilian police and was in danger of being killed by them. Domingo had been in Washington just a few days earlier and met with President Carter and, according to the rumor, Stroessner had taken his being received by Carter as a deliberate insult. So, as the rumor went, when Stroessner learned that Domingo would be flying to São Paulo, he'd arranged for the Brazilians to "disappear" him. Within an hour, the rumor went viral, and I started getting calls from reporters saying they'd heard from eyewitnesses that Domingo had been detained at the São Paulo airport and whisked away screaming. The crescendo of calls, including from aides to the Secretary, quickly built into a major uproar. One even came in from the National Security Council.

The minute I received the first call, I'd zipped a high-precedence cable to the Embassy in Asunción asking for information. But I hadn't received a response. And when I tried to get someone at the Embassy on the phone, no one answered. With nothing from the Embassy and the number of calls growing by the minute, I called López Escobar, the Paraguayan Ambassador, to ask if he knew, or could find out, what the hell was going on. He realized immediately that, since Domingo had just met with President Carter, any retaliation against him would cause a firestorm that could seriously damage or even destroy relations between our countries. So, while he insisted that he was sure Stroessner wouldn't do anything that dumb, he agreed to call Asunción immediately and ask that the rumor be investigated. He got back to me in less than an hour to say that both the Foreign Ministry and the President's office had called him back and told him that, to their knowledge, the reports were just rumors.

I quickly relayed López Escobar's response to my Office Director, the Assistant Secretary for Latin America, and just to cover my bases, to the Secretary of State's aide that had called me. But, given Stroessner's admittedly rotten reputation, I really did need something authoritative from our own Embassy as well. But follow-on cables and telephone calls continued to go unanswered. So finally, with media interest growing exponentially and the State Press Office now breathing hard down my neck, I did what I should have done in the first place. Domingo and I had been on a first name basis during my tour in Paraguay and I'd long made it a habit to keep a card file on all my contacts. So I went to my Paraguay file, pulled my card on him, and called his house. When his wife answered, I identified myself and asked if Domingo was there.

"Yes, Tim. But he's taking a shower. Can he call back?"

When I told her that I was hearing rumors that he'd been detained in São Paulo earlier that day, she said, "There must be some mistake. He had reservations to São Paulo this morning but missed his plane. So he's going tomorrow."

By then Domingo had finished his shower and came to the phone himself. And, after we exchanged greetings in Guaraní, he assured me there was nothing to the rumors and he was perfectly fine.

Relieved that my friend was OK, and having confirmed that the story was just a rumor, I promptly reported this back up the State Department food chain and went to get myself a much needed cup of coffee before the inevitable next media call came in. I didn't have long to wait. This time it was a Boston Globe reporter who, after repeating the story I'd been hearing all day, asked what we were doing about it. This time I was able to assure her that it was just a rumor. I'd just talked with Laino personally, and he was fine. But rather than saying thank you, she literally exploded over the phone, said she'd just got off the phone with an "impeccable source" in Asunción who'd told her Laino was in mortal danger. She screamed that I was a "fascist pig" and slammed the phone down so hard it would have hurt my ear if I hadn't already had combat-related tinnitus. Sometimes you can't win no matter how hard you try. And, on top of it all, now my coffee was cold. So, thanking the heavens that my Pariah days were nearing their end, I switched to tea. After two solid years of bureaucratic turf wars, I was more than ready to move on to my next job as Deputy Director of one of State's most prestigious offices.

FORTY-THREE

CRUDE, CRUD, AND CUBA

In my Foreign Service days, it was considered gauche to mention State's internal pecking orders, every though every FSO knew them by heart. One of them was geographic— Europe first, then Asia, the Middle East, Australia, and New Zealand, with Africa and Latin America vying for hind teat. This particular one was once beautifully illustrated by an off the cuff comment by that illustrious product of Euro-think, Henry "The Kiss" Kissinger, who, when asked by a reporter how important Latin America was to our national security, derisively called it "a dagger aimed straight at the heart of the Antarctic." Apparently the prospect of being incinerated by nukes (the Cuban Missile Crisis) or overrun by ten or twenty million Mexican refugees (a second Mexican Revolution) was less of a threat than a few tons of crud floating down the Rhine.

But there was a second pecking order that was even more important to FSOs, functional "cones," political first, economic second, administration third and consular last. There'd once been a fifth, commercial trade promotion, but it had been so far down the pecking order that State had given it to the Department of Commerce, free. So I was surprised when my next assignment was as Deputy Director of European

Regional Political/Economic Affairs, EUR/RPE, as it was both political and European.

EUR/RPE was responsible for an alphabet soup of international organizations, from the European Union (EU) and the International Energy Agency (IEA) to the International Atomic Energy Agency (IAEA) of later Iraq and Iran fame, the Organization for Economic Cooperation and Development (OECD), and the economic side of NATO. I was especially heartbroken to discover my new job required me to go to Paris several times a year as a spear carrier for senior officers attending conferences, or to Brussels to consult with NATO or EU officials. But I tried to make the best of it.

As is almost always the case at State, whenever you stick your middle finger in a new light socket, new problems jump out and bite you, and my new job was no exception. When I arrived at my new office, memories of the 1967 Arab oil embargo triggered by the Six Day War were still raw and the Cold War still dominated our strategic thinking. And, since Europe and the US both run on oil, one of the biggest challenges was to find new or at least more secure ways get crude out of the Persian Gulf if the balloon were to go up. I assumed there were others wandering around Foggy Bottom with a much better grasp of the matter that I would ever have. So at first I just sat and observed, until I was suddenly hit by a flash of *déjà vu*. The 1960s Vietnam-era-threat to the Strait of Malacca while I was a Marine working Southeast Asia morphed in my mind into a threat to the Strait of Hormuz, which might turn serious if someone started popping caps or tossing around anti-ship missiles there. So it wasn't a surprise when one afternoon, as I was contemplating my navel while waiting for the coffee maker to finish perking, an idea struck. Instead of using every carrier battle group we had to try to keep a piece of water fifteen miles across open, why not just go around it? When I looked at a map of the Middle East and its oil facilities, two possible partial solutions struck me. If you double-tracked the trans-Arabian pipeline you could move twice as much crude across the Arabian Peninsula, load it into tankers in the Red Sea, and take it through the Suez Canal to the Med. And if you had a pipeline from Abu Dhabi to Muscat, much of the rest could also bypass Hormuz.

With these ideas in mind, I called a friend from my Itaipú days at Harza Engineering. He gave me the phone number of a top engineer in Texas who specialized in oil pipelines, and I called him to ask what I thought was a simple question. How much would it cost to double-track the trans-Arabian pipeline? I had no idea how seriously he'd taken my innocent question until he called me back on Monday morning, said they'd put a team on the question over the weekend and come up with an estimated cost and done a preliminary design sketch. They were sending them to me by special courier that very day.

In light of the work they'd done, it would have been churlish not to use it for something. So I wrote up my ideas, attached the study I'd received, and launched them up the Memo chain until, barely tweaked by anyone above me, they landed on the desk of General Haig, then Secretary of State. He liked them so much that he got fired the next day, causing my scheme to be still-born. I like to imagine that had they been acted on, today's worries about the impact of hostilities in the region on crude supplies would have been markedly diminished. But, like so many other things, I'll never know for sure.

A second matter got me in trouble. Keep in mind that, at the time, the Cold War was very much in vogue. One day I was asked what I thought of an idea floating around in the Pentagon to create a new three-Division Army Corps specifically designed to fight in the Persian Gulf just in case the Soviets decided to send a few spare mechanized divisions south to capture its oil fields. When I thought through the concept, while I had no objection to the Army getting a few more divisions—a country can never have too many of those—I simply couldn't imagine any scenario in which Soviet forces would be pouring down through Iran and Iraq toward Saudi Arabia and the Emirates without our getting at least a little nervous about our Western Front in Europe. Following this reasoning, I then couldn't imagine any scenario in which, with a possible war brewing in Western Europe, any General or Admiral in his right mind would send a full corps of his strategic reserves to the Middle East. This would be especially true, since its ocean supply lines would be vulnerable to attacks by, for example, a Soviet sub or ten. I wrote up my thoughts and sent them to the Assistant Secretary for European Affairs who promptly sent it over to Defense, where it caused one hell of a reaction. One of my Army contacts quickly called me to warn me not to go over to the Pentagon for a while, because lots of people there were steaming mad at me. Not because I was wrong: Because I was right. They weren't willing to say so on the record, but several Defense planners later told me off the record that my critique had torpedoed an end-around attempt to obtain additional forces.

Another issue involved NATO and Cuba. Today, in its search for a new mission, NATO deploys forces to all sorts of hotspots, from the Balkans to the Middle East. But before the fall of the Berlin Wall, whenever the question arose of our playing together outside of Europe, the knee-jerk response of NATO planners was always, "We're a regional alliance, not a global one. Do it yourself." But, when I looked at NATO's potential problems in case of a general war, I couldn't help but turn a bit Latinocentric. There's a saying in the military, "Amateurs talk tactics - professionals talk logistics." So when I asked myself whether the rest of the world would play an important role should NATO get into it with the East Bloc in Europe, the answer was a resounding yes. Modern combat burns up supplies at an incredible rate. In any conflict that lasted more than just a couple of days, NATO would quickly need more, lots more, of almost everything. That "almost everything" would have to come primarily from the United States, most of it via the Gulf of Mexico on ships, and—hold onto your hat—everything coming out of the Gulf would have to pass within strike range of Cuban jet fighters and high speed Komar torpedo boats that could reach them in minutes. That made Castro's Cuba one of NATO's biggest problems because the Florida Strait would be even more important to NATO than Hormuz.

So the question became, in case of an all-out war, what would we have to do to remove the Cuban threat. The obvious answer sent chills down my spine. Were a general war to break out in Western Europe, the bulk of American military forces we would send to reinforce those already there would most likely have to go by convoy, as they did in World War II. Given the Soviet submarine threat, the most defensible ocean space where they could form up was in the Gulf of Mexico. They would then enter the Atlantic via the Florida Strait. So there would be only two ways to protect them against a possible Cuban effort to stop them. One would be for us to send a major part of our strategic reserves to Florida to stand by in case a threat from Cuba developed. But sending a giant slice of them to Florida, just in case Fidel Castro decided to act like himself, would be unacceptable. The alternative was equally bad. To our way of thinking, it would be irrational for Castro to take on NATO or the United States. But Castro proved during the Cuba Missile Crisis that he was perfectly capable of acting irrationally. So the first time one of his jets lifted off or a Komar missile boat headed out to sea, we'd have to take out Cuba, no matter how. And even if Cuba did choose to sit out the conflict, NATO would still have major supply problems. One of its most critical needs would be a dependable supply of the fuels and lubricants, without which a modern armed force can't maneuver. But almost all of Europe's crude oil came then, as it still does now, from the Middle East on ships. In those days, the tankers would have to sail within range of land-based Soviet aircraft or submarines, meaning they would be at extremely high risk, while sailing around the Cape of Good Hope, the only alternative route, would expose them to Soviet submarines for several weeks. And even were they able to reach Europe, its refineries might well have been put out of commission before they arrived.

So the next question was how could we deliver sufficient supplies of refined fuels, gasoline, JP4 jet fuel, diesel, essential lubricants, and so forth, to keep NATO in the fight? The giant tankers used to move crude petroleum can't carry refined products like gasoline or jet fuel because they don't have the necessary degaussing (electric spark prevention) systems to eliminate this threat. As a consequence, there are actually two very different types of ocean-going tankers, big tankers that carry crude and smaller ones that carry product. And only three high-seas fleets of product carriers existed, one that carried product from Singapore and northern Indonesia to Japan and the Pacific basin, one that operated in the Caribbean and Gulf of Mexico, and one, our domestic littoral fleet, that we would need to serve our own security interests. Since Singapore is on the wrong side of the globe and we wouldn't be willing to make our coastal fleet available, we would have to use the Caribbean fleet. And they too would have to be protected. And guess who sits astride several of the key passages between the Caribbean and Gulf of Mexico—Cuba. Gads, how quickly things can get complicated.

Regardless of how you cut it, Cuba, even though it is outside Europe, was vital to NATO's ability to fight the Warsaw Pact. At least this time when I sent my thoughts up the Memo chain, the Secretary didn't get fired. Instead I was authorized to lay my argument out to NATO planners during my next trip to Belgium, which I did. Much to my surprise, within months of my next visit, NATO modified its strategic plan to include defense against threats to its supply lines emanating from Castro Cuba. Then, just as I was getting into the swing of things, I got promoted and my boss got transferred. While still in Paraguay/Uruguay affairs I'd been informally alerted by someone very much in the know, that I was to be promoted. And being promoted would make me over-ranked for the Deputy Office Directorship. So I'd accepted the number-two job in European Regional Political/Economic Affairs with the understanding that, when I was promoted and its Director left, I would move up to his position, which would then be at-grade for me. Instead, when the Director left and I was, as expected, promoted, I wound up with a new boss. EUR/RPE was the desk for the Ambassador to the European Union, Tom Enders, and Enders insisted that an officer of his choice be made the new Director. So I went looking for another job, preferably within the European Bureau, until something else suddenly came up.

FORTY-FOUR

Cubanisimo!

Shortly after arriving in DC from Amsterdam, when I called on Nevada Senator Laxalt to thank him for appointing our daughter Barbara to West Point, he'd asked me to drop by from time to time while I was in Washington, which I'd been doing. Mostly we talk Nevada politics, not foreign affairs. So I was surprised when, shortly after Reagan's election in 1980, Laxalt called me to say he'd been asked to head the transition team at the State Department and wanted me to go see him.

Now, the career diplomatic service is a strange animal. Essentially it's a corps of professional nonpartisan and unelected political operatives, and this makes political partisans on both sides of the aisle distrustful of them. In my experience Republicans think all Foreign Service professionals are left-wing liberals, if not closet Marxists, and most Democrats are certain they're all right-wing reactionaries, if not out-an-out fascists, so neither believes they're to be trusted. While the Republicans Reagan brought in with him were no exception, Laxalt knew me personally and was comfortable enough with me to ask me a few questions. His first question was what I thought of the system of appointing political rather than professional Ambassadors. I think my answer surprised him,

"There's no such thing as a professional Ambassador. The difference is that professionals are the product of office politics while appointees are the product of party politics. Some of the best Ambassadors have been political appointees, and a few of the worst have been professionals. But, that said, by and large the professionals are measurably better."

Laxalt then asked me how many people they would need to appoint to take full control of the State Department's daily operations. When I said several hundred, he blanched and said they couldn't possibly come up with that many. Everyone in the partisan political world wants to be an Ambassador, and most would be happy with a cabinet or subcabinet post. But none of them want to be an Office Director. I responded that Foreign Service Officers are professionals, so there should be no need to make all that many political appointments. The important thing would be to listen to them and give their counsel full consideration, then make your own decisions, give them clear instructions and let them do their jobs. Regardless of their personal politics, with rare exceptions, and those could, or at least should, be weeded out, they would all do their best faithfully to execute the policies of the sitting President, regardless. The key was their professionalism.

Personally I'd never quite figured out whether I'm a Demican or a Republicrat. For that matter, I still haven't. But, professionally, as a Foreign Service Officer, it was my job was to implement the policies of the President of the moment regardless, even when I might privately disagree with them. As a result when, during the Carter years, I had zealous liberals call me fascist pig and during the Reagan years I had conservatives call me a Communist son-of-a-bitch. I took both epithets as evidence that I was doing my job fairly well.

A few days after my chat with Laxalt, Lyn Nofziger, one of Reagan's top political aides whom I'd known since his days in

California, called me from his new White House office to urge
me to take a job that had just become vacant, that of Deputy
Coordinator for Cuba Affairs. As soon as he hung up, I called
Laxalt to fill him in on Nofziger's call and say I wasn't really
interested in the job. His response was, we're determined to
solve the Cuba problem, but we need ideas and someone
to help push them through. The only limits to what we do
are that no one should get hurt and they shouldn't cost any
money. Though I didn't say so to Laxalt, those limitations told
me they weren't really ready to do what needed to be done.
With a man like Fidel Castro you can't accomplish anything
without spending money or risking casualties.

When it came to Cuba, given those limitations, while
Reagan's team wasn't intentionally looking for some Kabuki
Theater, it was close. And the more passionate people are
about a cause or policy the more they blame the messenger for
the message, which is why many FSOs avoid jobs like the one
they wanted me to take. In the case of Castro's Cuba, almost
anything you do can make someone spitting mad. And every
one of them has a Congressman, a political organization, a
lobbyist, and a typewriter (yesterday's version of a laptop).
So my biggest reason for not wanting the job was that it was a
potential career killer. I'd been there once before when I volunteered for Vietnam and wound up getting burned. But with
Laxalt and Nofziger on my case, I couldn't say no. So I reluctantly accepted.

Today all of this is history. But at the time my problem was
how to keep my new boss, Myles Frechette, from learning the
real reason I took the job. No doubt he would have still treated
me politely. But the slightest hint that I was there at the urging
of Nofziger and Laxalt would have made the situation very difficult, because my first loyalty had to be to him, not them. And

their having intervened in my assignment would have cast a permanent shadow of doubt over my motives. I've seen Myles many times over the years since we worked together and we're now good friends, not just office colleagues. He even did the foreword for this book. But this will be the first time he hears from my own lips the real story and may explain a few things that happened while I was his deputy, like getting calls directly from the White House from time to time.

During my very first day on the job, my phone began to ring off the hook, but it wasn't the White House. Almost every major reporter and TV anchorman in Washington was calling to welcome me to the Cuba desk, which told me my predecessor had probably been one of their "anonymous sources," something I was not about to be. I have a great respect for the professional press and, in other jobs I've often dealt actively with the media. But not this time.

My administrative assistant apparently had an unlimited supply of yellow sticky notes, because she made a note every time a call came in and tacked it on the end of a yellow ribbon chain that quickly began to grow exponentially. By end of my first week it went off my desk onto the floor and was well on its way out the door. By the end of the second, when I hadn't responded to a single one of them, the calls slowly stopped coming in. Apart from strongly suggesting that my predecessor had been a major media source, the outpouring of mock warmth from reporters trying to cultivate me as a contact also told me one other thing. In European affairs I was dealing with questions of war and peace. But those weren't of much interest to the press, while Cuba was because, for the media, especially within the beltway, sexiness trumps reality. Fidel Castro and "Che" Guevara, not war and death, were the flavors of the century.

As for my job itself, Frechette asked me to take the lead on management of the office and on consular and economics matters. He also gave me the task of helping assure that two orders issued by President Reagan were implemented. One was to establish a program of radio broadcasting to Cuba. The other was to tighten the Cuba embargo. Despite the President's written orders, neither was popular among the bureaucratic masses, so when I arrived in Cuba Affairs both projects were suffering "Death by a Thousand Memos" and needed to be revived. So when, shortly after I arrived on the job, Nofziger called me to see how Reagan's two pet projects were going, I told him they weren't. Taken a bit aback, he asked me over to the White House for lunch so he could introduce me to Ollie North, who was responsible for the Latin America portfolio in the National Security Council. I told Frechette about the call, walked over to the Old Executive Office Building, checked myself through security, and went up to Nofziger's office. After a short chat, he took me to meet Ollie North. From then on, especially after I got a look at Fawn Hall, Ollie's secretary, I started going over to the White House for lunch every couple of weeks.

FORTY-FIVE

RADIO RUM AND COKE, AND THE ETERNAL EMBARGO

Complying with President Reagan's order to establish a program of radio broadcasting to Cuba was a challenge. Almost every office in the Federal bureaucracy was opposed to the project. But since the President had directed that it be built, none was willing to say so openly. Instead they were all stalling for time in hopes it would eventually just dry up and blow away. Among those trying to starve it to death were all sorts of strange offices I'd never heard of but had to be involved, like the independent regulatory office responsible for allocating radio frequencies. Since the new station wouldn't be able to transmit without one, if they refused to assign it a frequency, that could be a problem.

After reading in on the project, my first step was to sit down with Myles and tell him I thought the working name of the project, Radio Free Cuba, sucked—badly. Spanish for Radio Free Cuba was *Radio Cuba Libre*, which translates to "Radio Rum and Coke," and that was a stupid name that would make the entire project a laughingstock throughout the region and beyond. After a few minutes resistance, he agreed with me and came up with a new name for it, the one it now has, Radio Martí, after Cuba's national hero, José Martí. It was an excellent alternative for two reasons. First, it was a name with all sorts of historical implications. And second, it would really piss off Fidel, which it did.

There was also a uniquely American problem. Radio Martí would technically be a private corporation, so it had to be incorporated somewhere as a business, preferably in Washington, DC. But, while Congress had authorized millions to build and run it, not a penny of those funds could be used to pay its twenty-five dollar incorporation fee. That one sent me running to Jeff Smith. Later, Jeff became the CIA's General Counsel. But at the time he was the State Department's lawyer for Cuban issues, who came up with a solution. Get a grant from a private, nonprofit foundation. To get Reagan's multimillion dollar project up and running we were forced to obtain a twenty-five dollar grant from the Smith Richardson Foundation to pay the filing fee for its incorporation. Once it was incorporated, we signed the papers that legally created Radio Martí, Inc. on top of my office book case.

As the project moved ahead, public debate over Radio Martí became more and more heated and Cuba began threatening to retaliate by jamming a potentially broad spectrum of US commercial radio stations if it were to begin broadcasting. The declassified, Confidential Memorandum for the Record by James R. Duncan of the Office of the Under Secretary of Defense, reproduced below, suggests with chilling clarity what our reaction to that might have been. Of course, as is so often the case, we had a second ulterior, and until now secret reason for wanting to build Radio.

C05262899

~~CONFIDENTIAL~~

OFFICE OF THE UNDER SECRETARY OF DEFENSE

WASHINGTON, D.C. 20301 OS

POLICY

DECLASSIFIED IN FULL
Authority: EO 13526
Chief, Records & Declass Div, WHS
Date: JUL 25 2013

TRANSFERRED FOR DIRECT REPLY
DOD   4 FEB 1982

MEMORANDUM FOR THE RECORD

SUBJECT: Radio Marti -- TDY to Key West, 3 February 1982

Mr. Kenneth Giddens and I visited Key West on 3 February to
gather technical data for the Radio Marti transmitter facility
and to confer with RADM Robert P. McKenzie, Commander, U.S.
Forces, Caribbean.

RADM McKenzie summed up his attitude toward the project as
follows: "If there is anything I can do that will help Radio
Marti get on the air one day sooner, please call on me." All
of the officers we dealt with at Key West were similarly
motivated.

RADM McKenzie stated that the proposed transmitting facility
would have enormous value for psyop in the event of operations
against Cuba, and that he will vouch for that fact at every
opportunity. He directed his senior psyop officer on the spot
to ensure that this capability is fully embodied in psyop
contingency planning. We agreed that it will be highly beneficial to provide in some way for mutual advice and cooperation
between his psyop staff and the Radio Marti programming effort.

We also agreed on the importance of counteracting publicly-
expressed fears that Cuba will retaliate by launching a "radio
war" -- by pointing out, whenever the issue arises, that

    (a) U.S. use of 1040 kHz for broadcasting to Cuba is
        sanctioned and protected under international law;

    (b) Cuba has placed itself in a position of international
        outlawry with respect to broadcasting;

    (c) Willful Cuban interference with legitimate U.S. use
        of the radio spectrum can justifiably be regarded
        as aggression and dealt with accordingly;

    (d) It is the Cubans who ought to be deterred by fear
        of what the United States might do, not the other
        way around.

One important conclusion from the technical discussions on
Saddlebunch Key is that considerable time and money can be saved
if we can get tower foundations and guy line anchors installed
before late March, when seasonally high tides and rainy weather
begin to impede access to the site.

cc: Dr. Ikle
    General Stilwell ~~CONFIDENTIAL~~   John Duncan
    Mr. Sanchez   James R. Duncan   RZ
                                      13M-2908

    OSD Disposition Attached

author's collection

Radio Martí's potential role as a psychological warfare
platform.

As for Reagan's order to tighten the Cuba embargo, it too, had ignited a swarm of bureaucratic battles. But eventually, and despite continued resistance from almost every agency in Washington, I was able to produce a set of proposals that, albeit often with considerable reluctance, all interested parties and the White House were willing to approve. So I wrote them up in what was called a Decision Memorandum and sent it around for everyone to sign. Job finished, or so I thought, I began to relax until out of the blue, the personal aide to one of the State Department's new senior officers called me to say his boss wouldn't sign it, because the recommendations in it were appalling and completely unacceptable. I was shocked, especially because his boss was a brand-new Reagan political appointee, so I pressed him, "Are you sure?"

"Yes!"

"Have you talked to your boss about it?"

"I don't have to. I know how he thinks, and he'll never agree!"

"Really?"

"Yes!!

"Are you absolutely sure?"

"Yes, absolutely!!!"

Finally, realizing that my attempts to engage him in cheerful repartee were just making him more and more angry, I said I'd be right down to talk with him about it. At first he insisted he was much too busy to see me. But when I persisted, he said, "It'll be a waste of your time. But if you insist, come down and I'll tell you 'hell no, we won't go' to your face."

My welcome assured, I strolled down to his office. It turned out that he was a political appointee with no experience whatsoever except as a personal lackey of his boss and that he had a particularly low opinion of career FSOs.

The harder I tried, the more he dug in his heels until, in the end, he flatly refused even to send the paper into his boss. At that point I was so pissed, to keep myself from punching his lights out, I did a smart about face and walked out. Several Foreign Service colleagues who worked in his office told me later that he'd been extremely pleased with himself and had started strutting around the office gloating about how he'd faced down yet another "striped pants cookie-pushing State Department leftie," implying that they should take their cue from what he'd done to me and stay out of his way.

His victory dance lasted about fifteen minutes. I was so steaming mad that the minute I got back to my office I called Lyn Nofziger on his direct line and asked cheerfully, "Why in the @#* did you appoint a Castro-loving leftist mole to take over Economic Affairs? I just had a run in with his aide and he's softer on Castro than anyone I've ever met! The @#*er is trying to block the tightening of the embargo we talked about just last week."

Lyn burst out laughing and asked me what had happened, so I told him. About five minutes after we hung up, my phone rang. It was Reagan's appointee calling me personally to congratulate me on the brilliant ideas in the memo, all of which he enthusiastically supported, although he had a few more ideas and wanted to discuss them with me if I could spare a few minutes to come down to his office. I promptly did so. As his aide stood by with a stunned look on his face, I explained that everything in it had already been approved by the White House and suggested he just sign it and present his new ideas later.

As an aside, the Cuba Embargo is a sterling example of myth trumping truth. The myth is that, because of the embargo, the United States does not engage in commercial trade with Cuba, and because we don't, try as they might, the Cubans have been unable to grow their economy. The truth is that every country in the world, from Canada to China, with the sole exception of the United States, has always traded with Cuba and so have we, albeit on an embargo-restricted scale. In fact, an important part of my job was to review and approve licenses authorizing the export of certain goods to Cuba, including any health-related items they couldn't get somewhere else in a timely fashion. There were also exceptions for items related to such things as air-traffic safety, search and rescue operations, and related communications.

author's collection

Washington, DC. After retiring from the Foreign Service, when in Washington, I made it a point to touch base with Nofziger. Lyn unexpectedly handed me this photo over one of our many lunches at the Old Ebbett Grill.

Personally, I considered the embargo then, as I do now, as more political than practical, especially after seeing what was really going on during my first visit to Cuba. Cuba's dollar stores were well stocked with American goods, dozens of US flag yachts were anchored at the Havana Yacht Club and most of the "Canadian" tourists wandering around Havana had southern accents. Today the United States is Cuba's biggest supplier of imports, mostly foodstuffs. But even then, while trade was much smaller, it did exist.

One fascinating example involved replacement parts for an undersea cable between New York and Cuba owned by ITT that had been the prototype for the first trans-Atlantic one. I understand that it's since been modernized. But at the time, its terminals in both Cuba and New York were still using vacuum tubes. Since they were no longer being made by anyone, whenever a tube blew, the cable's operators had to have a replacement custom built by an expert at restoring antiques.

Few people outside those directly involved realize that the Cuba embargo is governed by a World War I law, the 1917 Trading with the Enemy Act, that gives the President the power to enforce it or not. Up until 1996, when the President's authority became limited by a second law, the Helms-Burton Act, a sitting President had to make an official decision every year to continue the embargo. So every President since 1960 had the authority to end it, but none did. Each did, however, have a different position when it came to its implementation. When, in 1981, when Reagan gave orders to tighten it, the job of complying with his orders fell to the State Department, which is where it became my job to find ways to follow his orders, not ways to obstruct his decision.

We'd already pretty much emptied our quiver of bilateral measures, so at first I couldn't see how that could be done. Then one afternoon an idea popped into my head. If there weren't more ways we could screw the Cubans directly, why not screw them indirectly via our friends who were still trading with them, which pretty much included everyone. After a bit of discussion, Myles said he liked the idea. So we took it to Tom Enders, then Assistant Secretary of State for the Americas. Enders didn't just like it. He loved it, mostly because the Canadians would be among those we screwed. I never did learn what he had against the Canadians, but he was a former Ambassador to Canada, so they must have pissed him off while he was there, and he wanted to get even. Regardless, green light flashing brightly, I went hunting for friends to screw.

My first step was to collect data on what Cuba was exporting to other countries, which turned out to be mostly sugar, nickel, cigars, tobacco and AK47s. There wasn't much we could do about the AK47s. But we could do something about the others. The question was how to "persuade" our friends to stop buying stuff from Cuba, or at least get them to reduce their purchases. The answer was to extend the embargo to include products being imported into the United States from them that had so much as a smidgen of whatever they were importing from Cuba. For example, it takes lots of sugar to produce Canadian Club whiskey and Polish hams, and both Canada and Poland were buying sugar from Cuba, which was OK as long as not so much as a granule of Cuban sugar was used to produce what they exported to us.

I still remember an especially poignant letter from the distillers of Canadian Club assuring us, cross their hearts and hope to go broke, that they meticulously excluded Cuban sugar from the whiskey they exported to us. They did, however, complain that having to do this was a bit of a pain in the ass. As a former commercial officer, I could feel their pain. So I tried to be helpful by suggesting one way to make sure they were complying would be to put radioactive isotopes in whatever Cuban sugar they bought so we could trace it, just in case. Maybe they could even use that as an advertising slogan: "Drink Canadian Club— You'll Glow in the Dark." But for some reason they didn't cotton to the idea, perhaps because their marketing people thought that the risk of glowing in the dark after imbibing radioactive isotopes along with their booze might unsettle some of their customers.

Nickel was easier. Behind the headlines, a constant exchange of information takes place between embassies in Washington and the State Department. Mostly this is just a way for each to keep the others informed about what's going on, so one of the routine chores of a Desk Officer is to meet with officers from foreign embassies. While I was on the Paraguay/Uruguay Desk, no Embassy in Washington seemed interested in our relations with either country. But they all seemed to want to know what was up between us and the Cubans, including with regards to the embargo because of its impact on their commercial interests. In diplomacy just like in real life, money matters.

Dealing with the Japanese was especially enjoyable, because every month the same junior officer from the Japanese Embassy would invite me to lunch to pump me for information, and I love Japanese food. One of our meetings took place shortly after we began looking for ways to tighten the embargo. Since nickel is a major Cuban export and is used in all sorts of manufactured products, I'd asked one of the national labs if there was a way to determine whether nickel of Cuban origin, even if just a trace, was in a given product. To my surprise, they gave me a qualified yes. Using gas chromatography you can spot even trace quantities of Cuban nickel because it contains markers that identify its place of origin.

So during one of our lunches, between bites of superb sushi, I casually commented that we had a new system that could tell us if a product entering the US contained Cuban sugar or nickel, although we wouldn't be able to tell pre-embargo nickel from post-embargo nickel. When he looked rather quizzical (his English wasn't all that good, but more likely he didn't want to believe what he'd just heard), I explained that, for example, we'd be able to spot an automobile with bumpers that contain even a tiny trace of Cuban nickel and stop it from entering the US. The same would hold true, or course, for other things, like computer parts and electronic devices. That afternoon he called me seven or eight times to clarify certain points about what we might do. I assumed he was preparing a reporting cable to Tokyo. Shortly thereafter, just has we'd expected, the price of Cuban nickel suddenly dropped, since risk reduces market value.

To give my readers a taste of the sort of daily back and forth that goes on between the State Department and our missions on the embargo, I'm including below the text of a once SECRET/EXDIS, now declassified cable I wrote. Addressed to Ambassador Mansfield in Tokyo, it was part of our effort to use nickel as a lever to increase embargo pressure on Cuba via one of our friends, in this case Japan (EXDIS stands for Exclusive Distribution).

(transcribed from the original by the author)

"[SECRET—DECLASSIFIED AND RELEASED IN FULL]

DRAFTED BY ARA/CCA: TCBROWN: EN
APPROVED BY EA: JHOLDRIDGE
ARA: TENDERS
ARA/CCA: MBFRECHETTE [to protect their privacy, I've removed others]
P 022111Z AUG 82
FM SECSTATE WASHDC
TO AMEMBASSY TOKYO PRIORITY
S E C R E T EXDIS STATE 214469

EXDIS [DECAPTIONED]

E.O. 12356: XDS-3, 7/28/2002 (HOLDRIDGE, JOHN H.)
TAGS: ESTC, CU, JA
SUBJECT: CUBA EMBARGO: NICKEL AND JAPAN
FOR AMBASSADOR MANSFIELD FROM ASEC HOLDRIDGE

1. (SECRET ENTIRE TEXT).

2. THE UNITED STATES HAS RECENTLY ENTERED INTO CERTIFICATION ARRANGEMENTS WITH FRANCE AND ITALY TO ASSURE THAT CUBAN NICKEL IMPORTED BY THOSE COUNTRIES DOES NOT SUBSEQUENTLY ENTER THE US IN VIOLATION OF THE CUBA EMBARGO. THESE ARRANGEMENTS COVER BOTH NICKEL AS SUCH AND NICKEL CONTAINED IN MANUFACTURED PRODUCTS SUCH AS STAINLESS STEEL OR CHROME.

3. WE HAVE NOT YET ASKED JAPAN TO ENTER INTO A SIMILAR AGREEMENT EVEN THOUGH JAPAN IS A MAJOR PURCHASER OF CUBAN NICKEL AS WELL AS AN EXPORTER TO THE US OF ITEMS CONTAINING NICKEL. THERE ARE INDICATIONS THAT JAPAN, IF ASKED, MIGHT CHOOSE TO STOP IMPORTING CUBAN NICKEL RATHER THAN ENGAGE THE US FORMALLY REGARDING OUR EMBARGO RELATED CONCERNS. YOU SHOULD SEEK AN EARLY OPPORTUNITY TO MAKE THE FOLLOWING POINTS TO THE APPROPRIATE CABINET LEVEL INTERLOCUTOR.

4. WE ARE SERIOUSLY CONCERNED WITH CUBAN ACTIVITIES CONTRARY TO OUR NATIONAL INTERESTS AND IN THAT CONNECTION MAINTAIN AN EMBARGO AGAINST CUBAN EXPORTS TO THE US IT IS ILLEGAL FOR ANY CUBAN PRODUCT TO ENTER THE US DIRECTLY OR THROUGH A THIRD COUNTRY, EVEN AS AN INPUT TO FINISHED PRODUCTS OF ALMOST TOTALLY NON-CUBAN ORIGIN.

5. IN REGARD TO CUBAN NICKEL WE ASCERTAINED THAT IT WAS BEING INCLUDED IN PRODUCTS ENTERING THE US FROM THIRD COUNTRIES, AND WE HAVE CONCLUDED RATHER COMPLEX CERTIFICATION AGREEMENTS TO STOP SUCH IMPORTS FROM FRANCE AND ITALY.

6. WE HAVE NOTED THAT JAPAN IS AN IMPORTANT IMPORTER OF CUBAN NICKEL AS WELL AS AN IMPORTANT EXPORTER TO THE US OF

MANUFACTURED GOODS CONTAINING NICKEL. WE HAVE BEEN GIVING SOME CONSIDERATION TO ASKING JAPAN TO ENTER INTO A SIMILAR ARRANGEMENT. WE UNDERSTAND JAPAN HAS COMPLETED ALL ITS 1982 NICKEL PURCHASES FROM CUBA. DOES JAPAN PLAN TO MAKE ANY FUTURE PURCHASES FROM CUBA THIS YEAR OR 1983, 1984 OR BEYOND?

SHULTZ"

Another case involving a Spanish electronics company was even more dramatic. It was building a large semiconductor plant in Cuba. While that wasn't a welcome development, as long as they didn't use American products to do so, it wouldn't violate the embargo. But when we took a closer look, lo and behold, they were not only using American patents, they were secretly shipping American-made manufacturing equipment to Cuba, including some items of strategic concern. At first, rather than acting immediately we simply let them know that we were aware of what they were doing, giving them an opportunity to change their ways. But they didn't. So the day before the plant in Cuba was to be dedicated, we designated the company as an Enemy Agent under the Trading with the Enemy Act. While this may sound rather ho-hum, it was anything but. Let me put some flesh on it.

Designation as an Enemy Agent has a ripple effect. It does not make the designee an outlaw. But, once it is designated, any "American person" that deals with it is committing a felony and is subject to criminal prosecution. The company had an office in Chicago, so shortly after it was designated, its Chicago office manager called me to ask what it meant. My answer was simple. Henceforth, no company that operates in the US can legally deal with your company. When he then said he'd been asked by his headquarters to go to Europe to discuss the problem, I asked him how he planned to travel, since it would be a felony violation of the Trading with the Enemy Act for an airline that flies to the US to sell him a ticket.

"Then I'll fly from Canada," he said.

"How do you plan to pay for your ticket?"

"I'll use my credit card."

"I hope it's not American," I said, "because letting you withdraw company funds from a bank to pay your monthly bill will be a felony, too."

Not surprisingly, his tone of voice began to change from "damn the bureaucracy, full speed ahead" to one that was less certain and a bit more nervous.

So I asked him a few more questions. "How are you going to operate when the water company can't sell you water, the electric company can't sell you electricity, the phone company can't let you make calls, and the janitors can't even clean your office?"

By then he was thoroughly shaken, "So how can I do my job?"

My answer was simple, "You can't."

After a suitably pregnant silence, I suggested that he contact the Office of Foreign Assets Control (OFAC) of the Treasury Department and ask for a special license. "Although you'd better move fast, because your company may be going bankrupt."

Frankly, I was privately appalled by the ability of the United States government to put a company out of business without so much as a by your leave. But that's how it worked. While it was a large company, it was not terribly important to Spain on the national level, so we expected the political fall-out from our designating it as an Enemy Agent to be minimal, and were right. And, in any case, its attempts to bypass the Cuba embargo were so extraordinarily blatant that our taking action was easy to defend and had little effect on our bilateral relations. But had we invoked the embargo on certain other companies, the political fallout could have been disastrous. One case in particular comes to mind, that of PEMEX, Mexico's iconic national oil company.

In mid-1981, we received reliable reports that officials of PEMEX were trying to buy spare parts in the US to help Cuba repair an oil refinery that dated back to the pre-Castro period. Originally built by an American company using imported equipment and machinery, it had been nationalized by the Castro government without compensating its owners. So we had cut off its supply of spare parts. But, in this case, because PEMEX was a truly major player both in Mexico's economic and political systems, it was exponentially more politically sensitive should we designate it under the embargo. Many of its operations, including its refineries, involved properties Mexico had nationalized subsequent to its Revolution, Mexico's oil workers union, the Sindicato de Trabajadores Petroleros de la Republica Mexicana (STPRM), was a major far-left political force and a number of the union's leaders had been instrumental to Castro's success. And, as if that weren't enough, PEMEX is a key pillar of the country's economy, plays a major role in its self-identity, and is an iconic symbol of its having successfully wrested its oil industry out of the hands of "Yanqui imperialistas." So we were facing a dilemma - designating PEMEX would risk setting off a monumental political battle between the US and Mexico. But ignoring what it was doing would have been a violation of US law.

At the time, while I was aware of its importance, I didn't know anyone that had ever worked for or had close connections to PEMEX, so I had no personal interest in the company.

But, in the interest of full disclosure, since then I've come to know several Mexicans with very close connections to PEMEX. The father of "Pepe" Puente, whom I mentioned earlier several times, was a top official of PEMEX; Puente himself, a second generation Marxist revolutionary, was the subject of a chapter in my book, *When the AK-47s Fall Silent*; one of "Pepe's" closest childhood friends, Cuauhtemoc Cardenas, who did its foreword, a former Mayor of Mexico City and twice an unsuccessful candidate for President, is the son of Lazaro Cardenas, the President that nationalized PEMEX; and Noel Guerrero, the guerrilla warfare expert that was the first leader of Nicaragua's Sandinista Front and once was "Che" Guevara' confidential aide was an employee of PEMEX.

To give my readers another example of how such matters were handled at the time, I'm including below the text of another embargo-related cable I wrote that has since been declassified, concerning the PEMEX problem. To protect their privacy I've removed the names of others that approved it before it was sent. As you can see, far from just a unilateral US exercise in anti-Castro pique, the embargo had then, as it does today, real world consequences, even for countries that are our friends.

(transcribed from the original by the author)

"[CONFIDENTIAL - DECLASSIFIED AND RELEASED IN FULL]
DRAFTED BY ARA/CCA: TCBROWN: KS
APPROVEDBY ARA/CCA: MRRFRECHETTE
ARA/MEX: F.CRIGLER R

O P 230011Z JUL 81
FM SECSTATE WASHDC

TO AMEMBASSY MEXICO IMMEDIATE
INFO USINT HAVANA PRIORITY
C O N F I D E N T I A L STATE 193599
E.O. 12065: GDS 7/20/87 (FRECHETTE, MYLES R.R.)
TAGS: ENRG, CU

SUBJECT: (C) REPORTED PEMEX ATTEMPT TO EVADE
THE CUBAN EMBARGO
REF: 80 STATE 342377

1. (C-ENTIRE TEXT)

2. DEPARTMENT HAS RECEIVED REPORTS THAT
    PEMEX HAS BEEN ATTEMPTING TO ACQUIRE US
    SPARE PARTS NEEDED TO REPAIR EQUIPMENT
    AT A CUBAN OIL REFINERY. CONSUMATION OF
    ANY SUCH ARRANGEMENT COULD REQUIRE
    DESIGNATION OF PEMEX AS A CUBAN AGENT
    FOR PURPOSES OF EMBARGO ENFORCEMENT.
    THE US IS BOUND IN THIS RESPECT BY LAW
    AND HAS LITTLE IF ANY CONFIDENTIAL
    FLEXIBILITY. DESIGNATION WOULD REQUIRE
    US FIRMS TO TERMINATE RELATIONS WITH
    PEMEX, OBVIOUSLY A SERIOUS RISK TO PEMEX
    INTERESTS AND OTHER MAJOR US-MEXICAN
    BILATERAL   RELATIONSHIPS,   INCLUDING
    ONGOING ARRANGEMENTS FOR PURCHASES
    FOR SPR.

3. EMBASSY   IS   ASKED   TO   COMMUNICATE
    INFORMALLY TO GOM, POSSIBLY BOTH FOREIGN
    RELATIONS AND PEMEX AT APPROPRIATE
    LEVELS, THE FOLLOWING:

4. WE RESPECT THE POSITIONS OF OTHER NATIONS ON TRADE WITH CUBA BUT ASK THAT OTHERS IN TURN RESPECT OURS. (WE HAVE RAISED THIS WITH GOM IN DECEMBER, 1980, SEE REFTEL, AND PASSED COPIES OF OUR EMBARGO REGS.) USG HAS RECEIVED INQUIRIES FROM US FIRMS REGARDING OUR EMBARGO BECAUSE APPARENTLY PEMEX OFFICIALS ARE SEEKING TO PURCHASE US ORIGIN SPARE PARTS FOR USE IN REPAIRING OIL REFINERY IN CUBA.

5. THIS WOULD BE IN VIOLATION OF US EMBARGO LEGISLATION AND COULD, IN ACCORDANCE WITH US LAW, FORCE DESIGNATION OF PEMEX AS A CUBAN (PURCHASING) AGENT. DESIGNATION WOULD SEVERELY RESTRICT RELATIONS BETWEEN US FIRMS AND PEMEX WITH RESULTANT NEGATIVE IMPACT ON BILATERAL ENERGY RELATIONS. THIS WOULD BE PARTICULARLY UNFORTUNATE GIVEN MUTUALLY BENEFICIAL POSITIVE RELATIONSHIP THAT EXISTS. THERE IS LITTLE LIKELIHOOD THAT THE PURCHASE OF GOODS FOR CUBA IN VIOLATION OF THE EMBARGO WILL ESCAPE US ATTENTION. WE ASK THAT PEMEX OFFICIALS WHO MAY BE UNFAMILIAR WITH PERTINENT US LAW BE MADE AWARE OF US EMBARGO RESTRICTIONS AND OF SERIOUSNESS WITH WHICH US VIEWS BREACHES.

HAIG"

FORTY-SIX

DOING THE GUANTANAMO FLIP-FLOP

When it comes to Cuba, the biggest myth of all was then, as it still is today a half-century or so later, that the United States and Cuba do not have diplomatic relations with one another. Nothing could be further from the truth. True, we don't formally exchange Ambassadors so we don't recognize one another at the Head of State level. But we do have diplomatic relations. In fact we have lots of diplomatic relations. Cuba has two Embassy-size diplomatic missions in the United States, one at the United Nations in New York headed by an Ambassador, the other in Washington, DC, in the form of an Interests Section, headed by a top level Cuban diplomat. We ourselves have only one mission in Havana, the US Interests Section of the Swiss Embassy. But it's by far the largest diplomatic mission in Cuba. Not only is it housed in the pre-Castro American Embassy building on the Malecon, Havana's beach front promenade, the Head of USINT, as it's known, lives in a mansion originally built as the residence of the American Ambassador. And mansion it is! I know. I've stayed there.

The truth is that, despite our admittedly considerable political differences, whether we like it or not, we're next-door neighbors, so we have to cooperate with one another on lots of things. For example, we have shared concerns for the safety of flight, controlling contagious diseases and rescuing people in distress, to name just three. Take safety of flight. Commercial and private airplanes flying to and from Latin America and our east coast fly over Cuba because that's the safest and shortest route. They routinely obtain Cuba's permission to do so and maintain constant communications with air controllers in both countries. Aircraft flying to and from Canada do likewise. The same goes for safety of ocean navigation. When, for whatever reason, someone sailing near Cuba gets in trouble and needs to be rescued, both countries often need to cooperate. And contagious diseases don't stop at borders.

Still, when it comes to Cuba-US relations, some burrs under the saddle never seem to go away. One of the biggest is Guantanamo Bay, one of Cuba's major ports. The US base at the mouth of the bay is officially a Naval Coaling Station. In my day there was a small pile of coal in front of its headquarters building just in case a passing coal-fueled Navy ship might need some, and our lease agreement with Cuba allows us to occupy it in perpetuity - which was not a problem until Fidel Castro came along. Needless to say, neither Fidel nor his half-brother Raul has ever been ecstatic about our having a military base in Cuba, leased or not leased, and most certainly not in perpetuity. We, on the other hand, think it's a pretty good deal, and see no reason to leave.

But just like any lease, to stay you must pay your rent on time. And therein lay one of the tasks I inherited. If we didn't pay our rent promptly our landlord, Fidel, would legally be able to evict us. So one of my jobs was to assure that we always paid the rent on time, with a certified Treasury check no less. But since cashing it would mean that Cuba recognizes our lease as legitimate, Castro never cashed it. So it was just added to a slowly growing pile of un-cashed checks. That was just one of many oddities I discovered during my stint on the Cuba Desk.

An aside: Fast forward to 2012 and Guantanamo is still very much in the news, which is why I was perplexed when President Obama promised to close the post-9/11 detention facility there on the grounds that the United States should never hold unconvicted persons in its prisons. To take that position he would not only have to reverse major decisions made by two of his Democratic predecessors, John F. Kennedy and Jimmy Carter, he'd also have to reaffirm two decisions made by his Republican predecessors.

Not that US policy toward Cuba hasn't flip-flopped a dozen times before, it has. Perhaps the best example of our doing policy somersaults over Cuba involves family travel. Cuba. In 1962, during the Missile Crisis, when Fidel Castro showed he would rather ignite a nuclear holocaust than risk his Revolution, Kennedy responded by imposing today's economic embargo. In Kennedy's case this included a ban on family reunification travel. In 1977, fifteen years later, Jimmy Carter reversed Kennedy's travel ban and legalized family reunion visits. While today Carter revels in calling the Cuba embargo a moral abomination, he was President during the pre-Helms-Burton period and could have abolished it entirely with a stroke of his pen, but he didn't. Instead, he took just one baby step by softening Kennedy's approach to family reunification travel, apparently in hopes that, in response, Fidel would soften his rule. Initially his baby step was widely applauded, even by Fidel, who initially welcomed Carter's initiative, since by then he'd come to believe his own propaganda claim that his Revolution had become irreversible. And besides, he needed some more Yankee dollars.

To all appearances, the regime's propaganda had, by then, convinced most Cubans still on the island that when their compatriots fled to America they'd found themselves in an implacably racist country that denied them freedom and pushed them down into abject poverty. So when, taking advantage of Carter's decision, those selfsame relatives began arriving in Cuba to visit family, fat, happy, prosperous and loaded with presents for them, the stark difference between what Cubans had been told and what they could see with their own eyes generated a powerful wave of popular unrest, exactly what Carter said he'd wanted. But Carter had violated two basic principles of international relations. A bilateral policy cannot work unless both sides accept it, and the leader of one country cannot make decisions that are binding on the leader of another. In this case, Fidel Castro had the power to slam the Cuban travel doors shut at a moment's notice, and while he welcomed the Yankee dollars, he wasn't about to let them undermine his Revolution.

While not yet visible to outsiders, by early 1980 the unrest being generated inside Cuba by the sudden influx of relatively well-to do family members was approaching the boiling point. On April Fools' Day, it boiled over when five men managed to enter the Peruvian Embassy in Havana under a hail of police bullets and gain political asylum. The government tried to keep news of what had happened quiet, but word of it spread like a pandemic across Cuba, setting off a political avalanche. Within days, ten thousand more Cubans had reached the sanctuary of the Peruvian Embassy, and a heated international diplomatic stand-off had developed. By April 15, the situation was spinning out of control. So, apparently in an effort to reduce the pressure, Fidel opened an escape valve by announcing that any "counterrevolutionary *gusanos* (worms)" wanting to flee his paradise were free to do so immediately via the small port of Mariel. Taking him at his word, more than a hundred thousand Cubans promptly headed for Mariel to do just that, only to discover that Fidel had "forgotten" they'd need boats to leave. With tens of thousands of their fellow Cubans stranded in Mariel, this triggered yet another avalanche, this one from the United States, as flotilla after flotilla of small boats raced to their rescue and began bringing them to Florida. By October somewhere around one hundred and twenty-five thousand "Marielitos" had reached the US, and a million more, ten percent of Cuba's entire population, were reportedly jamming the highways trying to join them.

At that point, apparently realizing he had badly misjudged his own people, Fidel slammed the Mariel door shut. The vast majority of the "Marielitos" that did reach the United States went on to become valued members of American society. But some did not because, in an act of impressively petty "revolutionary" malice, Fidel had exploited the Mariel exodus to empty his prisons and mental institutions and send their inmates to the US hidden among the innocents, creating a legal problem essentially the same as that posed by holding terror suspects in Guantanamo Bay today.

None of the criminals Castro sent to the US had committed crimes here, much less enjoyed the benefits of the American legal system. But many were extremely dangerous, and releasing them onto America's streets would create a "clear and present danger". But, since Fidel wasn't about to take them back, and no one else wanted them, Carter was forced to choose between two evils. He could either release thousands of violent criminals onto the streets of America, putting American lives in jeopardy, or hold them in American prisons, without due process, because they were deemed to pose an imminent threat to the American public. Faced with that choice, Carter slapped them in jail to rot.

When Reagan assumed the presidency, some 2,746 unconvicted Marielitos were languishing in American prisons by edict of Carter. When I became Deputy for Cuban Affairs, I found all 2,746 of them sitting right on top of my in-box. By then Ronald Reagan had reviewed Carter's Cuba policies and, by and large, had begun to change some of them. But not when it came to the unconvicted Marielitos in US jails. In that case, Reagan was conflicted, since continuing to hold them constituted a major exception to due process. But after taking a close look he came to the same conclusion as Carter and left them in jail.

But Reagan didn't ratify Carter's post-Mariel decision to return to a policy of sharply restricting family reunification travel to Cuba. Instead, he ordered that all restrictions on family reunion travel to Cuba be lifted. When it fell to me to find ways to implement his decision without opening the tourism flood gates, my suggestion was to allow family reunification travel up to the "third degree of consanguinity" on the premise that, if someone couldn't dig up at least one second cousin somewhere in Cuba, they probably weren't really going there to visit close relatives.

To my pleasure, the idea was promptly codified. The "third degree of consanguinity" family reunification door was kept open by both of Reagan's successors, George H. W. Bush and Bill Clinton, but later slammed shut by George W. So I was rather pleased when Obama decided to reopen Reagan's door of travel to Cuba per the "third degree of consanguinity" clause. It was his opposition to Carter's decision to keep potentially dangerous suspects in jail, due process or no, in his case Islamic fundamentalist terrorists in Guantanamo, that took me aback, especially since history had proven Carter right. When a number of criminal-minded Marielitos were released by a judge, they'd promptly launched crime waves in New Jersey, Pennsylvania, Florida, and elsewhere. Many were then rearrested, but only after murdering, raping, robbing, and committing sundry other sordid felonies, not to mention creating one of our most violent criminal gangs, Los Marielitos. The violent criminal so brilliantly portrayed by Al Pacino in the iconic 1983 Brian De Palma-Oliver Stone film *Scarface* is a chillingly accurate dramatization of what Los Marielitos became. I can only pray that if the even more potentially violent terrorists now being held in Guantanamo are released, they don't do the same – or worse.

FORTY-SEVEN

MARTINIQUE MAGNIFIQUE — AMERICA'S FRENCH CARIBBEAN MISTRESS

But, as I've said several times before, all things, including Foreign Service assignments, must come to an end. So in 1983, as the bureaucratic sun began to set slowly on my tour as Deputy for Cuba, I began alternatively salivating and gagging over the available onward assignments. None really grabbed me until a notice appeared on my desk saying the position of Consul General in Martinique was coming available. I leaped out of my chair, raced by my startled secretary, bounced down four flights of stairs three steps at a time, and ran to the office of the one man that would most influence who got the assignment, the Bureau's chief administrator. It was a good thing I ran, because within minutes there were a half-dozen other pretenders to the throne of Martinique lined up behind me for the same reason. After begging and pleading, not to mention springing for a good lunch, I won out and was offered the job. Since I spoke Spanish but not French, at least not intelligibly, the Department sent me to the Foreign Service Institute for a six-week intensive language conversion course where two instructors took turns beating up on me for eight hours a day until I surrendered and began babbling in semi-coherent French. In my copious spare time, I also did my best to brush up on our current policy on the French Caribbean and surrounding area, which was fairly easy, since, as far as I could tell, we didn't have one. After briefing in, off Leda and I went to the Caribbean, land of sun, sand, sea, and subversion, sans children for the first time, since Barbara, Rebecca, and Tamara had married while we were in DC, and son Tim was a student at American University.

The job came with a furnished mansion designed by a disciple of Le Corbusier that sat on a low cliff overlooking the city and harbor, plus a car and driver, cook, maid, gardener, twenty-four-hour armed guards and guard dogs, and a seemingly endless supply of the paper plates and plastic eating utensils my predecessors had apparently used when entertaining. It also came with bathrooms that had toilets that tended to bounce around when you sat on them and doors that tended to fall off their hinges if you strained too hard. In addition, there was also a downtown office where I was expected to work once in a while. It was located in the heart of Fort-de-France on a delightful mob-magnet of a central square named after Monsignor Romero, the martyr-bishop of San Salvador, where I'd previously served. This being the day of the car bomb, my predecessors had made things easy for anyone interested in blowing the Consulate up by choosing as its digs a second-floor office suite, some of which, including my office, was cantilevered five feet over a sidewalk the locals regularly used as a parking lot.

For the first couple of weeks I was busy settling in, so I didn't notice this until, one night at about two in the morning, my wife and I were awakened by a large explosion. Rolling over, we said to each other almost simultaneously, "Bet that was the

Consulate," rolled back onto our pillows, and were almost back to sleep when the phone rang. The call was from the French Gendarmes, who asked politely, "Monsieur le Consul General, would you care to see what just happened to your Consulate?"

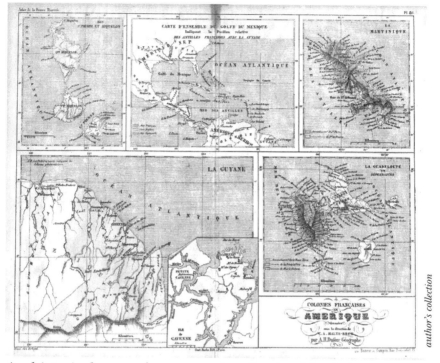

author's collection

An historical map of my consular district, Martinique upper right, Guadeloupe lower right and French Guyana, with their geographic setting in the upper center. The islands upper left, St. Pierre and Miquelon, surrounded by Canadian territory, were covered directly from Paris.

It was an invitation I could hardly refuse. So I immediately slipped on some clothes and walked down stairs to wait for the car they were sending for me. When I arrived at the

Consulate I immediately noticed two things. One was that the bomb had been small, more welcoming salute than serious effort to cause major damage. The other was that, small or not, it had exploded directly beneath my desk. The message was clear enough, "Welcome to Martinique, Yankee imperialist enemy of mankind!" It was just the first of dozens of terrorist incidents in my consular district during my years there, a far cry from what I'd expected in such an idyllic setting. Still, in return for living in one of the most beautiful and fascinating places in the world, having to drive around the occasional burning car and change hotel rooms every night to avoid the fire bombs, was a price worth paying.

One of the most interesting parts of the job was dealing with the French who, I must admit, have a few odd quirks, like eating snails, frog legs, and ground-up goose liver. I soon discovered that dealing with my own Foreign Service colleagues back home in Foggy Bottom could be even more challenging than dealing with the French, since they tended to take umbrage whenever the French tried to tell us our flies were unzipped or that we might have been less than totally right about something, which, in their view, was most of the time.

The French, of course, see Americans differently, more like country cousins, well-meaning but rather crude and unsophisticated folks that need help from time to time. They even think they, not the British, helped us win the Revolution, and delight in pointing out that they haven't fought a war against us since the French and Indian flap in the mid-1700s, which was for them just a side bar to the much more challenging Seven Years War. As for my fellow Americans, they seemed to think Parisians were typical of all the French, meaning they were as difficult to get along with as New Yorkers, when in fact most of the French had pretty much the same jaundiced opinion of Parisians that Americans did. I myself eventually concluded that what most irritates Americans about the French is that they're as arrogant and self-centered as we are, and we can't stand people like us. Still, as long as I didn't take them too seriously all the time, I found they could be fun. And even if I hadn't, my job was to get along with them and try to convince them to get along with us.

Besides, compared to the smarmy Parisian bureaucrats I'd dealt with during earlier incarnations, the local officials and business folks I found myself dealing with were downright homey. This came home to me when, after just a few weeks, the Préfet (Governor) of Martinique became comfortable enough with me to ask me personal questions like, "Monsieur le Consul General, why do you speak French with a Spanish accent?" A few months later he asked me if I were French-Canadian, although to the metropolitan French that's not necessarily a compliment. I knew I'd arrived when he stopped asking about my accent and began telling me incomprehensible jokes in street argot.

Martinique also gave me glimpses of some all but unknown events in American history. Hanging on my office wall was a copy of a letter from the Committee of Secret Correspondence to William Bingham (Binghamton, New York is named after him) dated July 3, 1775, a year and a day before the Declaration of Independence. It consisted largely of detailed instructions concerning military stores, small arms, cannons, powder and shot, and even uniforms that France had already agreed to supply to our revolutionary forces. The letter opened for me a window into an unknown page of my own country's history. It identified Bingham as having been appointed as an official representative abroad of the emerging United States more than a year before Benjamin Franklin was appointed envoy to

France. That made Martinique the oldest diplomatic mission we had, since it had been continuously manned since 1775. As for Bingham, he seems to have been an excellent choice, since he'd been the British Consul in Saint Pierre (then the capital of Martinique) since 1770, knew the language and many of the French officials involved, and was intimately acquainted with all the best routes for smuggling arms from there to his fellow rebels. Apparently he'd been using them himself for several years to smuggle rum from the Caribbean to the Colonies. He even seems to have had lots of smarts since after the Revolution he helped found the Pennsylvania Bank and became one of the richest people in the new United States before retiring to England.

Bingham's pre-Franklin mission to France turned out to be just one of many historical links between Martinique and the United States, and far from the earliest at that. One dated all the way back to 1607 when the three caravels carrying the founders of the Jamestown colony, the *Susan B. Constant*, *Godspeed*, and *Discovery*, made their first landfall in the Americas on Martinique's eastern shores to replenish their fresh water supplies before sailing north, a voyage that was reenacted during my tour. Later, during the Civil War, because much of France's assistance to the Confederacy was being carried on ships sailing to and from the French Caribbean, the Union established a network of coast watchers on Martinique and there were several nearby naval encounters between Confederate and Union ships.

As a former Marine, one historical footnote was of special interest. The first Marine amphibious landing during World War II was initially planned to take place in Martinique in August of 1941, a full year before the invasion of Guadalcanal. France had fallen to Nazi Germany, the French possessions in the Caribbean were being administered by the Vichy government, and a number of French warships, including an aircraft carrier, had put in to Fort de France and were just sitting there. More importantly, several dozen frontline fighter aircraft that had been in the process of being ferried to Europe when France fell were also sitting at the Martinique airport, and the Vichy government was under pressure from the Nazis to make these ships and airplanes available to Germany. But, despite this, the American Consulate had been allowed to remain open.

Shortly before the landing was to take place the Préfet of Martinique, then Admiral Robert, received orders to close our Consulate and expel its staff. Since the Consul was traveling elsewhere, the Admiral called in the Vice Consul and passed along the order to him. The Vice Consul promptly returned to the Consulate and sent a message to this effect both to Washington and to American naval forces lurking nearby waiting for the invasion to begin. As the story was told to me by a senior French official, the next morning the Vice Consul went to the government palace and said to Admiral Robert, "I agree that one of us will need to leave. But if you look out the window toward the harbor entrance you'll see some American warships entering the harbor. It's you that may wish to leave, not me."

The ships entering the harbor were part of the convoy carrying the Marine expeditionary force, all kitted out in tropical uniforms complete with shorts and pith helmets. As it turned out, Admiral Robert, reportedly with a sigh of relief, gave way, so the Marines didn't make their landing. But rather than returning them to the United States, in its infinite wisdom Washington chose to divert them elsewhere, which is how an expeditionary force of Marines wearing tropical uniforms and pith helmets found themselves in Iceland, the first Marine unit deployed to the European front during

World War II. But I hadn't been assigned to Martinique to study the past but to deal with the present.

While I was Deputy Coordinator for Cuba, one of the major strategic developments in the Caribbean I'd followed closely was the growing Cuban presence in Grenada, something that had weighed heavily in my favor when I asked for assignment to Martinique. Still, during my briefings in Washington, one point was repeatedly emphasized. Mine was to be a watching brief, since it was French policy to hold the United States at arm's length in the Caribbean. When I arrived in Martinique in September of 1983, that same message was reiterated to me by every French official I met, albeit much more diplomatically. Since Martinique, Guadeloupe, and French Guiana, the three *départements* of France for which I had responsibility, were in the Americas whether anyone liked it or not, I thought it was a dumb policy. But who was I to say? After all, I'd been responsible for implementing a few dumb American policies myself. So respecting a dumb French one shouldn't be a problem. Besides, a month after I arrived we invaded Grenada, and everything changed. With bigger policy fish to fry, neither Washington nor our Embassy in Paris realized just how big a regional game changer Grenada was. But the French did. And this set the stage for some of the most bizarre bureaucratic encounters of my diplo-years.

The Consulate in Martinique was an odd duck to begin with. As Consul General, I was responsible for three *départements* (provinces) of France that were officially under the jurisdiction of the Embassy in Paris. But, because they were in the Americas, I reported to the Assistant Secretary for Latin America, not to the Ambassador in Paris. It was also a "diplomatic in interest" post, meaning I was officially a Chief of Mission, and therefore responsible for all US government activities in my district, from Social Security pensions to intelligence matters. That gave me independent reporting authority, so I didn't need the approval of Paris or anyone else before sending messages. Of course, neither Paris nor Washington really gave a damn what I did, as long as I didn't do anything. This all probably sounds just about as nit-picking and bureaucratic as it gets, and you're probably wondering why the hell you should give a damn. And for about two weeks after I arrived in Martinique, I felt pretty much the same way, until I sent a message that lit the fuse of the Ambassador in Paris and set him off like a skyrocket, causing a series of bureaucratic snits that wound their way all the way up to the desk of the Secretary of State.

As I mentioned earlier, while in Cuban Affairs, I'd worked with Ollie North on the embargo, Radio Martí, and other Cuba issues. So before I left Washington, he'd asked me to come over to his National Security Council to discuss how we might con the French into helping us with a couple of other regional problems, such as drug interdiction and Grenada. Once on the ground in Martinique, I'd talked with the local French civil and military authorities, who seemed willing to cooperate, and sent a message to that effect back to North. I should have known better I suppose. But I assumed that, since the White House was responsible for more than just Martinique, this initiative had been discussed with the European Bureau at State, and they in turn had kept Embassy Paris informed. So, naïve me, I sent an information copy to Paris, causing the Ambassador to explode since, in fact, he hadn't been kept informed. How dare an officer in his Mission talk directly with the French on behalf of the White House about sensitive matters without his being consulted in advance! It wasn't entirely bureaucratic nonsense.

After all, the Ambassador to France did have legal responsibility for them.

Without going into detail, suffice it to say that my innocent efforts to keep Paris informed caused a full-blown bureaucratic hurricane and led to some negotiations between the Latin American and European Bureaus that made the Korean War peace talks look straightforward—until they finally reached a compromise that would have made Machiavelli happy, "To hell with it. Let's both screw the guy in the middle," meaning me: And thus emerged a hybrid mutant agreement known among the cognoscenti as the Treaty of the Seventh Floor.

Under the terms of this bureaucratic abortion, I was instructed to serve two masters and make both happy by complying to the letter with their orders while simultaneously complying fully with those of the NSC, which gave me three bosses. And if I screwed up, it would be my head, not any of theirs. To which overture I responded, "Yes, sir, yes, sir, three bags full, sir!" (of what, I didn't say.) Meanwhile, I was cursing the lot of them *sotto voce* and wondering if there might be a way to get a local voodoo witch doctor to cast a hex on the lot of them.

Still, orders are orders. And besides, just as I suspected might happen, once their pissing contest was over, the Ambassador in Paris and the European and Latin American Bureaus in State began trying to woo me onto their teams. They would have been better advised to look for ways to rein me in instead, which they would have done if they'd known me better. It was to be the only time in my career when there was more sucking down going on than sucking up, and I saw no reason not to take full advantage of it. As a result, rarely has anyone in such a lowly position ended up having so much freedom to make policy, or so much fun doing it. As they say in Chicago, one should never waste a crisis. Our Grenada "rescue mission" provided the catalyst.

Within weeks of Grenada, the Préfet of Martinique, the senior French official in my district, called me in to tell me that France had decided to reverse its stand-offish policy. Henceforth not only would they not hold the United States at arm's length, they would try to wrap us in a smothering embrace, and he'd just received instructions from Paris to begin this process at our relatively low local level by informally exploring with me what sort of gestures we might be willing to make to demonstrate our approval of France's presence in the region.

As soon as I got back to my office I wrote a message reporting his approach. When, unlike the reaction to my earlier missive, I didn't receive a response from either Washington or Paris. And, since silence implies consent, I took this as a green light for me to respond positively to the overture, went home, stood in front of a mirror, and began brainstorming with myself about what we could do. Ideas in hand, or head, I then sat down with the Préfet and the French Commanding General, Caribbean, to discuss them. Since Puerto Rico, Martinique and French Guiana were all within the operational areas of both the French and American regional military commanders, they didn't need permission from Paris or Washington to act on many them. And since France had, and still has, more military forces in the Americas south of Florida than we do—an Army regiment in Guadeloupe, the 33rd Marines in Martinique, and the 3rd Foreign Legion Regiment (*3ieme Régiment Étranger d'Infanterie*) in French Guiana—they had the assets with which to do things.

So I made it my primary mission to take full advantage of France's reversal of policy in the region. Since that would require taking some serious initiatives, I'd have to be careful *not* to tell Washington or Paris everything. Before long Martinique began receiving more attention than it had since World War II. On the intelligence front, it wasn't long before CIA Director Bill Casey and I became episodic pen pals. On the military side, Lyle Lane (the DCM in Costa Rica while I was in El Salvador and, later, Ambassador to Paraguay while I was his Desk Officer) was Political Advisor to the dual-hatted SACLANT/CINCLANT (SACLANT for Supreme Allied Commander, Atlantic; CINCLANT for Commander-in-Chief, Atlantic). With Lyle's encouragement, his boss, Admiral Wes McDonald, the one wearing both hats, cheerfully began sending warships and special operations units my way. On the law enforcement front, everyone from the Drug Enforcement Agency to the Coast Guard also happily jumped aboard.

Promoting military-to-military relations quickly became a key part of my efforts and, given my background, was also lots of fun. During my years in Martinique the number of US Navy ship visits more than tripled, senior American military and diplomatic officers regularly came calling, and I was able to arrange for several joint US-French regional military operations where none had gone before. Initiatives on the law enforcement front were also successful, and I was able to negotiate a *carte blanche* agreement for Coast Guard vessels and aircraft to use French ports and airfields without prior permission from Paris, something that, up until then, had been a major barrier to their making regular calls there.

As I mentioned earlier, within months of my arrival in Martinique, the issue of Grenada had been resolved by President Ronald Reagan using that most traditional of all American foreign policy instruments, the Marines. Not that Washington had bothered to keep me informed before, during, or after it was executed. They hadn't. But the French had. General Beal, the Commanding General, French Military Forces/Caribbean, had his own assets closely follow the movements of American ships and aircraft involved in the operation and called me regularly before, during, and after it took place to keep me up to speed on how the invasion was going. He even called me once to say that he'd just been swimming at a local beach and noticed some American military aircraft flying nearby. But, since he'd been standing in the water and the airplanes were also over water, he'd concluded that they hadn't been violating French airspace, so he hadn't bothered to report this to Paris. That was, of course, his way of telling me some American warplanes had violated French airspace by taking shortcuts across French territory, but they didn't mind.

During my first trips around the district to introduce myself to French officialdom, I'd made it a special point to visit the Colonels of all three regiments. So as soon as the news got out that we were considering some possible military-to-military initiatives, all three returned the favor by reaching back out to me. The Colonel of the 3rd Foreign Legion in French Guiana was first off the blocks and called me to say he'd like to host some joint US-Foreign Legion training in deep forest operations. When Colonel Duval of the 33rd Marines called me to say he wanted to play too, I suggested a joint American-French Marine amphibious exercise on the Puerto Rican island of Vieques and some joint training of American Rangers at the French Ranger training school at Fort De Saix. In his case, I asked for a favor in return.

At the time, both our second daughter, Rebecca, and her then husband were Marine Sergeants and wanted to come visit us, and bring the two-and-a-half grandchildren they'd blessed us with, with them. But there were two problems. Rebecca was six months pregnant, and her husband was due to reenlist during their visit, so he would need to be sworn in for it to be official. There wasn't much I could do about Rebecca's pregnancy. But I sent a message to the Commandant of the Marine Corps asking authorization to swear my son-in-law in, which he quickly granted. When I mentioned this to Col. Duval, the commander of the 33rd French Marines, he smiled.

A couple of days before I was to swear in my son-in-law, Duval called me, offered to make the Regiment's Hall of Honor available for the ceremony and suggested when it would be available. Needless to say, I thanked him. The day before the swearing in was to take place he called me twice to remind me of our arrangement and called me another couple of times the day of the ceremony to remind me of the exact time we'd agreed on. With Rebecca and her husband in uniform and the two-and-a-half grand-daughters, we all squeezed into my armored Peugeot, and off we went up the hill to Fort De Saix. As we drove in we were greeted by not just the Colonel but the 33rd Marine's Regimental Band and an Honor Guard. Rarely, if ever, had a United States Marine Sergeant received such an honor. The ceremony went beautifully, ending with a champagne toast to the newly sworn. I later wrote an article about the event that was published in the Marine Corps' *Leatherneck* magazine and Colonel Duval had it translated into French and published in the French Marine Corps' magazine, *L'Encore*. Since there are no female French Marines, Col. Duval told me later that he'd been particularly impressed by Rebecca being a Marine Sergeant. But what had totally blown him away was her being pregnant and dressed in a Marine maternity uniform. But, while these were all good clean fun, none had the pizzazz of two other gestures. One involved our invading a French island. The other involved the battleship *New Jersey*, the American Ambassador to France, and my posterior anatomy.

author's collection

Fort Desaix, Martinique, 1985. Our second daughter, Marine Sergeant Rebecca in the maternity uniform Colonel Duval found so impressive, standing in front of the shield and flags of France's 33rd Regiment d'Infanterie de Marine (33rd Marine Regiment).

FORTY-EIGHT

INVADING FRANCE

While Grenada and the subsequent reversal of France's policy in the region had made my own suggestions doable, the most audacious one was the brainchild of Préfet Saborin of Guadeloupe, who asked if we would please invade Marie-Galante, a small island under his jurisdiction. I'd visited the island, and it was a nice backwater sort of place. But it hardly seemed of sufficient strategic importance to merit an American invasion, and I said so. He explained that, while small, Marie-Galante it was fast becoming a royal, post-Grenada pain in the ass for the French, thanks to the Mayor of its largest town, Gran Bourg. Apparently he was a disciple of Grenada's late unlamented Maurice Bishop and was trying to rebuild Bishop's New Jewel movement with Marie-Galante as its base. So, backed by the French regional military CINC, General Beal, he was asking if we would be so kind as to join the French Army in invading the damn place and scare the living crap out of him. After having gone out of our way to squelch the pro-Castro machinations of the New Jewel movement in Grenada, I agreed that it would be a shame to have it rear its noxious head elsewhere. So what he was proposing seemed like a good idea. Besides, how often do you get a chance to invade France without having a De Gaulle looking over your shoulder? So I contacted Admiral MacDonald and asked if he might send me a Marine Force Reconnaissance planning team to look into the idea, which he did.

I can still see the shock on the face of the Marine Recon Team's commanding officer when I suggested that the best way to respond to the French request might be a joint US Marine-French "ostentatious recon" operation. I don't think he'd even heard of such a thing, much less been asked to make a public show of force, especially not inside France. But he swallowed hard and got with the program, no matter how bizarre he thought it was. He suggested a joint nighttime Marine-French HALO (high altitude-low opening) parachute drop onto the island from aircraft flying so high and far away their motors wouldn't even be audible on Marie-Galante. And so it came to pass that the morning after they jumped, the Mayor of Grand-Bourg de Marie-Galante woke up to find his home and his town, in fact his entire island, "under the protection" of American Marines and French Army forces against a hypothetical threat. That very day the Mayor got religion.

As for French Guiana, in response to the Legion Colonel's suggestion, small units of Navy Seals and Marine Recon units began visiting the European Union's favorite corner of South America to engage in joint training exercises on the Legion's Deep Equatorial Forest Training range. The California-sized virgin triple canopy rain forests in French Guiana are among the most pristine in the world, almost totally uninhabited and almost impassible, especially during the rainy season. When, once a year, the Legion sent a foot patrol to check the province's borders with Brazil and Suriname, for all but about twenty miles of their thousand mile trek, they had to cut their way through exuberant growth with machetes. Because there were very few places along the route where a helicopter could land, they also had to carry most of their supplies with them. Even for elite units, the terrain was challenging. But Marine Recon and Navy Seals like challenges, so both began sending teams to train alongside the Legion.

Toward the end of my tour as Consul General, the Préfet of French Guiana asked me to come down for a visit by the Minister of the DOM/TOMS, France's Ministry of Overseas Departments and Territories (*Departements d'Outre Mer et Territoires d'Outre-Mer*). And since the Minister would be accompanied by his spouse, he mentioned that he'd be pleased if Leda, whom he'd met during an earlier visit, were to come with me. Since the visit coincided with the return of both a Marine Recon unit and Navy Seal detachment from a joint deep forest trek, the Legion Colonel also asked me to be guest of honor at a ceremony marking their emergence from the wilds. When we arrived at the Legion's Kourou base, the Marines and Seals were in formation alongside their Foreign Legion colleagues, so freshly out of the forest they hadn't even had time to bathe. The minute the Marine's platoon leader heard I was a former Marine myself, he stripped off his sweat soaked Force Recon t-shirt, and gave it to me. It's still one of my prized possessions, although Leda insisted on washing it before putting it away.

After the formation, the Legion Colonel asked me to sign the Regiment's *Livre d'Or* (Book of Honor) and made me a *Fils du Régiment* (Son of the Regiment), invited us for a glass of champagne, and presented me with the engraved silver coaster pictured below, in honor of the occasion. As we sipped our champagne, I asked him what his impression was of the Marines and Seals. He said that both had very impressive high tech equipment, especially their communications and navigation gear, and the Marines had done well enough. But the Seals had had a hard time because they weren't in good enough shape to keep up with the Legionnaires. Having started in Marine life as a private in a recon type reserve unit and been around the occasional Seal detachment, it was hardly what I'd expected to hear, and his comment so intrigued me that I went back and spent some time talking with the men in both units. It didn't take me long to conclude that the problem wasn't the men. The men in both groups were equally impressive. The problem was their leadership. The Marine commanding officer was worn out but still gung ho and enthusiastic. The Seal's commanding officer was also worn out. But unlike his Marine counterpart, he had a negative attitude that had clearly undermined the moral of his men. For me, it was yet another example of why leadership counts.

The joint US/French Marine amphibious landing in Puerto Rico also went well. The only problem had been transport to Viequez and from ship to shore, since the French didn't have any amphibious operations-capable ships in the region. But it was the exercise in gunboat diplomacy that proved the most memorable, thanks to a rear guard problem.

author's collection

author's collection

Kourou, French Guiana, 1985: Silver coaster given to "*Mr. C. Brown, Consul General Des Etats Unis aux Antilles Guyane on January 22, 1985* by the Colonel of the 3rd French Foreign Legion (authors' collection).

FORTY-NINE

THE AMBASSADOR, THE BATTLESHIP, AND MY ASS

Of all the initiatives I'd managed to gin up in response to the French request for gestures of support for its presence in the Caribbean, the most grandiose involved the American Ambassador to France, a battleship, and my posterior anatomy. When the Préfet of Martinique had called me in, he'd said, "Monsieur le Consul General. We would very much like the United States to make a few gestures indicating that it welcomes the continued presence of its French friends in the Caribbean. *Peut-etre* (maybe) you have some ideas?"

The first thing I blurted out was, "How about inviting the American Ambassador from Paris to visit us here?"

"Pas mal! (not bad)!" he'd responded. And thus began my biggest, and potentially most painful, adventure ever in gunboat-and-tux diplomacy.

Martinique may have been the oldest American diplomatic post in the world but, until I arrived, no American Ambassador to France had ever made an official visit to it. So I'd inadvertently but officially committed myself to correcting that historic omission. On my next visit to Paris I dangled before Ambassador Galbraith the earthly delights of a grand tour of the French West Indies. His Deputy Chief of Mission clearly thought it would be a monumental waste of his time and tried to dissuade him, but the Ambassador was delighted with the prospect, so we began working on dates for his visit, and the longer I looked at the calendar the longer his visit grew, until it turned into a nineteen-day tour of my entire consular district. It would begin in Martinique, then go on to Guadeloupe, French Saint Martin's and Saint Barths and end in the most remote part of the European Union, French Guiana, with visits to the Foreign Legion base, Devils Island, and the Kourou space center.

I'd created a monster that would devour my entire yearly representational budget—until Rotary International came to my rescue. Being an active Rotarian myself, I turned to my Rotary comrades, telephoned the presidents of clubs through-out the district, and offered them the superb opportunity to host magnificent events that would dazzle the Ambassador during his tour—at their expense, of course. To my delight and relief, every one of them leaped at the chance and quickly began organizing gala dinners, lunches, and receptions in all sorts of out-of-the-way corners of France's Caribbean confetti of empire.

Of course, when it comes to sucking up to an Ambassador, too much is never enough. So, ever a glutton for punishment, I then started looking for yet more bells and whistles to add to his grand tour, and ideas began popping into my head so fast I didn't have the sense to turn them off until it was too late. One involved David Rockefeller's private retreat on Saint Barths, just across the private bay it shares with the Rothschilds. Maybe he'd let the Ambassador use it for a short respite during what was clearly going to be a long tour? Rockefeller's estate manager in New York was not at all pleased when I called to ask. But, since before calling him I'd confirmed that it would be available on the dates I proposed, he couldn't find a way to say no. After all, he'd invited me to stay there during an earlier visit to Saint Barths, so I knew it could be made available for the Ambassador. Which is how, one day, I found myself sitting next to the American Ambassador to France enjoying a lunch of newly caught lobster, quail eggs, and caviar served by the Rockefeller's butler. As an aside, Ambassador Galbraith's visit went so well that his successor as Ambassador to France, Joe Rogers, came a callin' years later. In his case, they even launched an Ariane rocket when he visited French Guiana.

But Ambassador Galbraith's grand tour of my district was just half of my idea. The other half was to gin up a concurrent exercise in gunboat diplomacy and when it comes to gunboat diplomacy, the bigger the guns the greater the diplomacy. Why not have an American warship, perhaps a destroyer or Coast Guard cutter, drop by during the Ambassador's visit to liven up the event with a show of military muscle. So I'd also called Admiral McDonald's Political Advisor, my old friend Lyle Lane, and asked if his boss might have a boat that could come down and visit me April 15. Being a good diplomat, friend, and ally, and always looking for an excuse to come to Martinique, he responded, "Let me get back to you." I suppose I should have mentioned that April 15 would coincide with the first ever visit to the French Caribbean by an American Ambassador to France. But, somehow, in the excitement of the moment that slipped my mind. And by the time Lyle called back to ask if the USS New Jersey would do, it was too late. As an aside, realizing that the arrival in Martinique on the same day of both the American Ambassador to France and the New Jersey might raise a few eyebrows, I tried to reassure both the Embassy in Paris and the Department of State that it was purely coincidental. To this day, I still suspect they found this hard to believe. Be that as it may, the Ambassador and the French were both delighted

All in all, the concurrent visits by Ambassador Galbraith and the New Jersey seemed a reasonably positive response to the Préfet's request, except for one thing. I hadn't counted on developing piles the week before the festivities were to begin. As you may imagine, the prospect of sitting on them for almost three weeks trying to smile in front of the Ambassador and a few hundred others was a bit worrisome. So I contacted a discrete French doctor and made two furtive visits to his office—and I do mean furtive—for him to perform the appropriate surgery. Much relieved, I promptly began feeling more and more comfortable. But being the cautious sort, I thought to myself that since the New Jersey had a doctor aboard why not have him check my behind as well, just to make sure, which is how the Ambassador and the Captain of the New Jersey both came to be standing in my office preparing to make formal calls on top local officials when, to my surprise, my secretary knocked lightly on the door and beckoned for me.

It seemed a rather strange time for her to interrupt me, so I assumed it must be of some importance, and it was. The doctor from the New Jersey was outside with a corpsman and was prepared to examine my posterior anatomy. I wasn't sure if I should send him away, perhaps never to see him again, or invite the Ambassador and Captain to wait outside. I chose the latter. Both the Ambassador and the Captain were clearly a bit bemused, but they politely agreed to leave my office and wait for me outside, as the doctor and corpsman, both resplendent in dress uniforms, slipped into my office.

• L'ambassadeur des U.S.A. au Port de Pointe-à-Pitre

Prêts à partir pour visiter les installations portuaires à bord de la vedette du pilotage, MM. Rivier, président du port autonome, Souriceau directeur, Galbraith ambassadeur des U.S.A. et Brown, Consul général...

Voir en page 3

author's collection

Pointe-a-Pitre, Guadeloupe. Ambassador Galbraith also visited Guadeloupe, the second island Prefecture in my district. Here we're being shown around by the Port's Director MM. Rivier.

Smiling, the doctor suggested that I dropped my pants, which was more complicated than you might think since I was wearing a suit and tie. But, being a former Marine and accustomed to taking orders, I complied and dropped both my pants and shorts down around my ankles and assumed the proctoscopal position so he could make a proper analysis. So there I was, bare-assed but still in coat, dress shirt and tie, bent over the most efficient piece of available furniture, a leather reading chair aiming my nether parts at the doctor so he could probe between my gluteus maximus. The entire scene was so beyond ludicrous that I couldn't keep from laughing. Now I don't know how much the average person knows about how the gluteus maximus function when their owner is laughing, but the harder the laugh the more difficult it is for anyone to take a good look at their anal sphincter, or at least that's what the doctor kept telling me in an attempt to calm me down. Happily all turned out well. My piles had been properly cauterized, the doctor declared me fit to sit, the Ambassador and Captain didn't insistent on the details, and we made it to the Préfet's office just in time, proving that the best things in life often come in the end. Despite its painful beginning, Ambassador Galbraith's grand tour went very well, so much so that towards the end of my assignment his successor as Ambassador to France, Joe Rodgers, followed his footsteps to Martinique. His visit went equally well, although that time I wasn't able to gin up a battleship or poach on David Rockefeller's lobster patch.

F I F T Y

THE TERRORIST'S VACATION

About halfway through my tour, the new Préfet of Guadeloupe, Yves Bonnet, was greeted much as I had been, when a bomb went off under his Basse-Terre office. Former Director of France's *Direction de la Surveillance du Territoire*, the DST, Bonnet was in the Caribbean taking a break after having arranged for Green Peace's ship, *The Rainbow Warrior,* to be sunk in New Zealand's main port, Auckland, by limpet mines planted by French frogmen. Even though it was true that the *Rainbow Warrior* was being used by some anti-nuke types to harass the French whenever they wanted to pop a nuke at Mururoa atoll in French Polynesia, their test site, the Kiwis had taken umbrage at France's action. So the French had sent Bonnet to Guadeloupe, partly to get him out of the political line of fire until things cooled off.

But, while giving him a well-deserved break in the Caribbean, the press versions of the bomb attack on Bonnet's office didn't add up. So I decided to go see what had really happened. According to the media, the bomb had been set by Luc Reinette, the leader of a local separatist group called the Caribbean Revolutionary Alliance (ARC, *Alliance Révolutionnaire Caraïbe*). But the way they described how he'd done it seemed so stupid I found it hard to believe. Reinette had reportedly used his personal credit card to rent a car and dutifully put a copy of the rental contract with his name and address on it in the glove compartment per the rental company's instructions. He then put a home-made bomb barely big enough to scorch the walls of the prefecture in the back seat, parked the car underneath the Préfet's office, set the timer, and caught a bus home. The only thing he got right was the detonator.

Needless to say, the Gendarmes didn't have a problem identifying him as the author since his home address was on his car rental contract. They simply went to his house, picked him up and slammed him in the local hoosegow. But what surprised me most was that, reportedly, he'd consulted with his lawyer before committing his act of terrorism. Reinette was a teacher, and, while he wanted to set the bomb, he didn't want to endanger his government career. So before he'd committed his mini-act of terrorism, he'd asked his lawyer for legal advice on how he could blow up the Préfet's office without risking his pension. He'd been told that committing it while on an officially approved vacation wouldn't endanger his status. Even for France that seemed weird. Weird yes, but, as it turned out, true.

And that was just the beginning. Once in jail, Reinette became a tourist attraction, or so it seemed. Apparently his fellow-travelers couldn't understand why anyone should be persecuted for committing such a reasonable act, so they began to stage well-organized daily demonstrations outside his prison, orchestrated by his lawyer, demanding his release. It may have been a novel approach to defending one's client, but it worked. During one of their get-togethers the demonstrators stormed the prison and released Reinette, who promptly raced to the international airport, jumped into a small plane that just happened to be sitting on a runway with its engine running, and disappeared, never to be seen again, at least not while I was there.

I wasn't to learn the ending of "The Saga of Luc Reinette" until almost a year after I left Martinique and was well into my next assignment as Senior Liaison Officer (SLO) to the Nicaraguan Contras in Central America, trying to clean up the mess left by the Iran-Contra scandal. Early one day, while I was sitting at my desk inside a vault inside a vault inside the Embassy in Tegucigalpa, trying to figure out what the hell was happening in the Contra War, my phone rang. It was Préfet Lacroix calling from Martinique to tell me rather gleefully that they'd just recaptured Reinette.

They'd received a report that Reinette was planning to return to Guadeloupe in a private plane from his hiding place somewhere in South America. Since the plane was too small to make it without refueling, his pilot had filed a flight plan with a stop in Guyana, supposedly to refuel. As soon as the French learned this, they sent their Ambassador to Guyana in to see its President, Forbes Burnham, to let him know what was happening and to suggest that Guyana might not want the kind of problems France would cause should Reinette be allowed to remain. So, when the plane landed in Guyana, it was allowed to refuel but ordered to get the hell out of Dodge as soon as possible, once it had. As a gesture of friendship, Forbes Burnham also gave the plane's onward flight plan to the French Ambassador, indicating that its next stop was to be Saint Lucia, the island nation just south of Martinique.

Lacroix explained that things then began to move so fast, he didn't have time to consult Paris. But, since he knew what they would want him to do, he took matters into his own hands and issued orders for a platoon of *Gendarmes mobile* to board a transport aircraft as quickly as possible, fly to Saint Lucia, and detain Reinette the moment his plane landed. He then called Saint Lucia's Prime Minister, George Compton, to inform him that a French terrorist was expected to land there momentarily and a platoon of fully armed *Gendarmes* was en route to Saint Lucia with orders to detain him. But even though they were authorized to use deadly force if necessary, he was sure they would meet no resistance. So, he went on to say to the undoubtedly rather shocked Prime Minister, that wasn't what he was calling about. He was calling because he had some very good news. Saint Lucia was a good friend and neighbor, and tourism was rapidly becoming its main source of income, so Paris had just authorized funds to pay for lengthening the main runway of its only airport and modernize its facilities.

Having spent my first year as Mr. Contra banging my head against the stone wall known as Washington, I couldn't help but envy how efficiently he'd handled the matter. I thanked him for the call, congratulated him profusely on a job well done, bid him adieu, went back to contemplating the unholy political mess cascading across my own desk and almost broke down and cried.

I suspect that Lacroix called me in part because he knew that Bonnet hadn't been Reinette's only target while I was in the French Caribbean. I'd been one too, as he had rather rudely informed one day by showing me an assassination list drawn up by the local branch of Reinette's ARC outfit. My name was on it in fifth place and the French were taking it seriously enough to assign a squad of plainclothes guards to protect me. The list incensed me. Not because I was on it, but because they'd ranked me fifth and that was an insult to my country. How dare they put the American Consul General fifth!

A short while later, I spotted one of the list's "secret" authors at a reception, sidled over to him in the usual unctuous diplomatic way, and joined him as he ogled a couple of mini-skirted young ladies. As we took in the view together, I casually mentioned to him that I'd just seen an assassination list with my name on it and felt terribly insulted, because whoever had written it, rather than putting me first as would have been proper for someone of my status, had listed me fifth. My message sent, I then walked away to ogle some other young ladies in even shorter mini-skirts.

Shortly after this little chitchat, the Préfet sidled up to me again and told me not to worry, because the terrorists had made the mistake of putting the Mayor of Fort-de-France, Aimé Césaire, first on their list. While not well known in the United States, Césaire was one of France's most famous poets, a member of the *Académie française*, and founder, along with Léopold Senghor of Senegal, of the Negritude movement. And his people, knowing full well who'd drawn up the list, had taken a direct approach. Rather than trying to be cutesy, they'd simply hauled in ARC's local leader and told him they knew the names, addresses, and daily routines of all of the organization's members, plus those of their wives, children, mistresses, mothers, fathers, aunts, uncles, and all their cousins, not to mention their girlfriends and boyfriends. And should anyone so much as touch a hair on Césaire head, all of them would disappear.

Still, I did manage to harvest one benefit from the experience, if you consider an armored Peugeot a benefit. After a few weeks sandwiched between French security agents like the ham in a *croque-monsieur*, their chief asked if, rather than assigning a half-dozen people to me at their expense for the rest of my tour, might I not ask my own government for an alternative, which I did. The immediate response from Washington was positive. They might not have a nickel for tribute, but they always seemed to have a stray million for security, so they would have my official Pugeot armored.

Soon, six hundred pounds of what was needed to armor it arrived, and we put it in the garage to await the impending arrival of the Seabee who would install it—and waited, and waited, and waited.

Now, quite frankly, bullet-proof car windows sitting in a garage don't provide a hell of a lot of protection. And being constantly escorted by body guards, no matter how professional, can be a drag. So after several months of pushing, shoving, tweaking, and trying to get the Department to send a Seabee down in this life, not the next, I got fed up and called Ollie North, who was still in the White House. One showed up within the week, having been assigned the arduous task of spending three or four weeks in Martinique installing Lexguard bulletproof windows and steel plates in my pet Peugeot's doors. He did a superb job, although he may have been a little bit slower than normal, since we'd housed him in a four-star hotel just down the mountain from the residence that had a great gourmet restaurant with an unobstructed view onto its topless beach.

FIFTY-ONE

SWEDISH COLONIALISM

At this point, I must make a confession. I once overdosed on lobster. But I had an excuse. It was Sweden's fault. The gastronomic capital of my consular district was the tiny island of Saint-Barthélemy, Saint Barths to those in the know. It wasn't far from the much better known tourist island of Saint Martin, but getting there was an adventure. While there was ferry service, the quickest way was by air, even though landing at Saint Barths required making a kamikaze dive over a mountain onto its ultra-short airport runway, then immediately slamming on the brakes and reversing prop so you wouldn't skid off into the bay. But it was worth it. Dotted with tiny boutique hotels and restaurants so good that Craig Claiborne, then the *New York Times'* restaurant critic, took his annual gourmet vacations there, its tiny capital of Marigot consisted of a string of fairy-tale buildings arrayed around a yacht harbor like a miniature tropical version of Monaco. The harbor itself was dominated by Fort Saint Luis, a fort-let dating back to the 1770s that had since been modernized. At least in my day, it sprouted an array of radio masts and intercept discs that would have made a Soviet intelligence trawler Captain salivate, all aimed in the direction of the then open, but since closed, US Naval Base at Roosevelt Roads, Puerto Rico.

Having dealt officially with modern-day Swedish politicians and found to be, at times, obnoxiously self-righteous and prone to denouncing the United States as immorally imperialistic, I was pleased to find that this delightful tropical island had once been a Swedish colony. The reality that today's egalitarian *uber alles* Sweden has an imperialist past came home to me with a flourish one day when I received an invitation to be a guest of honor at Saint Barth's anniversary celebration of its transference from Sweden to France. Having made an earlier, official visit, I accepted with relish. Since it was part of his prefecture, I also called Bonnet to let him know I'd be visiting his district. He said that he, too, had been invited to the festivities as an honored guest. But Paris had instructed him not to accept, because "France does not celebrate the former colonial presence of other countries on its territory." I could tell by the tone of his voice he was disappointed when he asked if I was going to fly up via Guadeloupe. If so, he wanted to have a short chat at the airport.

True to his word, when I arrived in Pointe-à-Pitre to change planes, Bonnet was there to greet me and a few others on their way to Saint Barths for the festivities, including the Swedish Ambassador to Venezuela and his American wife, and more importantly, Sweden's Minister of Public Works. The Minister's appearance on the scene seemed to bother Bonnet since, while he was under instructions not to attend the festivities, it would be a major protocolary *faux pas* not to honor the Minister with his presence. His dilemma was clearly weighing heavily on his mind as we walked to the small plane that would take us to Saint Barths. As we reached it, Bonnet turned to me for protocol advice. He wanted to know if, in light of the unexpected presence of the Minister, he was obligated to accompany him despite his earlier orders, since when he'd received them Paris hadn't been aware that a Swedish Minister of Government would be attending. The instant I nodded yes, he turned to his driver and told him to grab the bag on the back seat of his car and toss it in the airplane, because he was going to go to Saint Barths after all. Since I'd been told in advance that the Ambassador and Minister would both be accompanied by their wives, Leda was with me, and off we all went.

I was surprised to find that the islanders were more interested in me than in the other guests. At one event I was surrounded by local residents who began asking for my autograph. They knew the Préfet and the Swedish Ambassador and Minister were there. But having a representative of the United States join them was, apparently, the icing on the cake. Still, just to be on the safe side, I was careful to sign with a flourish that was different from my normal signature on the off chance there might be a stray visa form hidden beneath something I signed. As for the festival itself, it lasted for several days and was fun but exhausting. So, on the third day, we Honored Few took a break and went to a three-star restaurant for a snack. When the waiter brought us the menus, we looked at each other and said, almost plaintively, that we hoped they have something besides lobster. I love lobster. But having it for breakfast, lunch, dinner and hors d'oeuvres for three days in a row had been a bit much. And guess what? Lobster was included in every entrée on the menu. What one must do for country.

FIFTY-TWO

SOLVE HAITI? WHY?

One of my biggest disappointments during my years in Martinique was the State Department's rejection of another of my policy "initiatives" (they called them schemes), this one involving Haiti. My proposal was simple. France made the mess in the first place, so let France clean it up. While they all spoke French Creole as their mother tongue, had shared colonial histories and believed in the occult, France's Caribbean provinces, Martinique and Guadeloupe, were well governed, modern, and prosperous, while Haiti seemed to be subject to perpetual disasters.

The similarities between Haiti and it's French Caribbean cousins was driven home to me several times during my days in the Franco-tropics, including once when my wife and I were returning from a movie via a shortcut, a narrow but quite passable paved road that saved about twenty minutes driving time by cutting directly across a deep ravine rather than going around it. We'd taken it going with no problem. But on our way back, when we reached the bottom of the ravine my headlights revealed a half casket sitting at an angle in the middle of the road adorned with burning candles and a dead rooster. It was one of the methods by which the local quimboiseurs—witch doctors—communicated with the dead or, in this case, the living, like us. I don't believe in such nonsense, of course. But discretion is the better part of valor, especially when dealing with the occult. So, just to be on the safe side, I immediately turned around and took the longer route home. But apparently the State Department didn't feel the same way about sorcery as I did. When I proposed moving the Consulate from its place of honor as Martinique's easiest target for bombers to a safer location that had a cliff on one side, a cave on another, and the home of a particularly well-known and much feared local quimboiseur on another, they just giggled.

Another incident that underscored just how closely linked the French Caribbean and Haiti are took place when the local French spooks asked for help locating two far-left Martiniquaise members of the French National Assembly who'd gone missing. They suspected they'd slipped off to Cuba to consult with their political friends in Havana before heading for Paris to cast votes in the National Assembly, and wondered if I might check and see if they'd transited Miami. I sent off the query quickly but, before I could get a reply, my French contact called to say that I needn't worry. They'd found their illustrious parliamentarians. They were in Haiti consulting their favorite voodoo houngans, or quimboiseurs—not in Havana consulting with Castro—on how to vote on some legislation pending in Paris.

In 1986, during the third year of my assignment in Martinique, "Baby Doc," the second Duvalier dictator of Haiti, was overthrown, and the situation there became even more chaotic than usual. Not only was it a basket case, it looked like the bottom might fall out of the basket. On a post-Baby Doc trip to Guadeloupe, I'd discussed Haiti and the possibility of

France helping stabilize the situation with Lucette Michaux-Chevry, a remarkable woman and Guadeloupe's most popular politician. She'd just been appointed Minister of Francophonie. And, not long after she was sworn in to that post, asked me to go see her.

During her inaugural visit to Paris, she'd raised the question of Haiti with officials there, because its instability was constantly causing problems in France's two French-Creole provinces, and been told informally that France was prepared to explore doing a number of things in Haiti at its own expense. One was to reform the public education system, which was atrocious. Another was to train the country's civil administration and a new core of Haitian gendarmes to give the country an effective police force. A third was to provide troops to establish and maintain security while all this was being done, perhaps the 33rd Marines from Martinique. But before they formalized any of these ideas, France wanted two things. First, they wanted our prior approval of their involvement, since they were sensitive to our strategic interests in the region. Second, while France would pay their expenses, they would need American sea support and airlifts to help them move their troops to Haiti, since they didn't have the local capability to do so.

The offer sounded pretty good to me, since it might help resolve one of our major problems in the hemisphere at someone else's expense. So I was intrigued, to say the least. But it wasn't something I would have expected to be transmitted so informally by a Junior Minister who had just been appointed via a Consul General. So, before transmitting anything to Washington, I talked with the Préfets of both Guadeloupe and Martinique and spoke separately with General Beal, the French Commander in Chief, Caribbean. All three had been made aware of the initiative by their superiors in Paris. They said that France was, in fact, prepared to engage actively in Haiti. But they had also been made aware of the fact that, because this would be so innovative and new, before preparing a detailed plan and discussing it formally at the level of our capitals, Paris wanted to sound us out very quietly at a lower level, meaning me.

Satisfied that the French were reasonably serious, I wrote up the idea and sent it to Washington with, stupid me, strong recommendations that since it would solve one of our major foreign-policy problems in the region at virtually no cost to us, it was worth serious consideration. I even added that if it were to blow up in France's face, it would be them, not us, with egg on their face. In response I received a rather terse message from the State Department, which, while politely written, essentially told me to tell the French to shove it. I learned later the proposal hadn't been given any serious consideration beyond the Latin American Bureau, where several senior officers suffered from such Franco-phobia they probably didn't even eat croissants.

FIFTY-THREE

FRENCH GUIANA — EUROPE'S WILD, WILD WEST

Far and away the most exotic place in my district was *Guyane française*, French Guiana, a California-size piece of the European Union planted squarely on the northern coast of South America. Because it is an overseas province of France, rather than a colony, it's officially part of the European Union. At the time, it had a population of slightly more than a hundred thousand, almost all living along its Atlantic Coast. Its only cities were its capital, Cayenne—named after the pepper or vice versa—and Kourou, home of the European Space Administration's version of Cape Canaveral. Few Americans know much about the place, which is perfectly understandable since it is well off the beaten tourist track. It's only well-known feature, and its most infamous attraction, is Devils Island, made famous by the movie *Papillion*, even though in French its name is *Isle de Salut*, Health Island. Go figure!

Among other things, it was one of the few places remaining in the world where vaccinations against yellow fever were mandatory because, although no cases have been reported in recent decades, the virus might still be carried by monkeys in its forests. So a tiny island offshore housed an advanced medical research station dedicated to developing a yellow fever vaccine, just in case. At the time, the only American business there was a shrimping company licensed to operate in its near shore waters. The 3rd Foreign Legion I've discussed earlier was the province's primary defense force and I made it a point to visit the Kourou Space Center the Legion was guarding every time I visited French Guiana. Since I'd shown more than a little interest in its operations, the Director began to invite me down for satellite launches, and I would go down to watch them whenever possible.

author's collection

Kourou, French Guiana, 1986. Euro Espace's Ariane rocket launching pad in French Guiana from which both European and commercial satellites are sent into orbit.

During one of my visits, one of French Guiana's members of parliament, who was also there for a launch, invited me to go with him to visit some nearby constituents. Leaving my rented Citroën at the Space Center, I jumped into his car, and we headed for France's wild-west with him driving like a bat out of hell, dodging the occasional caiman and flying through the mandatory torrential downpours. Suddenly he hit the brakes, turned sharply to the left, and started racing down a dirt track.

About a kilometer down the road, we reached a clearing in the tropical forest surrounded by ten or twelve native huts standing on stilts above open ground floor spaces where most cooking and daily life took place. Stopping at one of the huts where a heavyset, bare-breasted woman was stirring something in an iron pot big enough to cook two or three missionaries, he embraced her, kissed her on both cheeks and introduced us. Not being familiar with the customs of Paramaca Indians, I settled for a simple *bonjour*. He explained that she was the headman's wife, and he was asking where he could find her husband. It turned out that he was just a few yards away, squatting in the middle of the road clad in a loin cloth, near where Lord knows how many naked children were swimming in a river.

It felt like I was back in Southeast Asia visiting a tribal village in the Philippines, Thailand or Vietnam, except for a couple of things. The headman's wife was stirring the pot with just one hand because she had a telephone in the other and was chatting with a friend, the headman was squatting in the road watching satellite television, and all the dugouts canoes had outboard motors. They may have been Paramaca Indians living much the same way as their ancestors. But they were also citizens of France and their votes counted just as much as those of the haughtiest professors at the Sorbonne. And my friend was running for office. There was another, even closer link in French Guiana to my past in Asia—several villages of Hmong tribesmen.

During earlier visits to French Guiana, I'd seen Hmong dressed in traditional tribal attire just like those I'd visited along the Thai-Lao border decades earlier during my Marine years. They were from villages that had fought alongside the French against the Pathet Lao. So rather than abandon them to their fates, France arranged for them to have safe havens in Northeast Thailand. While this worked for a while, for the Hmong they were little more than refugee camps. So the French moved them again, this time to French Guiana, which is how I found myself in South America chatting away in Thai with Hmong tribal leaders, to the wonderment of my French hosts.

After France withdrew from Laos, thousands of other Hmong had continued to fight the Pathet Lao as allies of the United States. Years later, when our own efforts to keep the Pathet Lao from taking power in Laos failed, we too, resettled many of them, in our case to the United States mainland. I'd seen lots of Hmong in Fresno, California, during visits to family there and had been told that they'd resisted assimilation, spawned a number of criminal gangs, and become a major problem in general. That was a very different outcome from what had happened in French Guiana. There the biggest problem they were causing was that their fresh produce was pushing some importers of Brazilian products out of the market. The main difference between the way the French had handled their resettlement and the way we had was clear, at least to me. Rather than trying to force them to integrate into an urban life that was contrary to their tribal origins as we had done, the French resettled them in villages that largely replicated their traditional settlements, separate but not isolated, rural not urban, agricultural not commercial.

In French Guiana the Hmong were free to wear traditional tribal dress, speak Hmong, live in traditional style houses, and, by and large, settle problems among themselves. They were free to assimilate into French society if they wished at their own pace, but not pressured to do so. Not that they were entirely free to duplicate all of their traditional lifestyles. They weren't. For example, while they could farm land that was allotted to them they were not free to clear new areas or to cut down trees without permits, as they had done in Laos. They were also required to comply with French public health and educational requirements. The results of the latter were especially impressive. Hmong children were required to go to French public schools and to study the national curriculum up to and including taking France's "bacs," its annual national baccalaureate exams. The French were astonished by the results. The first year French Guiana Hmong took the bacs, two of them ranked among the top students in all of France. We had taken an essentially opposite approach in the United States. We too had welcomed the immigration of Hmong. But we hadn't kept them together as communities. We'd settled them in urban not rural environments; and pressured them to assimilate into our culture. Our approach had triggered a defensive reaction, up to and including the emergence of violence-prone gangs. By not pressuring them, France had harvested just the opposite. It was a lesson worth learning.

FIFTY-FOUR

Drums Along the Maroni

My last experience in French Guiana came just before I left Martinique for Honduras and my next assignment. There was a rebellion brewing next door in Suriname, so I went down to see what was going on. I took our son, Tim, with me, since by then he'd graduated from American University, passed the Foreign Service Entrance Exams, been accepted, and was just hanging around our swimming pool waiting for orders. The Préfet and the Legion Colonel arranged for us to see what was happening on the ground and to meet some of the refugees that had begun to flow out of Suriname across the Maroni River into France.

Most of the refugees were being housed in Grand-Santi, a tiny village on the French side of the river and the only way to get there, since there were too many shallow rapids for anything larger, was by canoe up the river. We soon found ourselves in a motorized canoe, sailing up the Maroni with a Gendarme escort. Grand-Santi's original residents were Boni tribesmen, descendants of black Africans that had reached Suriname but escaped before they could actually be enslaved. The refugees were Bosch, another group of re-tribalized black Africans, descendants of slaves that had returned to the bush after being freed when slavery was abolished, making the two more cousins than brothers.

Grand-Santi was not, in fact, very grand. But it was fascinating, a truly distant and exotic corner of the European Union. The community had a tiny clinic run by Catholic nuns and an equally tiny detachment of Gendarmes. We'd been advised by the State Department's medical office to take Fansidar, a type of anti- malaria pill especially formulated to ward off the region's chloroquine-resistant mosquitoes that carried a strain of incurable malaria. We could, as an

author's collection

Grand-Santi, French Guiana, 1987. Our son, Timothy, now a senior FSO in his own right, in front of a typical Bosch home.

alternative, take chloroquine, although it was much less effective against the local mosquitoes. It seemed a simple enough choice, until they added that we should be prepared for a few possible side effects of Fansidar, such as double vision and minor brain hemorrhages. That left us with a rather Hobbesian choice—risk contracting incurable malaria or risk having brain hemorrhages. Since during my years in Thailand I'd already had a couple of bouts of malaria, I chose to take Fansidar. My son took the chloroquine. When we reached Grand-Santi we were still vibrating from the out-board canoe trip, quickly fell into mosquito-net protected cots provided by the Gendarmes and slept soundly, until we were awakened the next morning by howler monkeys playing in the nearby jungle. We spent most of the day talking with the nuns and Gendarmes and, through interpreters, with some of the refugees.

The biggest French concern appeared to be not to let the refugee Bosch stay in French Guiana for more than three months because, under French law, that would qualify them for permanent refugee status. As for the refugees, while they weren't in bad shape, they were definitely afraid to go back home. They also hadn't yet found out that if they managed to stay on the French side of the river for three months they would become eligible for French residency and welfare payments for the rest of their lives.

The biggest surprise came in the form of an invitation from the Gendarmes to dine at the local restaurant, since I hadn't seen anything that even vaguely resembled one. As night fell, our hosts took us to an open-air pavilion that had four tables, eight benches and an open-air kitchen. It was less elaborate than the better restaurants in France—no walls, pigs and naked little children running back and forth beneath our feet, and no menu, since the main course was always the kill of the day, in this case a capybara, or water pig. And yet the meal turned out to be one of the best I've ever had. It began with soup made from river and jungle greens, followed by roast capybara, then came a cheese course, and finally a fruit tart, all accompanied by excellent wines. Only the French! It turned out that the cook was from Saint Lucia, the Caribbean island nation just south of Martinique, although how she wound up in Grand-Santi I'll never know. It almost made me forget why I was really there, but not quite.

A rebel Surinamese soldier, Sergeant Ronnie Brunswjik, was recruiting a force of the disenchanted, giving them some arms, and training them in preparation for launching an attempt to overthrow the Surinamese government. He hadn't yet launched his "Jungle Commando" into battle, but it was clear to me that his strategy would be dictated almost entirely by the terrain. The précis of the situation I sent to Washington was straightforward. Brunswijk would wait for the end of the rainy season and then launch his force straight down the Maroni. His first objective would be an island that housed the only readily available logistical supply facilities. He'd then move down the river to capture the Surinamese town of Albina, then wheel west and head for the capital city, Paramaribo, on the only available all-weather coastal road. I even suggested that if someone were to stand on the French side of the river opposite Albina they'd be able to watch the attack. The only thing I didn't predict was that Brunswijk would burn Albina to the ground, a spectacular event witnessed by a fellow American from another agency after his bosses took up my challenge. While I was proud of having accurately described Brunswijk's campaign in advance in detail, in light of what came next, maybe I shouldn't have been.

FIFTY-FIVE

SECRET/EXDIS/CONTRA

As my years in Martinique came to an end, the fickle middle finger of fate was to flip me off toward Nicaragua yet again. As you hopefully recall, my very first overseas assignment involving my country's foreign affairs had taken me to Nicaragua in 1956 when I was barely seventeen years old, when the Somoza dynasty was on the second of its three legs. Since then the third Somoza had been overthrown by Sandinista revolutionaries with the active help of Castro's Cuba and the Carter administration. Once in power, the Sandinistas began efforts to transform Nicaragua into a Cuban-style worker's paradise and publicly declaring themselves allies of Cuba, the Soviet Union and the Warsaw Pact, and sworn enemies of the *imperialistas Yanquis, enemigos de la humanidad* — Yankee imperialist enemies of mankind, meaning the United States.

The Sandinistas efforts to transform Nicaragua had ignited a peasant uprising in the country's Segovian Mountains where almost half of all Nicaraguans live. And a small trickle of support for the rebels Jimmy Carter had authorized during his last days in office had been transformed by his successor, Ronald Reagan, into a major covert operation and our theoretically secret support for them had become front page news, even in Martinique. What was not in the news was that, despite the Iran-Contra imbroglio that was the scandal of the day, Congress had given Reagan funds to continue covert support to the Contras, as the rebels were called. Congress had added as a condition precedent to approving these funds that henceforth the Secretary of State had to take personal responsibility for seeing to it that there were no more Ollie North-esque attempts to make end runs around its authority.

While, at the time, I didn't know Reagan had obtained secret funding to continue support for the Contras, when a call went out from State for a Foreign Service Officer volunteer to head up a "project" in Central America, I was pretty sure what it was, and had no interest in sticking one of my more valuable appendages into yet another political meat grinder. But, once again, Lyn Nofziger called me, told me the job being advertised involved working with the Contras, said "they" hoped I'd volunteer, adding that Laxalt seconded his request. And, once again, I couldn't say no. So despite my fear that the assignment could end my diplomatic career, I volunteered.

After being thoroughly vetted for the job by everyone involved in the Contra program from the CIA and White House's National Security Council to the State Department's Inspector General and the Director General of the Foreign Service, I found myself back in Washington. This time I was being briefed in on what was to prove the most demanding, complex, least successful, and by far the most politically charged assignment of my diplomatic career as the Senior Liaison Officer (SLO) in Central America to the Nicaraguan Contras, and head of a secret compartmentalized office, unique in the history of the Department of State.

author's collection

To Tim Brown – With special gratitude for your friendship and support. Best Regards,

Ronald Reagan

Washington, DC 1987. This photo reached me via Lyn Nofziger during the second year of my tour in Honduras as the State Department's Senior Liaison Officer (SLO) to the Nicaraguan Resistance, the Contras, in Central America.

author's collection

Tegucigalpa, Honduras. Interpreting for Senators Dodd and McCain.

From 1987 through 1990, I was to be "Mr. Contra," a professionally challenging political nightmare. During those years, I met, briefed, and escorted what seemed like half the Members of Congress and all their staffers, many of them several time. Here I'm serving as interpreter for Senators John McCain (R-AZ), one of the Contras' biggest fans, and Christopher Dodd (D-CT), one of their strongest critics, during a meeting with Honduran President Azcona and Army Chief of Staff General Regalado to discuss the Contras. McCain is on the left, Dodd is shaking hands with General Regalado, and Honduran President Azcona is partly hidden behind the General. As usual, I'm smack dab in the middle.

For four years, messages entering or leaving my office would be classified SECRET/EXDIS/CONTRA and reach only a handful of people in Washington. Unfortunately, one of them was Ana Belen Montes, both the top Cuba/Nicaragua analyst at the Defense Intelligence Agency - and a Cuban spy. Toward the end of my assignment I was recommended for the National HUMINT (Human Intelligence) Award, possibly the first time a Foreign Service Officer was ever recommended for it. But then, FSOs don't normally voluntarily enter active battlefields, nor does their reporting lead to major changes of policy, deployment of the 82nd Airborne or air strikes. But that's another story.

SECRET UNCLASSIFIED

PAGE 01   TEGUCI 20104 01 OF 03 072234Z
ACTION INR-07

INFO   LOG-00   ADS-00   CIAE-00 ARA-00   NSAE-00 SSO-00   HA-09
       INM-08   INRE-00 RP-10   OES-09   MMP-01   OIG-04   /048 W
       ------------------256366   080115Z /61
O 072230Z NOV 89
FM AMEMBASSY TEGUCIGALPA
TO SECSTATE WASHDC IMMEDIATE 6939

EXCISE

SECTION 01 OF 03 TEGUCIGALPA 20104

E.O. 12356: DECL: OADR
TAGS: KPRP, HO
SUBJECT: NOMINATION FOR NATIONAL HUMINT AWARD --
         SPECIAL LIAISON OFFICE OF EMBASSY HONDURAS

REF: STATE 272977

1. (S- ENTIRE TEXT)

2. EMBASSY TEGUCIGALPA WISHES TO NOMINATE ITS SPECIAL
LIAISON OFFICE FOR THE NATIONAL HUMINT AWARD. WE ARE
AWARE THAT THE DUE DATE HAS PASSED BUT HOPE THIS
NOMINATION CAN BE GIVEN FULL CONSIDERATION.

3. THE SPECIAL LIAISON OFFICE (SLO) OF EMBASSY
TEGUCIGALPA IS UNIQUE IN THE FOREIGN SERVICE. IT WAS
ESTABLISHED IN THE SPRING OF 1987 AS A COMPARTMENTALIZED
OFFICE TO WORK DIRECTLY WITH THE NICARAGUAN DEMOCRATIC
RESISTANCE -- THE CONTRAS -- IN HONDURAS. IT IS
RESPONSIBLE FOR DAILY LIAISON WITH THE ARMED RESISTANCE
FORCES OF THE ERN/NORTH AND YATAMA, THOSE RESISTANCE
POLITICAL ELEMENTS BASED IN HONDURAS, AND SELECT
HONDURAN GOVERNMENT OFFICIALS. IT HAS BEEN DEEPLY
INVOLVED OPERATIONALLY IN THE ACTIVITIES OF BOTH THE
ERN/NORTH AND YATAMA WITHIN THE LIMITS OF LEGAL
AUTHORITIES. SLO, BECAUSE OF ITS COMPARTMENTALIZED AND
SENSITIVE NATURE, HAS REPORTED ALMOST EXCLUSIVELY
THROUGH ITS OWN SPECIAL CHANNELS -- EXDIS CONTRA
-- HANDLED AS A LIMITING VERSION OF
NODIS IN THE DEPARTMENT AND WASHINGTON IN GENERAL.

b1

9. THE CHIEF OF THE SPECIAL LIAISON SECTION, TIMOTHY
BROWN HAS PRODUCED OVER 350 REPORTING CABLES DURING THE
PAST 27 MONTHS. THESE COVERED THE ENTIRE SPECTRUM OF
SLO REPORTING BUT THREE SERIES ARE OF PARTICULAR NOTE.
IN MARCH OF 1988, MR. BROWN PREDICTED THE SANDINISTA
INVASION OF THE RESISTANCE STRATEGIC HEADQUARTERS AND
SUPPLY AREA AT BOCAY, HONDURAS BASED ON VISITS TO THAT
HEADQUARTERS PRIOR TO THE ATTACK. DURING THE INVASION,
HE PRODUCED COMBAT SITUATION REPORTS ABOUT EVERY
FOUR-SIX HOURS ON INFORMATION FROM CONTACTS HE HAD
DEVELOPED INSIDE THE RESISTANCE COMMAND STRUCTURE. THEY
WERE USED AT THE WHITE HOUSE, THE DEPARTMENT OF STATE,
THE DEPARTMENT OF DEFENSE AND THE CIA TO MAINTAIN
TACTICAL MAPS ON THE BATTLEFIELD SITUATION AS THE BATTLE
EVOLVED. THEY WERE ALSO USED BY THE HIGHEST LEVELS OF
U.S. GOVERNMENT AS A BASIS FOR ITS PLANNING AND THE
EVENTUAL DEPLOYMENT OF A REGIMENT OF THE 82ND AIRBORNE
AND BY THE HONDURAN GOVERNMENT AS A BASIS FOR ITS

UNCLASSIFIED

DECISION TO LAUNCH AIR STRIKES AGAINST NEARBY SANDINISTA
POSITIONS INSIDE NICARAGUA. SANITIZED VERSIONS OF HIS
REPORTING WERE ALSO USED TO BRIEF THE UNITED STATES AND
INTERNATIONAL PRESS. IMMEDIATELY AFTER THE SANDINISTAS
BEGAN TO WITHDRAW, MR. BROWN, ACCOMPANIED BY A
DEPARTMENT OFFICER AND OTHERS, REVISITED THE BATTLEFIELD
TO COLLECT AFTER-ACTION PHOTOGRAPHS, VIDEOS AND MATERIAL
EVIDENCE OF THE SANDINISTA INCURSION. THIS INCLUDED A
TRIP TO THE RIO COCO BORDER BETWEEN NICARAGUA AND
HONDURAS BY HELICOPTER AND TRAVEL ON THE RIVER IN
MOTORIZED CANOE W
HICH CAME WITHIN 1-1/2 KILOMETERS OF
THE ACTIVE BATTLEFIELD. MR. BROWN'S REPORTS WERE
MATERIAL IN CONVINCING A SKEPTICAL U.S. AND WORLD PRESS
THAT THE INVASION HAD BEEN REAL. ON ANOTHER TOPIC, MR.
BROWN REPORTED ON DEFECTS IN A U.S.A.I.D. HUMANITARIAN
ASSISTANCE PROGRAM IN ITS EARLY STAGES IN THE SPRING OF
1988. THOSE REPORTS WERE READ BY THE PRESIDENT, THE
SECRETARY AND MANY OTHERS RESULTING IN MAJOR CHANGES IN
THE INITIAL APPROACH TO PROVIDING THAT ASSISTANCE AND
CHANGED IT FROM A PROGRAM ALMOST CERTAIN TO FAIL TO ONE
THAT HAS WORKED WELL. HIS REPORTING ALSO WAS USED BY

THE ADMINISTRATION WITH THE CONGRESS IN THE FORMULATION
OF THE CURRENT LEGISLATION COVERING HUMANITARIAN
ASSISTANCE. OTHER SERIES OF REPORTS BY MR. BROWN HAVE
COVERED HUMAN RIGHTS, INTERNAL POLITICS INSIDE THE
POLITICAL BRANCHES OF THE RESISTANCE, YATAMA POLITICAL
ACTIVITIES, ATTEMPTS TO FORM AN ENGLISH-SPEAKING
NICARAGUAN/CREOLE POLITICAL/MILITARY MOVEMENT AND
PROPOSALS FOR POLICY APPROACHES TO NICARAGUA AND CENTRAL
AMERICA THAT ARE OFTEN PRECISELY ECHOED IN THE CURRENT
U.S. APPROACH TO THE REGION.

Penfold

Made in the USA
San Bernardino, CA
29 January 2015